A Piano
in The
Pyrenees

A Piano
in The
Pyrenees

Tony Hawks

EBURY
PRESS

3 5 7 9 10 8 6 4

This edition published in 2007

First published in 2006 by Ebury Press, an imprint of Ebury Publishing

A Random House Group Company

The Random House Group Limited Reg. No. 954009

Addresses for companies within the Random House Group can be found at
www.randomhouse.co.uk

A CIP catalogue record for this book is available from the British Library

 Mixed Sources
Product group from well-managed
forests and other controlled sources
www.fsc.org Cert no. TT-COC-2139
© 1996 Forest Stewardship Council
FSC

'Stayin' Alive'
Composed by Barry Gibb, Maurice Gibb and Robin Gibb
© Crompton Songs
By kind permission of Warner/Chappell Music Limited

'Stayin' Alive'
Written and composed by Barry Gibb, Maurice Gibb and Robin Gibb
Published by Gibb Brothers Music/BMG Music Publishing Ltd.
Used by permission. All rights reserved.

'Nature Boy'
Composed by Eden Ahbez
© Crestview Music Corp/Burke & Van Heusen Music Inc
By kind permission of Warner/Chappell Music Limited

Printed and bound in Great Britain by Cox & Wyman Ltd, Reading, Berkshire

ISBN 9780091903336

To buy books by your favourite authors and register for offers visit
www.rbooks.co.uk

Apologies

I would like to apologise for not having a 'Thanks' section at the front of this book. Frankly, these are very dull to read unless you happen to be one of the people getting a mention, and, let's face it, you probably aren't. However, if you do happen to be one of the people who have helped with this book in some way, then well done. Without you, this apology section wouldn't have been possible.

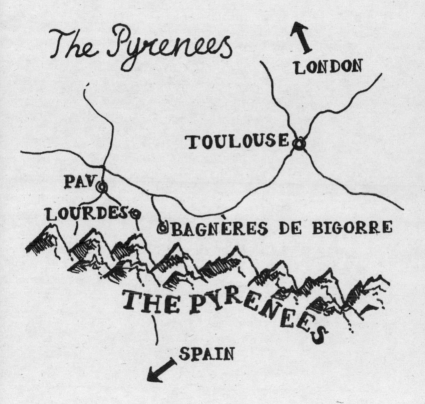

1

Not so Young, Free and Single

'What do you mean you're not going to play any more?' said Kevin.

The dressing room smelt, we'd just been beaten 8–2, and I was close to exhaustion.

'I mean exactly what I say,' I replied. 'No more five-a-side football for me. I'm forty-four years old and this is clearly a game for a younger man. Like you, for instance – you're forty-three.'

'Don't be too hasty about this,' said Brad, a mere forty-one.

'Yes, are you sure you don't want to think this through?' said Tim, forty-three.

'There's nothing to think through,' I said firmly. 'My body's hurting too much. I can still meet you guys in the pub after the game and do the boysy catch-up. I just won't bother with the football bit.'

'It won't be the same,' said Kevin.

Of course it wouldn't be the same. Life changes. It's supposed to change. I wasn't going to make the mistake of trying to hang on to something that ought be allowed to become a pleasant memory. (Or, in this case, simply a memory.) Nothing stays the same. Our bodies get older, our children get bigger (or, in my case, god-children), our pets die on us, our friends get jobs abroad and move overseas, our passions ebb and flow like the tides, governments rise and fall, and natural disasters destroy life with a callous contempt and an alarming regularity.

So why was giving up five-a-side football such a big deal?

'What are you drinking, Tone?' asked Tim from close to the bar.

Dave, the team's fifth player, had gone home to his wife and kids, so that left me sharing this smoky atmosphere with three of my oldest and closest friends.

'The usual please, Tim,' I replied before sitting down with the other two weary members of our heavily defeated team.

The pub opposite the sports centre was heaving, mostly with drinkers I recognised as being younger, if not healthier, than all of us. We watched the back of Tim as he fought for the barman's attention. He stood there: tall, good-looking – particularly from the angle we were now surveying him. His gentle, roguish sense of humour was something that had made him enormous fun in our younger days when, more likely than not, we would have been in a pub like this one with the sole purpose of trying to chat up women. Unlike me, Tim had settled down. He'd met Lucy when they were both jobbing actors specialising in poor quality adverts for German toothpaste, Belgian coffee or Norwegian shower gel. Shakespeare it hadn't been, but it had provided them enough money to get a nice house and the means to support their two boys, Archie and George.

'Tony, what's "the usual" again?' asked Tim, who had quickly popped back from the bar.

'A pint of lager,' I replied. 'Not one of the strong ones. Cooking lager please.'

'Righto.'

Tim's question revealed just how infrequently these vaguely sporting liaisons actually occurred. Many years ago, we'd played weekly in a five-a-side league, but now our busy lives prevented such frivolous indulgences. We were lucky if we managed three games a year. All the more reason, I would have thought, for my retirement from the game to have been accepted more readily.

'Well, I suppose you should listen to what your body's telling you,' said Brad, who was always the first to be conciliatory.

Brad looked younger than his forty-one years, boyish almost. I looked at him and remembered how much irritation his looks had caused me over the years. Too many girls thought he was 'cute', and it wasn't fair. I'd always taken some comfort in the fact that he wasn't a very good footballer (that's why we put him in goal), although regrettably my retirement from the sport now made that consolation redundant.

Brad's emotional life had always been much more complicated than mine. We'd met in 1985 as performers in a West End musical called *Lennon*, and at that stage Brad was already a father figure to Sarah, the daughter of Kate, the woman he lived with. He and Kate no longer lived together but they were great friends. In fact, Brad was now married to someone else – Claire – but then he didn't live with her either. Instead, they too were great friends, who happened to be waiting on a divorce. A pattern was beginning to emerge in Brad's love life, but this wasn't the time or the place to discuss it.

'Tony, if it feels right to stop the football, then you should do what you want,' continued Brad.

'Yes, but what do you want?' enquired Kevin.

'What do you mean?' I replied.

'Well,' said Kevin, somehow adopting the swagger of a courtroom barrister, 'if you had to pick two things you wanted – if you had to – what would you pick?'

I hesitated. This was a bigger question than was usually asked at these post-match debriefs. I resisted the temptation to opt for the easy way out – the humorous reply, so often the Englishman's refuge from confrontation with his true feelings.

'I suppose the honest answer would be,' I said, still accessing the last pieces of required data from a jumbled mind, 'the two things would be: meeting my soulmate, and finding an idyllic house abroad somewhere.'

'Where?' asked Kevin.

'Where what? If you mean where will I find my soulmate, then God knows.'

'No, where would you buy the house?'

'In France, I think. In the mountains somewhere – so we could ski in the winter.'

Kevin produced a satisfied smile of anticipation. Like me, he was a keen skier. He'd introduced me to the sport years ago in what now seemed like another lifetime. In 1982, he'd worked in a school in the French Alps as part of his university degree, and when I'd visited him he'd insisted I join in with the pupils' ski outing on Wednesday and Friday afternoons. Kevin had been my ski instructor, even though at the time he himself had no real idea how to ski. His tuition had taught me two things.

How to do an emergency stop when travelling at dangerously high speeds.

How to suspend all natural instincts for self-preservation or feel any concern for the safety of others who were foolish enough to be 'in the way'.

Kevin had been married, but despite a promising start, matrimonial bliss had somehow disintegrated, and for the best part of a decade he'd been adapting to the life of a divorced man. I guess, along with the rest of us, the five-a-side football had been one of the things that helped him through it all. Kevin is roughly the same height as Maradona, but despite his best efforts doesn't resemble him greatly in any footballing sense. He's a nifty little player, however, and although I wouldn't go so far as to say he was the best in our team, he was definitely in the top five.

'Why France?' asked Brad.

'Because I speak pretty good French, and I've been there a lot and always liked the place.'

'France is good,' said Tim, who'd finally arrived with a large tray of drinks and crisps. 'That's where we've got our place.'

I turned to him in shock. 'Your place?' I asked.

'Yes. I thought I'd told you, Luce and I have bought a run-down house not far from Limoges.'

'I didn't know that,' I said, still surprised. 'You sneaky bugger. I thought it was always going to be me who'd be the first to buy a house abroad.'

The fact that Tim had omitted to discuss the purchase of a French house with me wasn't so much a sign that we were best friends who'd drifted apart, more that he was a father of two and I wasn't. Our lives didn't really coincide any more. I went to drinks parties and he went to PTA meetings at the local school. On occasion, when I'd been heading off to a book launch or a cocktail party, I might have noted a soupçon of envy in his eye, just as he might have spotted the same in mine each time his children leapt into his arms when he opened his front door.

'Tim, why on earth did you buy a house in France?' I demanded.

'We see it as a good investment. Property is cheap. We'll do the place up and it'll make money. Plus, it'll be a fab place for family holidays.'

'It makes sense, Tony,' said Brad. 'You should do it. Of all of us, you're the one with the most disposable income.'

'Yes,' I said, still somewhat confused as to how the conversation had turned to this subject from that of my retirement as a five-a-side footballer. 'But just because it's disposable doesn't mean I want to throw it away.'

'You know that skiing weekend you have booked with Kevin next month?' said Brad.

'Yes.'

'Well, maybe you should take some time off to look at houses then.'

'No, Brad. It's a ski trip, and ski trips are for skiing.'

'Yeah, but you could take an afternoon off and—'

'No. That's final. The house thing can wait.'

And at the time I meant it.

It had been Kevin's idea to try the Pyrenees.

'We've skied just about everywhere else in Europe,' he'd said. 'It would be wrong not to give the Pyrenees a go.'

A comment that revealed the lack of research that had gone into our choice of destination. The plan hadn't gone much beyond flying to an airport called Pau Pyrenees. Only on arrival were we going to decide which ski resort to go to. We had indulged in this slightly anarchic approach to travel before and we both liked it, not least because we could occasionally revel in the following exchange with people we met on the journey:

'Where are you guys headed?'

'We don't know.'

What we did know was that there were plenty of ski resorts in the Pyrenees, some to the east of Pau and some to the west. Perhaps it was something of a metaphor for the current state of our lives, but we simply had no idea what direction we would take. We were both at a kind of forty-something crossroads. Kevin had been dating Nic for a couple of years now and they seemed nicely matched, but I had no idea whether he wanted to marry again. Happy though they seemed, would he risk the pain once more? And did he want to become a father? Kevin and I were close, but not geographically – we lived in different cities, and the only times we'd got together in the past couple of years had been on social occasions when a heart-to-heart hadn't been possible. Not being female, for us the subjects of marriage and fatherhood didn't fall into the category of small talk, sexual stereotyping requiring us instead to favour discussions about football or comments on the breasts of passing women.

If I was unsure what Kevin wanted, then I was just as uncertain of my own aspirations. Some of the questions Kevin was having to ask himself were less pressing for me since I wasn't even going out with anybody. I wanted to, of course I did, but my soulmate hadn't had the common decency to make herself known. When people asked me about the state of my romantic life, I tended to offer up a stock reply: 'I'm still interviewing for the position of Mrs Hawks.'

Up until this point I'd conducted a lot of interviews, some more fun than others, but I didn't seem to be any closer to making a permanent appointment. Was it because I enjoyed the freedom of being a bachelor too much? Or was it because the 'right person' hadn't come along yet?

'It'll happen when you least expect it.'

This was what I was always being told, usually by people that I didn't know very well and who might have been better off minding their own business.

The trouble was that I'd been 'not expecting' it to happen for such a long time now that I simply wasn't expecting not to expect it any more.*

I looked across at Kevin. He was reading the in-flight magazine, presumably for the same reason that other people read it – because they've left what they really want to read in a bag in the overhead lockers and they can't be bothered with the rigmarole of fetching it. We were an hour and a quarter into the flight and we knew that the mysterious Pau couldn't be far away. Our imminent arrival was marked by the aircraft gently tilting its wings and swinging us slowly to the right, a move that provided us with a new and breathtaking view to our left.

'Wow!' said Kevin, wide-eyed and child-like. 'The Pyrenees.'

We were getting a privileged aerial glimpse of a spectacular chain of mountains that stretched for four hundred kilometres along the frontier between France and Spain. Beyond its pristine white peaks there were lush meadows and deep canyons, fast-flowing rivers and secluded glens, an abundance of wildlife and

---

*A team of linguistic scholars has studied this sentence for weeks and they are still split fifty/fifty as to whether it makes sense or not.

plants. This was a playground for the nature lover. Fortunately, there were quite a lot of mechanical ski lifts too. Kevin and I would need something to keep us happy.

'Cabin crew – ten minutes to landing,' announced the captain, as if the rest of us would be landing at a completely different time.

Soon we were shuffling off the plane and filing through passport control. I glanced at Kevin's old passport photo and it reminded me just how long we'd known each other. We'd met a quarter of a century ago when we'd been at the same school. I hadn't deigned to talk to him back then, mainly because he was in the year below me and, worse still, he was quite small. He was beneath me in every way. However, after A levels I'd taken a year off and he hadn't, so we'd ended up starting at Manchester University at the same time. During our first term there I'd bonded with Kevin, playing an enormous number of games of table football, some for very high stakes – the loser had to do the other's laundry. Bored by my degree in drama, I'd left early to pursue a career in 'not having a proper job' whilst Kevin had hung on until graduation, subsequently carving out a successful career as a consultant in tourism and leisure.

'I think we should head for La Mongie,' said Kevin, consulting the guidebook as I made my first tentative manoeuvres in the hire car. 'It says here that it's the biggest skiable domain in the French Pyrenees.'

'Sounds good to me,' I replied. 'We'll find a nice hotel, treat ourselves to a slap-up meal, and then get up early to take advantage of a full day's skiing.'

'It's a top plan.'

And like a lot of top plans, it all went horribly wrong.

'What's the matter?' I called as I looked back up at Kevin, who was halfway down the slope, reaching down to his ski boot and grimacing.

We'd been skiing for less than half an hour. The conditions were excellent – a smattering of fresh snow the previous night, and although it wasn't a clear day, visibility was good.

'It's my ankle,' he called back. 'I thought it was going to be OK.'

Tentatively, and clearly in some pain, he skied down to join me.

'What do you mean – your ankle?' I said accusingly the moment he drew level. 'Since when did you have an ankle problem?'

'Since Thursday evening.'

'And what happened Thursday evening?'

'We played five-a-side football.'

'Oh no. You bloody idiot! Does this mean . . .?'

'Yes, I think it does.'

And that was it. Our long weekend of skiing ended there. Kevin was clearly in too much pain to carry on and I didn't fancy skiing on my own, despite my mate's reassurances that he'd be 'fine' if I did so. He wouldn't be 'fine' and I knew it. Besides, skiing alone has never been my thing. It's a sport that I've only really enjoyed if I can push myself to the very limits of my ability, and that means I need someone with me who can regularly pick me up and dust me down after each spectacular fall.

So we adjourned for a drink in a bar at the foot of the slopes, in a case of ridiculously premature après-ski.

'What are we going to do with our weekend?' I said, as brightly as I could.

I was trying not to reveal just how miffed I was. Why hadn't Kevin, like me, had the wisdom to hang up his football boots?

'We could go sightseeing,' he replied with an apologetic shrug.

'Kev, it's February. The only sights to see are covered in snow. Snow is going to make us want to ski, and we can't ski because you've got a bad ankle.' I scratched my head, enabling an idea to strike me, just as it does in cartoons. 'I know! There's nothing else for it! We'll just have to go to the nearest town and visit the estate agent instead.'

'What?'

'Look for a house. For me to buy. I think your ankle might be fate's way of telling me to become a French home-owner.'

'Fine by me. But don't these things need more research? I mean, you don't just come on a skiing weekend somewhere and then buy a house because your mate injures his ankle.'

'Of course not, but you've got to start looking some time, and what else are we going to do?'

'Fair point.'

I reached for the map.

'The nearest big town to here is Tarbes,' I said. 'Let's head there straight away. You have to admit, Mr Ankle, that anything is better than watching other people ski.'

Kevin agreed.

Tarbes is not an exciting place. For me, anyway, the distant promise of the mountains left it feeling like a town where you might stop for refreshments before continuing to where you really wanted to be. However, it was pleasant enough and it had what we wanted – an estate agent – just off the pretty main square.

'I'll let you do all that stuff,' said Kevin, as I prepared to go inside.

I could see that he was eyeing a Prisunic store, a kind of French Woolworths, with an obvious yearning.

'You're just going to buy lots of pants, aren't you?'

Kevin always did this. He likes buying his pants abroad. I'm not sure if it's a fetish or not, but if it is I don't know the name of it.

'I might do,' he said innocently. 'I'll see you back here in half an hour.'

'What exactly is it that you are seeking?' asked the smug-looking thirty-something agent.

I toyed with saying that I was seeking 'enlightenment and spiritual fulfilment' but then I remembered that estate agents generally aren't good at that sort of stuff.

Monsieur L'Agent was smartly dressed in a dapper suit, with a trendy hairstyle that looked neat enough to make the photo in the window at a unisex salon. But for his dark complexion he was not unlike most of the British estate agents I'd encountered – well groomed, polite and adept at a sycophantic charm, undoubtedly nurtured to maximise profit.

'I guess I want somewhere with views of the mountains,' I replied. 'Without too much renovation work to do, reasonably private but not isolated, and within striking distance of a good-sized town where there's quite a bit going on.'

'I think that we have one just like this. It is brand new – we only took the instruction the day before today.'

Yeah, yeah, I thought. When estate agents say they have something that is 'just like' your request, it has usually involved them indulging in liberal interpretation. 'Striking distance' can be covered by 'anything reachable in just under an hour on the day when there happens to be no traffic on the roads'. 'Private' means 'own front door', and 'not requiring much renovation work' is their way of saying 'sky not visible through first-floor ceiling'.

'Can we look at it now?' I asked.

'Sure,' he replied. 'Just sign this.'

He produced a document and pushed it towards me. It was full of complicated French, but I glanced through it quickly. It seemed odd that I was having to sign something so early on in the proceedings but I guess that the agent needed to be sure that if I wanted to purchase the property we were about to see then I would do so through them and not with any other agent. I didn't bother reading the contract in detail, partly because I wouldn't have understood most of it anyway, and also I suffer from Formophobia.*

'How far away is the property?' I asked, returning the signed form to the agent's outstretched hand.

'Twenty minutes,' he replied, smiling. 'And we can go right now.'

★ ★ ★

---

*Fear of bureaucratic paperwork.

'From the particulars, it does sound like it's exactly what I'm looking for,' I said to Kevin as our car sped along behind Monsieur L'Agent on the way to the house in question. 'Usually they just talk bullshit, but I've got a feeling that he won't be wrong on this one.'

Kevin looked thoughtful for a moment, holding on tight to his big plastic bag full of pants.

'Tony, if you ended up buying this place, what would you do in it?' he said, as the drive into the mountains became ever more picturesque. 'I'm playing devil's advocate here, but isn't there a good chance that you'll just end up sitting on your own and admiring the view?'

'I'll invite friends over,' I replied defensively. 'I'll have parties. We'll go skiing in the winter and we'll have mountain walks in the summer.'

'I see,' said Kevin, who was patently aware of my deficiencies as a social secretary. I'd once invited everyone I knew to a party on my birthday, and then failed to attend it myself. (I'd been invited on holiday at short notice and had judged that to be the far better option. I left the keys to my flat with a mate, and the party was alleged to have been a great success, some of the more unkind guests saying that it had gone better than it would if I'd been present.) Kevin looked over at me with a cheeky glint in his eye. 'Yes, I'll look forward to you organising all that.'

'I can do my writing there – and it'll be a good place to practise the piano, too.'

'What?'

'No neighbours within earshot. I've always wanted that – I can bang away on the keys to my heart's content.'

'You're going to buy a house in France so you can practise the piano?'

'Let's not get ahead of ourselves,' I replied. 'I haven't even seen the place yet. I might not like it.'

The omens were good as our car nosed over the brow of a hill, revealing a large sweep of imposing mountains on the horizon. They rose up like white-helmeted granite centurions standing guard over the scores of villages spread out before them like powerless minions in the lush green rolling foothills. Monsieur L'Agent's car took a left and we followed him down a snaking single-track lane past barns and farmhouses that all seemed to overlook striking landscapes.

'So far, this is doing it for me,' I said, sensing a kind of adrenalin rush building within.

After several twists and turns we started to find that the lane changed in character, private residences taking the place of farm buildings. Most of these were modern but all seemed to be built in the characteristic architecture of the region – two-storey houses with high gabled roofs peppered with small dormer windows. We turned one more corner and then followed Monsieur L'Agent into a steep driveway on our right, where we parked and got out of the car. The view took my breath away. The house was perched on the side of a hill with a 270-degree view of undulating greenery, all against a backdrop of dramatic snow-capped peaks.

'This is it!' I said to Kevin.

'Aren't you going to look at the house?'

'Ah yes, the house.'

The house wasn't an old tumbledown farmhouse ready for loving restoration, but a twenty-year-old property that looked ready for immediate habitation. Three things made it special – location, location, location.

'That is the Pic du Midi,' said Monsieur L'Agent, pointing to a mountain in the distance, and possibly sensing from my open mouth that a quick sale was far from out of the question. 'You can ski in this place.'

I didn't tell him that we'd already done so – for half an hour, earlier that same day.

'The villages you can see dotted on the hills are all in the area called Les Baronnies.'

'Yes. It's quite a nice view,' I said, trying not to look too enthusiastic and attempting to subdue an ecstatic grin.

'Also, there is enough flat land to put in a pool if you want. Now, let us go inside.'

Oh yes. Inside. I'd forgotten about the inside, so enchanted had I been by the scenery that was stretching out before us.

The inside was pretty damn good too. 'Ready to move into' would have been the estate-agent parlance to describe it, but it would have been justified in this case. It had all the features that you're looking for in a house – windows, doors, ceilings, floors, bedrooms, a bathroom, radiators, a nice wood-burning fire, and all in excellent condition. The kitchen was a little small but that was more than compensated for by the large living room that ran the length of the house and off which was a large balcony that overlooked the view. The fabulous view. Did I mention that at all?

'You shouldn't have put an offer in there and then,' said Kevin as we drove towards Bagnères-de-Bigorre, the nearest town. 'It makes you appear too keen.'

'Well, I am keen,' I argued. 'What's the point of not appearing keen if I am?'

'It hinders the negotiating process.'

Kevin was right, of course. I'd had enough experience in the world of courtship to know that an element of duplicity in the 'negotiating process' was vital. Only the inexperienced reveal their true hand, and they usually pay the price. I often wondered what kind of God had created the absurd human trait that finds 'keen' unattractive. A mischievous one, probably.

'And what happens if they accept your offer?' continued Kevin. 'You do realise you'll be buying a house in France?'

'Will I? By God! That hadn't occurred to me. I thought we were just outside Portsmouth. I wondered where all those mountains had come from.'

'You know what I mean. I love the house too – but I'm just

being a good mate and trying to stop you rushing into something that you might regret. Have you thought it all through?'

'Kev, sometimes in life you've just got to go for things. If you think too much, stuff doesn't happen.'

'Well, houses in France don't get bought, certainly,' Kevin pointed out.

Bagnères-de-Bigorre had seen better days. It was in an idyllic location, nestled in the valley between giant mountains, but it smacked of faded glory. All around were grand, venerable buildings desperately in need of a lick of paint.

'I like this place,' I said. 'Let's find a hotel and make this our base for the night.'

'Are you sure you don't want to visit some other estate agents in some other towns?'

'Of course I'm not sure, but life would be pretty boring if we were sure of everything.'

We checked into a hotel with a superficially majestic appearance that masked an interior that was borderline decrepit. This hotel had almost certainly been built when the town was at its most fashionable, back in the nineteenth century. In the early 1800s, Bagnères had become established as one of France's leading thermal resorts, the 'in place' for the likes of Rossini and Flaubert. Now, in the early twenty-first century, it was having to make do with a visit from Hawks.

I spent the rest of the day dragging Kevin around the town, reading to him from my guidebook as we went.

'It says here that in the twentieth century,' I announced as we stood before Les Grands Thermes, the elegant healing spa that conjured up images of the town's halcyon days, 'the Pyrenees became a haven for people who were on the run, either from the Republicans at the end of the Spanish Civil War, or from the conservative establishment after the failed '67 Paris revolution.'

'Hmm.'

'I mean, how romantic is that?'

Kevin pulled a face that seemed to mean 'not very', and I detected a hint of resentment that this cultural tour was preventing him from buying more pants. Ignoring this, I dived back into the guidebook and he braced himself for further trudging.

By dinner, he was exhausted.

'I feel like Britain's leading expert on this town,' he said, pouring us a second glass of a slightly heavy red wine.

'That's good. You'll appear very knowledgeable about the place when you come to visit me.'

'Yes, well, let's not get carried away. There's a long way to go yet,' said Kevin, looking rather serious. 'The vendors probably won't accept your offer.'

The hotel breakfast was rather disappointing. Coffee, French bread and a dollop of jam are often deemed by our Gallic hosts to be a sufficiently nutritious start to the day. I was mid-mouthful when I got the call that proved Kevin wrong.

'What is it?' he said, when he saw the look of horror on my face.

'Monsieur L'Agent says that my offer has been accepted!'

Suddenly, reality had kicked in. I felt weak. What had I done?

Kevin shook my hand, and I immediately began thinking about how I could get out of things. It wasn't too late to halt proceedings. A quick phone call to Monsieur L'Agent and it would fall to him to let down the vendors.

'I can still back out of this,' I said to Kevin as he picked at the crumby remnants of his breakfast.

'Yes, but I wouldn't do that if I were you,' he replied with an air of the statesman about him. 'I think you've got it at a good price and it's an excellent house.'

'Oh,' I said, now rather confused with this sudden approval. 'I thought you were of the opinion that I'd been too reckless.'

'Oh yes. You have been ludicrously reckless, but you should still go through with it.'

By now it was beginning to dawn on me. I worked out what

had caused the sudden shift in Kevin's role from confirmed sceptic to enthusiastic supporter. Two words summed it up.

Free holidays.

It all made perfect sense. As one of my oldest friends he knew that he would naturally fall into the 'keys are yours whenever you want them' category. Overnight, he'd realised that the biggest beneficiary of my hopelessly ill-prepared lurch into the world of overseas ownership would be none other than his good self.

'So you think it's a good deal?' I said, feeling a little emotionally drained.

'Oh yes,' he said with a cheeky grin. 'Just think – soon you will be the proud owner of a home in France.'

I didn't reply. I didn't need to. The big gulp said it all.

2

Célibataire

Back in England I pondered and deliberated. I fluctuated between thinking that this purchase would be the most foolish thing I'd ever done, and giving in to bouts of reverie that saw me lying on the cool tiles of the living-room floor in my Pyrenean home as the sun streamed in through the French windows. These daydreams were vivid – I could even hear the distant reverberating bells of grazing cattle and sheep, and picture the snow-capped mountains towering over them on the horizon. In these dreamy moments it all seemed irresistible. What a contrast to the frantic pace of life in London, with all its competitiveness, noise, pollution, flurry, stress and anxiety.

However, there were doubts too. Big ones. Surely buying a property overseas was the preserve of the married couple? Hadn't Kevin been right to ask his question: 'Isn't there a good chance that you'll just end up sitting on your own and admiring the view?' Also, at a time when more and more English people were moving to France and pushing up the price of property so much that it was becoming difficult for locals to buy, wasn't there a risk that I was going to be greeted by aloofness and resentment? Would a single forty-four-year-old man be accepted with open arms into a remote Pyrenean village?

Every night in bed, the doubts and the dreams fought it out in the battleground of my mind, until one further consideration started to tip the balance in favour of returning to France to sign the contracts.

The small matter of the piano . . .

It wasn't until I was at the back end of my adolescent years that I'd begun to fall in love with the piano. From the age of eleven I'd dutifully done my nightly twenty-minute 'piano practice', but this had largely consisted of routinely crucifying the classical pieces allotted to me by my music teacher. However, by the time I was sixteen, I had begun sitting at the keyboard for hours, experimenting with different chord sequences, composing little melodies and trying to hammer out boogie-woogie rhythms with my left hand. I started to teach myself, and I no longer felt bound by the shackles of the musical notation before me. I was playing the music of 'Tony' and whether it was any good or not didn't matter. I was expressing myself.

Soon I had made myself a little promise. One day I would find a romantic location somewhere and install myself therein with a piano, devoting my time to reaching my fullest potential on this instrument – a potential that at the time a combination of peer pressure and youthful foolishness was causing me to squander, hopelessly grappling as I was with the first throes of adulthood.

Maybe, just maybe, a quarter of a century later, it was time to honour that promise.

And that's as good a reason as any to explain why, two weeks later, I was driving down the narrow lane back to the village. I had been invited by Jean-Claude, the owner of the house, to come over to meet him and his family. We would share 'un café' before heading off together to the *notaire*'s office to sign the legal papers.

Rather inconsiderately, the UK and French authorities have completely different methods of interfering in the affairs of those who buy and sell properties. Stamp duty and the solicitor's fees all get rolled into one payment made to a fellow called the *notaire*. It's about 6 per cent of the purchase price, and frankly it's a bit steep, but that's the way it works, and who was I to question it? An occasional and quiet whinge would be the way I dealt with this inconvenience, much in the way that the British deal with most problems encountered abroad.

The system also differs in that the *notaire* represents both the vendor and the purchaser. One might imagine that this could open up the *notaire* to bribery – one party might seek favourable treatment by baking him a succession of delicious cakes. How could I be sure that the *notaire* who was allotted to me hadn't already been nobbled? How did I know that he wasn't one of those Frenchmen who allegedly hate the English? What could I possibly do to even things up if I had no access to decent baking facilities?

As I drove, my thoughts turned from worries about the *notaire* to concerns about the property I was actually here to purchase. As I turned the final corner, I felt a tingle of nerves. Well, more than a tingle. A veritable knot. What if I went off the place? The fear of the ghastly error returned with a sudden savagery. Being single, I'd had no partner with whom I could talk this whole thing through. Instead of endless pillow talk on the pros and cons of the purchase, I'd relied on 'trusting my gut', and now I was seriously beginning to wonder if it had let me down.

Immense relief greeted me, then, after that final turn on the narrow lane. Instead of regret, there was comfort. I loved what I saw. It may not have been the loveliest of days, and the view of the mountains may have been concealed by a blanket of grey clouds, but the house looked warm, welcoming, inviting and reassuring as it nestled neatly on the hillside. This felt right.

I stood on the front porch and rang the bell, perhaps for the last time if the next few days went well. Maybe on the next occasion I was here, I'd have a big bundle of keys and a list of chores as long as the garden.

The door opened and there stood a stocky, burly man. I was struck by an immediate thought. Rugby player. The house was in the heart of French rugby country, and there was no doubting that the man before me had indulged. His cauliflower ears bore testimony to a youth misspent grovelling around in mauls and scrums.

'*Bonjour, je suis Jean-Claude,*' he said. 'You are Tony, yes?'

I nodded and Jean-Claude shook my hand. It was a big, second-row-of-the-scrum-type shake. We sat down for drinks and I looked around the house. Although it wasn't decorated to my taste, it looked cosy and I could easily picture just how nice I could make it. Soon I was chatting to Jean-Claude's wife Annie and his thirteen-year-old son Jérôme, as well as being offered some rather delicious cakes that Annie had baked herself. This worried me a little. Could it be that the *notaire* had already been the beneficiary of this culinary talent?

After refreshments, Jean-Claude treated me to a technical tour of the house. Soon I was being lectured on radiators, boilers, ovens, fridges and fuseboxes. Everything was being explained at great length, but only a few centimetres were being taken in.

'*Il est simple, Monsieur Tony,*' said Jean-Claude as he leaned over a drain in the garden.

He was on his haunches, endeavouring to explain something which, despite his '*il est simple, Tony*', patently wasn't simple. A house's drainage system is a complex business even when related to you in your native tongue, but now my rusty A-level French was being severely tested by Jean-Claude's rapid-fire delivery of technical plumbing information, spiced up with a strange twang that I took to be a regional accent. I nodded profusely at the conclusion of each utterly incomprehensible sentence, thinking that not to do so would have been an act of rudeness.

Jean-Claude came across as a proud man, but an affable one who liked to laugh, particularly at his own jokes. I took each of his guffaws as a cue to smile politely, assuming them to be emitted at the conclusion of what he believed to be an extremely humorous remark. The explanation of the exact location of the septic tank was terminated with a comment of such hilarity that this also required copious giggling from both his wife and son – although this seemed to be more dutiful than spontaneous, an ersatz chuckle which appeared to be something they could produce on demand.

After the detailed house tour, Jean-Claude announced that we should leave right away for Bagnères or we would be late for our appointment at the *notaire*'s office. Another tingle of nerves. This purchase was getting ever closer to the point of no return.

The *notaire*, or rather our *notaire*, wasn't at all what I was expecting. He didn't seem a legal type at all. I felt he had more the demeanour of a maverick doctor – the type that gets struck off for seducing patients. Tie-less and in rolled-up shirtsleeves, he had a cheeky grin and a mischievous glint in his eye. In his bland office in a Bagnères backstreet, he ushered me to sit down. He kicked off proceedings with a menu of the bureaucratic courses that were to follow. Jean-Claude and his wife Annie were beside me, whilst Monsieur L'Agent was seated on the periphery of proceedings, ready to offer timely translations of big words. Appropriately enough, the whole thing had the air of the registry office about it – after all, I was on the verge of making a huge commitment.

For what was supposed to be a formal meeting in a lawyer's office there was an awful lot of jollity. Jean-Claude and the *notaire* laughed at each other's jokes and Monsieur L'Agent tittered obsequiously. I did my best to join in by smiling at everyone, but since I didn't really know what was going on and couldn't respond with a comment, this probably just made me look like a vacuous buffoon. Or a politician.

Irritatingly, the *notaire* found something about me deeply amusing, and every time he looked my way it was accompanied by a smirk or a snigger, followed by a comment that prompted laughter from all present. I felt like the new boy at school – totally ignorant of how things worked, unaware of who held what status, and nervous about what to do when laughed at. I was hugely relieved when the *notaire* finally got down to formal business and began reading from a document.

It began with the personal details of the vendor. Jean–Claude was announced as being a married '*fonctionnaire*' – a state worker or civil servant. This prompted approving nods all round.

I was next.

'*Monsieur Tony Orchs*,' announced the *notaire*. '*Ecrivain*.' (Writer.) All present turned and looked at me, raised their eyebrows and then looked at each other. Then the *notaire* said something, and everyone began chuckling. I smiled, but with the faintest hint of resentment. What could the joke have been? Had it been derogatory? Had it even been that funny? One thing was for sure, I would have to brush up on my French as a matter of urgency so that in future I could respond appropriately when this kind of banter kicked in.

'*Monsieur Orchs*,' continued the *notaire*. '*Demeurant à Londres, Angleterre – célibataire*.'

Upon delivery of this last word, he looked up, threw his head back and made a comment that drew the biggest laugh so far. Even Monsieur L'Agent, who'd been doing his best to be professional, laughed this time. I was getting a bit fed up now. Instead of smiling, I chose to adopt a gentle scowl. I didn't much like the way this meeting was being conducted. *Célibataire* I knew meant 'bachelor'. What was there to laugh about? Had the *notaire* made some comment questioning why I might still be a bachelor at my age? Had there been some homophobic questioning of my sexuality? What else, I wondered, could have caused such merriment?

I guess I was also irritated by the very word itself. *Célibataire*. What a terrible word for bachelor. To think the Académie Française in Paris is desperate to preserve the purity of the French language and to defend it against the increasing pressure of Anglicisation. What's the point of preserving a language that calls a bachelor like me a *célibataire*? It has all the wrong implications. Instead of coming across as a carefree, fun-loving man about town who has a new girl on his arm every month, it has the ring of a loser who can't get his leg over however hard he tries. '*Monsieur Orchs – celibate.*' How dare they! It was true that I'd split up with my girlfriend some months previously and I hadn't exactly been a Don Juan since then, but I'd got off with lots of girls in my life and I was still extremely capable of getting off with a lot more. I was tempted to stand up and argue this point, warning them to lock up their daughters when the sale was completed and I moved into town.

Fortunately a part of me reminded myself that this probably wasn't the best way to kick things off as an outsider trying to establish himself in a quiet little community.

My smouldering indignation was suddenly punctured by the voice of the *notaire* who had launched into a long passage of French 'legalese'.

'*Le vendeur en s'obligeant aux conditions générales qui suivent . . .*'
This continued for some time, and I had to stop myself day-dreaming. I had to keep reminding myself that this was important stuff that was legally binding and involved a lot of money. It was hard, though, because the *notaire* kept droning on about lead and asbestos inspections, service charges, local taxes and insurance. It really wasn't any fun at all.

Soon, though, when the *notaire* read out the price Jean-Claude was getting for the property, I became very interested, although the fun level dipped to an all-time low. It seemed that Jean-Claude was receiving considerably less than I was paying for the property. How could this be? I questioned it, and Monsieur L'Agent, who up until this point had been motionless, shuffled awkwardly in his seat. After much discussion, the agent explained that the discrepancy was created by his commission on the sale. It was 10 per cent. An awful lot of money, given that I'd walked into his office and bought the first property he'd shown me.

'What's this?' I protested to the agent. 'You can't charge this much, surely? That's 10 per cent – in Britain the agent takes no more than 2 or 3 per cent, and anyway the vendor pays that – not the purchaser.'

'But you signed the papers agreeing to this,' he replied.

'Did I?'

'Yes. Look.'

He produced the document I'd signed when I first went into his office. Oh dear. Immediately I knew that my formophobia hadn't done me any favours. If I'd read the form properly I would have seen that I was agreeing to pay a fat 10 per cent commission to a fat agent who did sweet FA. (He wasn't fat actually, but he bloody well ought to have been.)

I felt a knot of anger materialise in my stomach.

'I've been well and truly stitched up here,' I said, dispensing with the polite and simple English with which I'd addressed him thus far.

'Not so,' he said.

'Yes so,' I said indignantly. 'I am not happy about this level of commission. I'm not sure that I'm prepared to sign the papers now.'

Monsieur L'Agent looked suddenly concerned and he leant forward towards me to exclude the others.

'Do not worry about this,' he said, conspiratorially. 'This fee is negotiable. We will discuss it later. Also, you should know that under French law, the purchaser is entitled to a seven-day cooling-off period after signing the contract.'

I felt hugely relieved. If, in few days' time, I still felt that I'd been utterly shafted, I could back out and not lose my deposit.

So, when the *notaire* eased the large piece of paper towards me with both his and Jean-Claude's signatures on it . . . I signed.

I felt a bit sick, but I signed. The commission was negotiable after all. It was time to get tough.

I'm not very good at getting tough. It's so much less preferable to 'mucking about'. It was at times like these that I had to concede that I was an adult living in the 'big world'. To some extent I'd been cosseted from these kinds of situations, swanning around as I had done in a world of entertainment, happy in the knowledge that if things got a little bit tricky, then my agent would sort it. The irony of this situation was that this particular agent was well and truly sorting it. Sorting it so that a good chunk of my money ended up in his pocket.

After saying goodbye to Jean-Claude and the *notaire*, I stood in the rain outside the office with my newfound foe.

'OK, let's negotiate,' I said, trying to sound like a hard man from a Hollywood blockbuster. 'Maybe 5 per cent is a fairer figure for me to pay. And anyway – you didn't explain that the form I signed would give you 10 per cent and my French isn't that good.'

Monsieur L'Agent got shifty.

'I have to call my boss.'

He made the call on his mobile and I waited patiently for the outcome. After a few minutes of hushed exchanges, he folded up his phone and turned to me, rather sheepishly. The rain was falling hard around us on the dark backstreet, making me feel like a shady character in a film involved in some illicit underworld transaction.

'My boss says that the fee is not negotiable,' he said, displaying something not far from a hangdog expression.

'What rubbish,' I said. 'Of course it's negotiable. Call him straight back and give me the phone.'

'He does not speak English.'

'Never mind,' I said crossly. 'I can speak enough French to make my point.'

This statement turned out to be untrue. Arguing in French, I was soon to realise, requires a more comprehensive vocabulary than the one on which I could draw. As soon as I had taken the phone and stumbled to my first point, Monsieur le Boss, who was evidently a quick-tempered man, raised his voice and launched into a tirade that suggested he wasn't embracing my rationale.

It was such a shame that I'd signed a document agreeing to the very thing that I was now contesting. That didn't really strengthen my position. My only argument was that the document had not been properly explained to me and that I had almost been bullied into signing it. However, when it came to it, all the French words that would have helped convey this completely eluded me. I attempted to make my case, but my sentence stuttered and stumbled before it eventually ground to a halt.

'*Il faut expliquer que* . . . er . . . um, er . . . er . . . er . . . er . . . *il ya un problème* . . . er . . . *je* . . . er . . . er . . . er . . . *est-ce que* . . .'

My adversary would hardly have felt that he was up against a heavyweight debater. Oh how I longed for the vocabulary that the situation demanded: 'Look here, matey, if this commission isn't negotiable, which seems to be the main thrust of your recent ill-mannered and unprofessional diatribe, then how come your employee assured me in the *notaire*'s office that it was? Eh? Answer me that!'

But it was no good. The required words wouldn't come. Some were secreting themselves in the dark recesses of my memory bank, and some had simply never been there in the first place. The only half-baked sentences I did manage were shouted down by the manic ramblings of my foe. Realising that the argument was lost, I resorted to English, because, though I say so myself, I'm rather good at that.

'You are a greedy little man,' I said, puffing out my chest and handing the phone back to Monsieur L'Agent.

Not big. Not particularly clever. But it made me feel a bit better.

I'd calmed down considerably by the time I made it back to the village, but I was still cross. I felt cheated, and I was no longer sure that I was prepared to go through with the transaction. Also, the dispute at the *notaire*'s meant that I was now running twenty minutes late for lunch at Malcolm and Anne's. Surely they wouldn't mind? They'd probably been living in the south of France long enough to have developed a healthy regard for those who shun meticulous punctuality.

Jean-Claude had suggested I meet them. He'd announced rather excitedly over coffee that there was an English couple in the village who were 'très gentils' and who often came round to his place to watch big rugby matches on his TV. I had telephoned them to say hello and they'd immediately invited me round for lunch.

As I made the scenic ten-minute walk from Jean-Claude's to Malcolm and Anne's house, I decided that the village wasn't really a village at all. Kevin and I had driven round it after the first visit to the house and we'd discovered that it was more of a hamlet – a group of houses dotted around on the two sides of a pretty valley. There was no main street with shop, bar or post office. Rather ludicrously, however, for something of its size, it did have a small church and a *mairie*, or town hall. This meant that it was given the administrative status of '*un village*', complete with the trappings of a mayor and a deputy mayor, plus planning and social committees. All for a population of 130.

Having walked up the gentle incline past several of my potential neighbours-to-be, I reached a small fork in the road. I was immediately greeted by a boisterous gaggle of chickens, geese and ducks. It was almost as if they were questioning my very presence. 'What are you doing here? We're not sure if we approve of your sort – I mean, you're not from round here, are you, mate?' Foul fowl.

I left the noisy birds behind and turned left down the narrow lane that led down one side of the valley. Soon it would rise steeply again, leading the walker to the other 'half' of the village, but I didn't need to go that far. My destination was on my right, marked with a sign saying 'Gîtes de France'. For a moment I amused myself with the idea that Malcolm and Anne were advertising themselves as 'French gits', but I knew that it far more likely meant that they had converted a part of their house into self-contained accommodation that could be rented out in keeping with the regulations of the French Tourist Board. That must have been a fun process to go through, I thought, as I walked up the steep gravel path.

Soon I could see a couple in their mid- to late forties standing on the terrace in front of a house that bore a strong resemblance to the one I'd spent the morning endeavouring to buy. As I drew closer, the couple (who were now smiling and waving) became more clearly defined. They were both light-framed, and they sported deep suntans, shorts and stress-free expressions.

'Welcome to the village,' said Malcolm.

'Thanks,' I said, resisting an initial urge to point out that it wasn't really a village.

'Come and eat,' said Anne, directing me to a table on the terrace.

I sat down and basked in the spring sun, looking out across a view that included a different mountain to the one visible from my place, owing to the more westerly aspect of the house. As we tucked into charcuterie accompanied by tomato salad, it soon became clear that I was with two very kind people who shared my sense of humour and relaxed outlook. I felt confident that we would become friends.

Malcolm and Anne had done what many British people dreamt of doing – they'd left the rat race behind. Malcolm had been an accountant and Anne a teacher, and whilst neither had been unhappy in their work, they'd felt sure that they somehow wanted more. That 'more' had turned out to be a Pyrenean home and a relaxed lifestyle, financed by organising walking tours and renting out the apartment they'd created on the second floor of their tranquil home.

'Another glass?' enquired Malcolm, bottle of red wine poised in his left hand.

'Oh, why not?' I said, demonstrating a will of aluminium.

'So, how is the purchase going?' asked Anne.

I explained about the morning's fracas with the estate agents.

'You've got a two-week cooling-off period,' Malcolm reminded me.

'Yes, that's an excellent idea, that is,' I said. 'I need to reflect a little back in England. I'm still not certain that this is the right thing to do.'

'Well, if you do go through with it,' said Anne, 'you can rest assured that you've picked a terrific part of the Pyrenees. When Malcolm and I decided that we wanted to come out here, we spent nine months searching for the decent-sized town that we wanted to be near. After extensive research, we decided that it was Bagnères. Then we rented accommodation there and began the hunt for the right house in the right village.'

'And you're happy here?'

'It's wonderful,' said Malcolm.

'You couldn't have found a village made up of a nicer bunch of people,' said Anne.

This is exactly what you want to hear when you've just bought the first house you've seen, having done no research and made no comparisons with any other houses whatsoever. It was nice to know that my wild, irresponsible and reckless leap into the French housing market could receive such comprehensive endorsement. I appeared to have landed on my feet, even though I'd broken every rule in the book when it comes to buying property abroad. I hadn't even had the house surveyed. Well, I thought, why bother? I decided some time ago that I wasn't a 'make sure you have a survey done' kind of person. I like to think that I could see if a house was falling down. I had an eye for that sort of thing. If there happened to be any hidden dangers such as subsidence or rising damp, then I would rely on my guts to instil me with a healthy feeling of unease about the place. I was something of a hippy in this regard. I went for it because it felt right.

'It feels right here,' I said, as Malcolm and Anne cleared away the plates. 'But do you think I'll fit in here OK? I mean, an Englishman buying a house on his own – aren't they going to think I'm a bit weird?'

'I think you'll be fine,' said Malcolm. 'As long as you speak a bit of the language and turn up to some of the social events, they'll take you to their hearts.'

'Great,' I said, raising my glass, taking the final sip of red wine and staring off into the soothing horizon.

Momentarily it felt like I could peer into the future, and I could picture it all vividly – me seated at my piano, gazing into the mountains, poised and ready to compose my masterpiece.

'You look happy,' said Anne.

And she was right. I was.

3

White Van Man

Back in London I began to wonder what piano I was going to play in my new mountain retreat. It seemed that either I had to look around and buy one when I got there, or I could take my own piano out with me – the iron-framed upright with the tone and action that I loved; the piano that had provided me with hours of pleasure; the piano that felt as much like a friend as a hefty mass of wood, iron and ivory could possibly be.

Upon reflection I decided that I couldn't be unfaithful and get a new one. Besides, I would have enough on my plate when I got to my new home without having to drive to Toulouse to look at pianos, purchase one and then wait for delivery. That would lose me valuable practising time, and I wanted to start my new and strict training regime just as soon as possible.

Of course, the question remained as to how I was going to get the instrument out to France. There was the easy option of instructing a removal company, but this would be expensive and it seemed somehow soulless. I preferred the alternative of hiring a van and driving it down there myself. That way, I figured, would allow for some emotional attachment to the whole experience and it would somehow mean more when I sat at the piano and played it. I have often felt that in the course of making our lives easier (and by that I mean by hiring people to do the donkey work or unpleasant tasks for us), we miss out on experiences that can enrich our lives and enable us both to learn and to acquire wisdom. We live in a culture where people avoid strenuous tasks and hard manual labour but pay vast monthly sums to join gyms where they work their nuts off trying to get fit and lovely-looking. (I, by the way, have always managed to remain lovely-looking without recourse to such cold and heartless places.)

I started looking into hiring a van.

'Get a Luton,' said Ron.

Ron had started out as my builder, but fifteen years and a succession of extensions, kitchens and bathrooms had left him as someone I now considered a friend. Most of my other friends thought that rather odd. I'd crossed some kind of line that they thought ought to exist between builder and customer.

'Don't pay him for the job until he's finished the skirting boards,' would be the kind of thing I'd hear.

'I can't do that,' I'd reply. 'It's Ron. He'll finish them eventually.'

And he always did. I was never disappointed, provided I was prepared to accept that 'eventually' was a period of anything up to two years.

Through no real fault of his own, over the years Ron has acquired for me the unenviable role of 'sage of all things practical and mechanical'. Whenever advice is needed in the vast realms of human endeavour where my knowledge is minimal, Ron will get a call and will offer up his best. In spite of the fact that most of the time this involves him uttering the words 'Sorry, Tone, but I don't really know much about that', it has never stopped me returning for guidance. It's not that he's good, more that I don't know anyone better.

'Besides a piano, are you going to take other stuff down with you as well?' he asked.

'Yes. A settee, a couple of beds, a sideboard and loads of boxes.'

'Well, in that case it's got to be a Luton. You can get so much more in them – they've got loads more available square footage than your long-wheelbase high-top transit.'

Cleverly, Ron had spouted a lot of technical stuff that meant nothing to me. Never mind that I hadn't understood what he'd been talking about, it had sounded impressive enough for me to be convinced of its wisdom. Until someone came along and spouted some better mumbo-jumbo, then this would remain my position.

So, for now, a Luton van it was.

When I spoke to Tim, he thought it was a good idea too. So good, in fact, that he wanted in on the whole thing.

'If you're going to hire a van, can I bung some stuff in and come with you? My place is virtually on the way, we could stop there for an overnight, dump my gear and then carry on to yours.'

'Sounds great,' I replied. 'That would make the whole thing much more fun.'

'Do you think there'll be enough room?'

'I should think so because I'm going to hire a Luton and they've got loads more available square footage than your long-wheelbase high-top transit.'

'Are you sure you want to go ahead with this, even though the house isn't legally yours yet? I mean, what if it all falls through?'

'It won't all fall through. It'll be fine.'

'OK, your call. But how much is it going to cost?'

'Leave it to me, Tim,' I said. 'I'll get some prices and get back to you.'

The first few quotes seemed a little high: £520 for four days, plus mileage. A glance at the map reminded me just how far it was to the foothills of the Pyrenees, and I began to balk at the prospect of making both the outward and return journey in such a short period of time. It wasn't long, though, before I came up with a brilliant idea.

I would buy a Luton van.

It made perfect sense. I would find one that was old but reliable, one that I could use at my French residence for the summer, and then, depending on its condition and how much I'd paid for it in the first place, I could either drive it back to England and sell it, or simply dump it in France. The added advantage of this was that Tim and I could fly back, thus halving our driving workload and doubling the fun.

'Are you sure that buying is a good idea?' asked Tim, over the phone.

'It's a bit risky, but we should be fine. I'll get the van checked over before I buy anything.'

'All right. Go for it.'

In the following days I discovered that Luton vans in my price bracket (I'd given myself a budget of £1500 maximum) are most sought-after vehicles. Every time I answered an advert in one of the trade magazines I received the reply, 'Sorry, mate, but it went this morning.' Obviously those in search of second-hand Luton vans buy the papers the day the ads go in and then mobilise themselves to make a swift purchase and see off the opposition. The only ones available were upwards of three grand and that was too much to make the project economically viable.

After two weeks of being called 'mate' and hearing that vans had 'just gone', I began to reconsider the hiring option. That was until, almost as a last resort, I quickly surfed the internet and to my amazement discovered a Ford Transit Luton Van that seemed perfect. When I say perfect, it is important to remember that I was not looking for a van that was in fabulous condition since I only really needed it to be able to complete one journey. And so a broad smile came across my face when I read the following advert.

1983 Ford Transit Luton Van. Some bodywork damage owing to accident. MOT and tax one month remaining. Runs good. Click below for a photo.

When I saw the photo, I was genuinely excited. More excited than I had ever been before on viewing a really poor quality van. Perverse though it may have been, the van's shortcomings were the very cause of my exhilaration. Its dents, short MOT and tax, and age were all positive boons. After all, the intention was to dump this van as soon as I got it to the Pyrenees, so there wasn't much point in paying for luxuries like good bodywork and long MOTs if they were never going to be required. Plus there was the excellent news contained in the two-word description: 'Runs good.' Never mind that the advertiser had used an adjective when an adverb had been required, the vehicle was a nice little runner, and that mattered more than grammatical accuracy.

'Ron!' I called excitedly down the phone. 'If I give you twenty quid, will you come and look a van over for me?'

'I suppose so,' replied Ron, with little enthusiasm.

'It sounds like it's exactly what I'm looking for.'

'How much is it?'

'They're asking for £250.'

'Oh God.'

'Get round here for eight in the morning and we'll head off together from here.'

'Oh, all right.'

Ron was often available at short notice partly because he had no family commitments. He had a family – just no commitments. He'd been married before and he had three grown-up children, but the marriage had disintegrated when the children were very young and he'd played little part in their upbringing. After his second marriage had run into difficulties, Ron had begun to withdraw from the world and he now lived on a narrow boat that was moored alongside an island in the Thames. There was no bridge to the island and he had to row to and from his slender floating home in a bashed-up little dinghy. It was splendidly eccentric.

The downside of this arrangement was that he would spend long winter evenings holed up in a narrow boat that was as thin as its name might suggest, and that didn't even allow him enough headroom to stand up straight. Those of us that knew him well had become a little worried that in recent years he had begun to pass too much time in this confined space. Ron was slowly closing himself off to the world. He had become a kind of millionaire recluse, without the money.

The van was parked on the driveway as Ron and I pulled into the suburban Croydon address. It was slightly more bashed up than it had looked in its photo. The whole offside wing was twisted and gnarled. It looked like it had been through a mincer.

'Bloody hell!' gasped Ron.

'Let's not jump to conclusions,' I countered, putting a positive spin on things. 'Remember – beauty is only skin deep.'

'Yes, but there's such a thing as skin cancer.'

'Let's see how it runs. If it runs good, then that's all that matters.'

'Hmmm.'

I rang the front door bell and was greeted by Fred, a middle-aged man with grey hair who looked like he ran a business that made him worry a good deal.

'Morning,' he said cordially as he shook my hand. 'I'll start her up and I'll take you for a spin round the block.'

We moseyed over to the van, climbed into the cab and Ron and I waited in anticipation as Fred plunged the key into the ignition, looking surprisingly confident. Ron looked across at me resignedly as Fred turned the key clockwise, but to his tangible astonishment, the engine fired up and began to tick over, albeit somewhat noisily. Rather impressive, especially after what had been quite a cold night. I threw Ron an 'oh ye of little faith' look and he responded with the cursory raising of an eyebrow.

'You have to leave it a few minutes to warm up,' said Fred. 'And you need to keep the choke out. It's best to use this.'

Fred took a clothes peg from the dashboard and clipped it around the choke.

'The spring on the choke is bust, but this does the job OK,' he added, almost suavely, as if clothes pegs were a design feature.

Finally we set off. The van jumped forward noisily and slowly, but it worked its way through the gears well enough and it definitely went in the direction it was pointed in without any trouble. So far, so good.

Having negotiated a narrow road, Fred turned us into a deserted industrial estate where he began to open up the accelerator.

'What do you want it for?' he then asked, unwittingly expressing what Ron was clearly thinking.

'I need to take a load of furniture and a piano down to France,' I replied. 'So it needs to do one long journey at least.'

'Oh, this van'll definitely get you to France,' he said confidently. 'This van runs good.'

And with those words Fred nonchalantly spun us into a left turn. So nonchalantly, in fact, that he failed to notice the sports car that seemed to appear from nowhere.

'Fred! Look out!' I shouted.

Fred, whose mind had clearly been distracted by proud thoughts of how 'good' his van ran, suddenly saw the blue sports car directly in front of him and slammed on the brakes whilst heaving the steering wheel to the left. I caught a glimpse of the horrified face of the driver in the sports car as he took evasive action. Surely it was too late. A collision was inevitable. However, the van's brakes performed exceptionally well and for a split second it appeared that we would just miss each other. But then BANG!!

Time seemed to stand still. All I can remember is seeing the rear end of a sports car spiral out of view as a direct result of Fred's sizeable vehicle smashing into it. A moment of silent realisation. Three men sat in the cab of a stationary Luton van looking ahead into an open road, without daring to turn their heads to view the motorcar with which it had just collided. Ron looked at me. I looked at Ron. The minimal eyebrow movement said it all. I chanced a glance at Fred, whose skin had turned a pallid grey, almost matching his hair.

'Shit!' he said, under his breath.

Shit indeed, I thought, as Fred gathered himself and then slowly descended from the cab to go and inspect the damage that his leviathan 1983 Luton Transit had inflicted on the impish sports car.

'He must have written it off,' I said, still in disbelief.

'I don't want to be here,' said Ron with a nervous giggle and visible shiver, stating something which had always been the case but which had been accentuated by recent events.

Five minutes must have passed. Five quiet minutes. Ron and I said little. What was there to say? Although I was longing to see what damage Fred had done to the sports car, it didn't seem right to hop out of the cab and watch him whilst he tried to sort matters. All Ron and I felt able to do was sit and wait, and then see what mood Fred would be in when he eventually returned to the van.

The shocked hush of the cab was finally broken by the return of a surprisingly upbeat Fred.

'Sorry about that,' he said. 'These things happen. Still, it's all been sorted with a handshake.'

'What?' I asked, incredulously.

'Well, he agreed that it was his fault. He was on the wrong side of the road when I hit him. He's happy to pay for his own repairs.'

What a result for Fred, I thought. As far as I had seen he'd been at fault, but somehow he'd managed to talk his way out of it.

'What about the damage to the van?' I asked, my mind turning to more selfish concerns.

'Not too bad. The front right indicator is completely smashed and a bit of the bumper has fallen off – but I'll knock money off for that, obviously.'

And with those words Fred restarted the van and calmly drove us back to his house.

I was now faced with an interesting dilemma. Should I go ahead and buy the van? The engine seemed to work fine, but it had been a wreck when we'd arrived to view it, and now, only ten minutes later, its condition had deteriorated still further. Ron circled the van with the air of a predator, studying tyres and generally doing things that might justify a twenty-quid call-out fee.

'What do you think?' I asked him when he'd run out of things to prod.

'I think it's a piece of shit.'

'Oh.' I thought for a moment. 'Shall I offer 150 quid?'

Ron scratched his head. 'Not a penny more,' he said eventually, almost with disdain.

Fifteen minutes later I was driving the van back to my place. I was indeed proud, sitting up high in the cab of my new old vehicle. I'd never owned a van before and now I owned a bloody big one. I felt rather macho too. This was me, Tony, who up to this point in life had always felt rather intimidated by van drivers and the men who inhabited that world. Now here I was, one of them. Tough, brash, strong, self-sufficient, and able to wind down the window and shout 'Orrlright darlin'!' to adjacent blonde birds. It's true that this image was slightly tarnished by the fact that Ron was following behind in his car to check that I was all right, but nonetheless I was doing it – I was driving a big van, a van that I owned, and I was doing it damn well.

The wheels started to come off (thankfully only metaphorically) shortly after Ron left me to fend for myself when I stopped for petrol. Fred had told me that the petrol gauge had broken and that it was safer to fill her up 'as soon as poss'. I pulled in alongside the pumps, descended from the cab and headed for where I thought the petrol cap would be. Nothing. I looked on the other side. Nothing. I looked around, about, above, below, around again, but I couldn't find the bloody petrol cap anywhere. Like a fool I even checked the glove compartment (the handle came off in my hand) for a manual, but that really was overly optimistic.

At this point it is worth taking a moment to mention an unwritten rule of the road. Generally speaking, in this chauvinistic dominion it is deemed forgivable if a woman fails to locate a petrol cap. Sometimes even a man can be forgiven, provided that he is an artsy-fartsy, namby-pamby type, who clearly wouldn't make heterosexuality his specialist subject on *Mastermind*. However, there is a tacit understanding that those who drive around in large Luton vans are fully compos mentis with how their vehicle works. And by that I mean that they would be expected to throw the bonnet open at the slightest hint of engine trouble and sort the problem out with minimal fuss. Anyone in charge of a large van who fails in this regard lets the rest down very badly. It's not unfair to say, therefore, that it is generally accepted that the driver of a big Luton van ought to be able to find the petrol cap when he is in a filling station. Unaided.

I, however, was not coming up with any answers as to the location of the petrol cap, and cars were beginning to build into a queue behind me. In desperation, I looked around for help. I needed to ask someone but I was scared. I didn't want to admit that I was a bloke in a van who couldn't find his petrol cap. It would just be too, too, embarrassing.

There were two other van drivers on the forecourt and I took a deep breath and tried to determine which one looked less like he had a criminal record, which, as it happened, wasn't an obvious choice. I selected the stocky redheaded man on the grounds that his van was cleaner and that this might mean he was a more compassionate type. I was fully aware, however, that as soon as I opened my mouth I would lose all dignity.

'Excuse me,' I asked somewhat pathetically as he withdrew the pump nozzle from his shiny white van, 'but I've just bought that van over there and I . . . I . . .'

I was so embarrassed it felt like I wouldn't be able to cough the words out. I tried again.

'I . . . I . . . was wondering if you happened to know where the petrol cap is.'

The man looked over to my vehicle. He shook his head. 'You just bought that?'

'Yes.'

He shook his head. 'Bloody hell.' He just stood there looking at the van in amazement.

'You're looking at its worst side,' I said, noticing for the first time how unroadworthy it appeared. 'It's not so knackered on the other side.'

'I should bloody hope not.'

'Yes. Now, about the petrol cap. Any idea where it is?'

'Course I do. The cap sits on top of the tank on those things. It's on the passenger side underneath the vehicle. You'll probably 'ave to get down pretty low to see it.'

'Right. Silly me. Thanks.'

I walked away in disgrace, but at least I'd accessed the required information without getting beaten up. Nightmare over.

Or maybe not. Seconds later, having located the petrol cap, I then discovered that I couldn't remove it. All three of the keys that Fred had given me completely failed to release the obstinate cap, however much I wiggled, twisted and forced. Despair. I looked up behind me to see the queue of cars building, with frustrated drivers reversing, tutting and pulling their cars into different filling aisles. A child on a bike was laughing. The woman in the car immediately behind me grimaced. There was nothing for it but to suffer the humiliation of seeking help again.

I looked around me and I didn't much like what I saw. People were either consumed by their tank-filling duties or sitting in their vehicles looking decidedly pissed off with me because I was holding them up. So I decided there was only one thing for it, and I walked into the garage shop and got the attention of the last man in the queue. The stocky redheaded man.

'Excuse me,' I offered apologetically, 'but when you've paid your bill – would you mind helping me get my petrol cap off? It seems to be stuck.'

The man looked at me in seeming disbelief. His eyes were penetrating and fierce and I was relieved that we were in a public place. He hesitated and then drew breath.

'Yeah, all right,' he said begrudgingly.

Major relief.

'Thank you very much,' I said, trying and failing to sound polite but not wet, before adding unnecessarily, 'I'll be by the van.'

The man nodded solemnly, and I turned to leave. As I walked towards the door, I clearly heard another male voice declare a succinct and unselfconscious opinion of me.

'Tosser.'

I didn't turn to see who it was.

It was a relief to get the van home and shut the front door on it. The rest of the journey had been without incident, at least until I'd reached my house. Allowing myself to relax a tad, I'd begun the process of backing the van onto my driveway. With care I studied the wing mirrors and eased the vehicle towards the front of the house, but it wasn't long before I was reminded both of the height of the van and the presence of the tiled porch that overhung the front door. This reminder came precisely at the moment the van smashed into the porch, removing several tiles in the process. This had been the van's second accident in just under an hour and a half.

It would be important in the future to get this 'accident per hour' ratio down a little.

In the following days, the van posed outside my property, providing those in the neighbourhood with the opportunity to speculate on how and why my career had nosedived so spectacularly. In the meantime, I was not idle. I called Steve the mechanic (recommended by Ron) and charged him with the task of looking over the van and making sure it would make one long journey. Then I got on the phone to insurance companies and, despite huge difficulties finding any insurers who would provide breakdown cover for a van of that age, I did manage to find one who would cover us for France, but not the UK. Having bought the policy, I felt hugely relieved, because even if we only got the van as far as Calais, if it broke down then, at least we had the reassurance of knowing we could get towed the rest of the way.

When I arrived at his lock-up, Steve offered what was fast becoming a stock response for those viewing the van for the first time – a shake of the head followed by 'bloody hell'. However, after a full morning's work, he felt quite confident that it would make the journey. I was now armed with a new battery and alternator, and the front right indicator had been replaced, albeit with an indicator normally meant for a Ford Escort.

'It doesn't look pretty,' said Steve, eyeing the van with anything but a sense of pride in his work. 'But I reckon it will get you there.'

'Great,' I said eagerly. 'All we need to do now is pack it, and then we're ready.'

It was one of my former colleagues from the five-a-side football team who masterminded the loading of the piano. To my amazement, Brad had volunteered. I suppose I shouldn't have been surprised. For a creative type, Brad is good at practical things and enjoys solving problems. In the past he'd helped me build a little home recording studio, and quite an impressive shed for the garden. So he was someone I felt able to trust in supervising the daunting task of piano removal that lay ahead of us.

The plan had been to hoist it into the back of the van using four strong men, but Brad had other ideas.

'You don't need to bother anyone else,' he said. 'You and I can get it in there between us.'

I didn't like the sound of where he was going. Even though

mathematical statistics weren't my speciality, I strongly suspected that by reducing the available workforce by half, that would double the workload for us.

'Are you sure about this?' I enquired tentatively.

'Yes. We need to create a ramp,' he said, looking optimistically into the back of the van, which must have come up to at least waist-high on him. 'The piano's got wheels on it, so that way we can just push it into the back.'

In the hour that followed, Brad improvised with all kinds of stuff that he found in the house – steel bedframe, wooden shelving, gaffer tape and half-inch screws – to produce a feat of engineering which would have made, if not Isambard Kingdom Brunel, then certainly Heath Robinson, proud.

Moments later the piano was slowly and painstakingly pushed up the ramp and into its new temporary home. I gave Brad a high five in a peculiarly un-British way.

'We're on our way!' I said with a beaming smile. 'Next stop – the Pyrenees.'

4

The Incredible Journey

Tim and I had decided on an early start. We figured that if we could be on the channel tunnel train for 8.30am we could steam through France and make Limoges before nightfall, in time for a well-deserved dinner. I rose at 5.15am and felt particularly good about things. I was looking forward to going to France, and I was pleased that I'd be able to spend time with Tim. Apart from the odd game of five-a-side football we'd not been able to get together as much as I'd have liked in the past few years, his life having been saturated with the exhausting but joyous task of raising two small children. The hours in the van would afford us a wonderful opportunity to fill the unwelcome gaps in our friendship that the paraphernalia of life had caused.

'All set?' said Tim chirpily, as he rolled round to my place at 5.30am on the dot.

'I'm ready,' I replied. 'Let's do it.'

We loaded our overnight bags into the back of the van, checked that our various boxes and items of furniture weren't going to move about too much, pulled down the metal shutter and clambered into the cab.

'Here goes,' I said a tad nervously as I put the keys into the ignition. 'Fingers crossed.'

There'd been no need to worry. The little beauty started first time. I smiled at Tim, revved up the accelerator, popped it into first, and allowed the engine to haul us out of the driveway and onto the road. It was 5.40am and we were on our way, off to France with our metaphorical bundles in the back of the van – off to seek maybe not our fortunes, but something. Just what it was, neither of us really knew, but perhaps the journey would reveal that to us.

I made a right at the end of my road and slipped the van into fourth gear for the first time. We began to gather speed and I started to swell with pride. There had been those who had scoffed at this plan. A significant few had expressed their doubts as to the wisdom of the 'old van' approach, but already we were only a couple of hours away from victory. Even if we did encounter mechanical problems in France, the recovery insurance would kick in and we could be happily towed to our final destination.

Tim and I began our first conversation of the trip, experimenting with the volume levels that would be required on board such a noisy vehicle.

'Sleep well last night?' I called out, perhaps slightly louder than necessary.

'Like a baby,' he shouted back.

I didn't ask if this meant that he'd woken every two hours screaming and then fouled himself.

'For once I guess you were up before the kids.'

'Yup. They were still sleeping soundly as I—'

BANG!

A loud explosion beneath us. I felt all power die from the accelerator and all I could do was steer.

'What on earth was that?' I called across to Tim, who had gone pale.

'I don't know, but it didn't sound good.'

I tried the accelerator again. Nothing. I had no choice but to let the van drift gently and peacefully into a parking place that happily opened up for us in this busy residential street. I braked and the van drew to a halt. I stared ahead in disbelief.

'That wasn't a good sound, was it?' I said, turning to face Tim.

'No. I've heard that once before – on my mate Dave Dilley's car.'

'And what had happened?'

'The engine had blown up.'

A silence. I cannot speak for Tim, but I was suddenly swamped with an overwhelming sense of defeat. In just a matter of seconds my dreams had gone up in smoke, as a cough from Tim confirmed.

I turned the ignition key. Nothing. Absolutely dead.

'This isn't good,' I said, once again stating the bloody obvious.

And then we both sat in silence for probably another minute. Tim, out of respect, was probably allowing me the time and space to evaluate the situation. He knew full well that it had been my plan, that it was my van, and that it was me who had to come to terms with the humiliation.

'What are we going to do?' I asked, breaking a deafening silence.

'Hmm. Tricky one that,' shrugged Tim, who clearly wasn't about to adopt the mantle of 'situation saviour'. 'How long would it take us to walk back to your house?'

'About five minutes.'

'Well, shall we wander back, have a cup of tea and discuss the options?'

'Good idea.'

The TV programme *The Weakest Link* proudly boasts a 'walk of shame' in which contestants are filmed in close-up as they shuffle off the set when they are voted off the show. That 'walk of shame' cannot hold a candle to the one that I now walked. My walk home was longer (although not by a huge margin) and enabled the 'walker' more time to reflect on what had just occurred. Having proudly set off for a distant mountain range on the French/Spanish border, the vehicle in which the 'walker' had invested time, money and to some extent his credibility had exploded within a few hundred metres of his house. Each awful step took him past upsettingly familiar houses as the words of Fred, the previous owner, resounded in his head: 'Oh this van'll definitely get you to France.' Each agonising pace drew him towards the postbox at the end of his road and ever closer to his home and his kitchen kettle, still tragically warm from its all too recent use.

At the breakfast table Tim tried to be upbeat.

'We were lucky it happened here I suppose,' he pointed out. 'Rather than in the middle of Kent.'

He was right enough, but it was too early for me to view anything about this incident as 'lucky'.

'Is it worth getting the AA out to see if they can get it going?' he asked, mustering as much enthusiasm as such a sentence could allow him.

'Tim, that van is dead,' I muttered sadly and unequivocally. 'I think what we witnessed there was the big end going.'

I'd often heard this expression used – 'The big end's gone' – and even though I had no understanding of what it meant in terms of mechanics, I was completely sure that this was what had just happened to my van.

'That van is scrapheap bound,' I continued. 'I am not prepared to put a further penny into it. The only thing we can do is hire another one and start again.'

And in that moment I knew that my period of temporary madness was over and I had finally come to my senses. I was now doing what I should have done in the first place. It made no economic sense to carry on with this van. My outlay thus far had been:

COST OF RON'S WISDOM:	£20.00
COST OF VAN:	£150.00

FULL TANK OF PETROL:	£45.00
REPLACEMENT OF INDICATOR:	£50.00
NEW ALTERNATOR AND BATTERY:	£80.00
BREAKDOWN RECOVERY INSURANCE FOR FRANCE:	£50.00
2 x BUDGET RETURN FLIGHTS (since these would remain unused as we would now have to drive the hire van back):	£120.00
TOTAL COST:	£515.00

It's important to remember that this total of £515.00 had to be measured against the distance covered before the engine blew up. A measly 1000 metres. The van had effectively cost me 51.5p a metre. Calculated at this rate, the journey to the Pyrenees would have ended up costing about £515,000.

'I'll make another pot of tea,' I said, authoritatively.

And why the hell not? There were another two hours to kill before the van-hire people turned up.

It turned out to be quite an exhausting day. Once the reams of paperwork had been completed and the new van had been hired (and boy did it look new compared to what we'd just been in), we had an unenviable task ahead of us. We had to empty onto the roadside the contents of a Luton van that had taken hours to pack, before loading it all onto a new one. Just as Tim pointed out how 'lucky' we were to have a nice bright morning in which to complete the undertaking, rain clouds appeared, in preparation for drenching us and our gear at the most inconvenient moment. Fortunately the piano's second movement (pun intended) was simpler than the first, because we were able to drag it from one van to the other by putting the vans back to back. Anxious onlookers emerged, no doubt from Neighbourhood Watch. They looked on in both wonder and dismay as Tim waved his arms and guided me and the pristine Luton van into position, butting it end to end with the stranded, disgraced and completely shitty one. The whole operation gave everyone a brief glimpse of a downmarket version of a rocket ship docking with its mother station in space. However, on successful completion of the mission there were no whoops and hollers from Houston, just dirty looks from disapproving local residents, followed by some eager piano-wheeling from two rather desperate-looking figures.

We were on the road again at one o'clock, with a load comprising two tired men (one with an empty wallet and bruised ego) and a considerable amount of damp furniture and boxes. Initially we made good headway, but then, as if we were being karmically punished for past misdemeanours, we discovered that the M20 was closed between junctions 9 and 10. A huge detour was necessary through rural Kent, affording us a snapshot of the idyllic 'little England' that each year people leave in their droves for retirement in Spain, Italy, France and elsewhere. In spite of this briefest of glimpses of the tranquil England of cricket greens, oast houses and quaint villages, it didn't leave me thinking: why am I leaving for France when I can have this? Maybe this is because much of the English countryside doesn't really feel like the country – more like large green areas with easy access to motorways that can speed you into cities. The quaint villages aren't necessarily full of quaint villagers, and the nicest houses are invariably inhabited by CEOs and retired city traders. And even though it isn't crowded, it still feels like it's bang on the edge of crowded.

How marked the contrast then as soon as we emerged from the tunnel and began to drive through Normandy. The farrago of vans, lorries and cars that had so clogged the latter part of our British drive seemed to dissipate the instant we touched French soil. Quite where it all went remains a mystery but the roads were empty and, like magic, large vistas of green rolling hills opened up around us. Tired though we were, it felt good to be in a new country, especially in a nice safe vehicle with no fears of imminent breakdown, and with an engine volume that allowed easy conversation.

The fact that we hadn't hit Calais until 6pm local time did mean that we were hopelessly behind schedule. We pressed on heroically, however, circumnavigating Paris with some difficulty and finding ourselves, much to our surprise, eulogising on the merits of the M25. Paris lacks a simple peripheral motorway and the road signs that are supposed to guide you around the city are like coquettes that lead you on with the promise of your destination only to disappear at the moment your passions are most aroused.

By 1am we started to fade and left the *péage* in search of a place to lay our weary heads. Fortunately we were in a country whose entrepreneurs had taken it upon themselves to cater for the travelling motorist who chooses to push on into the night. France is well served by newly constructed budget hotels situated on industrial estates near major roads. They offer very little, but to be fair they only ask for 20–25 euros in return. Armed only with a credit card, the guest can struggle with a machine (in our case, bad temperedly) and then be given a slip of paper containing four digits that allow access to a small room. The accommodation is spartan but the bed is so welcoming to the exhausted driver that it matters little. However, what did matter on this occasion was that we were inheriting a room from the man with the smelliest feet in France. The moment we opened the door the smell was quite over-powering. We were immediately faced with a major drawback of these hotels: none of one's dealings are with human beings. However much Tim and I wanted to, it would have been fruitless to go back to the machine and bellow at it until it had the common decency to provide us with a room that didn't smell like a cross between a cheese shop and a rugby changing room. So instead we collapsed resignedly onto the disappointingly hard beds.

'Well, Tim, it's been an interesting day,' I said. 'What mark would you give it out of ten?'

Tim mused for a minute.

'I think a five would be fairest.'

And he was right. We had successfully avoided death, injury, robbery and assault and we were in a new country where we'd found a bed for the night and a roof over our heads.

We couldn't shut the door though. That would have been too risky. There was too grave a danger of passing away peacefully in our sleep as the first known victims of 'lorry driver's feet', so we had to sleep with our coats on and with the door wedged open, leaving ourselves hopelessly vulnerable to a random theft or mugging.

'I remember the last time you slept in that leather jacket,' said Tim, wriggling around in a futile search for comfort. 'It was in that dodgy hotel in Salamanca.'

'Oh Christ,' I said. 'Don't remind me about that weekend.'

It had all looked so promising. Many years previously the two of us had headed off to Spain for a long weekend and we'd ended up in the picturesque Spanish town of Salamanca. On the Saturday night we'd met two fabulous girls and we'd had the most amazing evening. They were both beautiful, spoke fluent English and, happily, Tim and I each fancied different ones so we weren't fighting over the same girl. Their interest was reciprocal. We drank wine, joked, laughed and danced into the night. It was incredible. Tim and I were smitten. So smitten in fact that we made no attempt to try and kiss the girls other than in a polite way when the whole magical evening drew to a close. What was the hurry when they were that gorgeous and that much fun? Besides, we were going to spend all of the next day and evening together. We had agreed that we'd all head off in our hire car to Portugal together.

At midday the next day, as arranged, Tim and I waited for Arantxa and Mercedes in front of the cathedral. We were ready for the most romantic adventure of our lives thus far.

The girls were late. No sign of them by 12.15.

OK, we thought. A woman's prerogative.

The girls were very late. No sign of them by 12.30.

OK, we thought. A Spanish woman's prerogative.

By 12.45, still nothing. We were running out of prerogatives.

At 1pm we began to wonder if there was another cathedral and we were at the wrong one. There was absolutely no way we could have misread the signals the night before. No question – the two girls had enjoyed an amazing night and, like us, they were well on the way to falling in love. There had to be a reason why they weren't there at the cathedral. They must have got held up in some way. There must have been some kind of incident.

Tim and I took a picnic lunch on the cathedral steps and continued to wait. We would not give up hope. We wandered the streets nearby. We peered into hotel receptions. Maybe the girls had overslept – after all, it had been getting light when we'd parted company the night before. But nothing. By 3pm there was no sign of them anywhere and there was nothing else for it but to give up, and so we plodded back to our car, distraught and heartbroken.

During the sombre car journey back to Madrid we discussed all the possibilities for what could have happened to Arantxa and Mercedes. In the end we decided that there was only one plausible explanation.

They must have been murdered.

Tim shuffled on his hard bed, turned towards me and frowned. I didn't know whether this had been brought on by the room's smell or the painful memory of Salamanca.

'Those poor girls,' said Tim, shifting onto his side ready to have a stab at sleeping. 'Funny how a double killing like that never made the papers.'

'Yes, it was very odd.'

'Goodnight.'

'Goodnight.'

In the morning, after a surprisingly good night's sleep, we made our way back to the van to continue our epic journey. As we walked past the credit-card machine with our bags, we waved cordially but we were ignored. No acknowledgement, not even a nod or a 'Have a nice day'. We felt used. Frankly, once those machines have swallowed and then regurgitated your credit cards, they don't give a toss. This was an example of twenty-first century 'progress'.

No wonder finding a house in a French village was so appealing.

Tim's house was in a picturesque rural setting with lovely hill views, but was much more of a 'project' than mine. It had been a ruin when he and Lucy had bought it, but extensive works were now only months away from completion. Tim had avoided all the drama and constant disappointment that usually accompanies such building projects by cleverly giving the job to one of his best mates, Matt, who had formerly been his partner in an amusing double act that had worked the London comedy circuit for a few years. Despite prospects for a promising career as an actor, Matt had thrown in the showbiz towel when his girlfriend Helen had become pregnant, and shortly afterwards they'd moved out to this region of France with barely a franc in their pockets, setting up home in a barn.★ Now, fifteen years later, Matt and Helen had fostered a successful building business, added two more children, and embraced convention by shunning 'barn life' and moving into a house.

They were working on Tim's property when we arrived and they greeted us with enthusiastic hugs and kisses, which suggested that fifteen years of living in France had meant they'd more than embraced the concept of French salutations. And perhaps they were pleased to see us, too.

'How was the journey?' asked Helen.

'Ah,' said Tim.

'Perhaps we should tell you about it over a cup of tea,' I said.

And a terrific cup it was, over which the story of the 'journey

---

★Their first born son would be lucky enough to be able to go through life leaving doors wide open, and when challenged with the question, 'Were you born in a barn?' would be able to reply, 'Yes.')

thus far' was related, much to Matt and Helen's amusement. Then a new plan was formulated. It was decided that Matt would travel with us on the next part of the journey. This would give me and Tim another driver, and Matt the chance to catch up on a decade of news. It had been a satisfyingly spontaneous decision, and one to which Helen had acceded with great generosity of spirit.

'The chance for you to be three lads together in a Luton van?' she'd said. 'How can I deny you that?'

'Three lads in a van' (and I use the word 'lad' more in reference to gender than age) turned out to be great fun. For us, the *autoroute* south now became 'Memory Lane' as we discussed stories from London's comedy circuit during the late 1980s, successful and unsuccessful sexual liaisons and past girlfriends, all of which were peppered with the occasional mention of football. And we laughed. How we laughed.

And then, somewhere along the seemingly endless stretch of motorway, perhaps between Montauban and Toulouse, the banter suddenly matured and became surprisingly philosophical and analytical. Tales of past conquests and humiliations gave way to more reflective discussions about life and love, and where we all were. Of course, we were all in a Luton van working our way towards the Pyrenees, but where were we on our life journey? And being the only one who hadn't followed the more conventional path of finding a partner and raising a family, my life invited the closest scrutiny. Matt and Tim fired question after question at me: what age had I been when my parents had divorced? What was my relationship like now with my parents? Why had I split up with my last girlfriend?

It was Matt who asked the hardest question.

'What about love, Tony? Have you ever been in love?'

A very tricky question indeed.

'Well,' I replied uncomfortably, 'I know it sounds an incredible thing for a forty-four-year-old man to say – but I don't think that I ever have. Of course, it depends how you define it.'

'What do you mean?'

'Well, there are lots of meanings for love, aren't there? I mean, you can love your sister and you can love your dog.'

'Yes, but you're not supposed to sleep with them,' said Tim.

'Maybe there were moments with Lianne,' I continued, ignoring Tim's facetious remark. 'And Clare. But the closest to really being in love was probably with Fi. Remember her?'

'Ah yes, Fiona!' said Tim with a smile, no doubt recalling the many fun nights the three of us had spent together over a decade before. 'Nothing ever actually happened with that though, did it?'

'Things almost happened – but the trouble was that she was still in love with her ex-boyfriend. In the end she went back to him. He lived in Ibiza.'

'Well, I'm not sure if it counts as being in love if it remains unreciprocated,' said Matt, taking on the role of adjudicator. 'So Fiona doesn't count.'

'I even wrote a song for her,' I mused, surprising myself with the frankness of my confession.

'Really?' said Tim.

'In that case perhaps Fiona should count,' said the adjudicator.

'Yes, I think she should too,' said Tim.

'Right,' I said. 'Whatever you boys think.'

'The main thing,' said Tim, 'is that you're ready to get stuck in again.'

'Agreed,' said Matt. 'What type of girl would be right for you?'

I shrugged. This was all getting to feel like I was on the psychiatrist's couch – but for the fact that I was sitting bolt upright and driving a big white van on a French motorway. The questions went on and, despite feeling a little under the diagnostic cosh, I answered each one as honestly as I could, and by the time we'd successfully negotiated Toulouse's *périphérique*, a conclusion had been drawn by my two amateur psychologists. Basically, I was a man who expected a great deal of a partner in a relationship and perhaps I needed to find a way to be more understanding and tolerant of weaknesses and faults. Secondly, it was agreed that often in the past I had been attracted to personalities who were ambitious and who needed to prove themselves in some way.

'What you need, Tone,' said Tim, elbow out of window, map of France open on his lap, 'is someone independent, who likes what she does but doesn't need to measure her success in terms of achievements.'

'Right,' I said, almost subordinately, as if there was a new hierarchy in the cab and I was now student to Matt and Tim's university tutor.

'Maybe,' continued Tim, 'you need someone simpler – more at peace with themselves, who can support and encourage you, but still with enough enthusiasm for their projects so as to maintain your interest in them.'

'Right,' I said with a nod.

'And with nice tits,' added Matt.

At least one of us had remembered that we were three blokes in the cab of a white Luton van.

'Perhaps you'll find someone in France,' said Tim.

'Yeah – a nice French girl,' Matt chirped boisterously. 'With nice tits.'

'Yes, thanks, Matt,' I interjected. 'Well, let's see what happens, shall we?'

And the van sped on.

Half an hour after Toulouse, the Pyrenees rose defiantly and majestically to our left. These snow-capped peaks have formed the natural boundary between France and Spain, the buffer between two cultures, and frequently the escape route for dissidents, freedom fighters and escaped prisoners of war. We were now in the French *département* of Hautes-Pyrénées, which before the French Revolution had been known as Bigorre. This was where my new home was situated. A home that was looking in fine form by the time we reached it. Tim and Matt approved of the location.

'Wow!' said Matt, whilst Tim offered a whistling sound of admiration.

I swelled with pride and went to knock on the door, an act that reminded me that I wasn't yet the legal owner. Soon Jean-Claude and family were helping us unload the van with a surprising and most welcome gusto and enthusiasm.

'*Ah, Tony – tu joues du piano!*' Jean-Claude observed on noting the instrument that slowly revealed itself from beneath tables, chairs and an assortment of bedding.

'*Oui,*' I replied, offering a few playful notes of blues as my accomplices began to shuffle it down the van.

'*Très bien,*' he said with a nod, whilst his wife and son looked on in amazement as if I'd just performed a magic trick.

The addition of French brawn (Jean-Claude's rugby-playing past now even more acutely evident) meant that the piano was off-loaded without further incident, and it was left to relax in its new home – the garage beneath a French house in the foothills of the Pyrenees. Here, I hoped, it would have time to acclimatise itself to its new surroundings so that when I returned it would be ready to ease my fingers across its keys, perhaps towards some inspirational melodies.

We spent a frustratingly short amount of time in what I'd now taken to calling 'nearly my house', partly because we'd arrived on a day when the family were anxious to leave for an outing. There was only time to give my two English psychotherapists a short tour, which involved a lot of nodding and smiling at Jean-Claude, who followed us at every turn. All too quickly we were climbing back into the van whilst the family waved us off, completely oblivious to the disasters that had befallen its predecessor and ignorant of the gargantuan effort we had made to get there.

'You've done well there,' said Tim, looking back at the house as we pulled away.

'Yeah,' said Matt. 'For someone who gave it about half an hour's thought, this is a bit of a result.'

I hoped they were right.

After drinks with Malcolm and Anne and a meal in town, we were back on the road again. It wasn't until shortly after we'd rejoined the motorway that I noticed my leather jacket was missing, complete with the diary nestling in its pocket. A quick search of the van confirmed that it was not on board – and I felt pretty confident that on departure I had stashed it in the cab by my feet near the offside door. Irritatingly, I could only conclude that it had fallen out of the cab when I'd opened the door to collect the ticket for entry to the *péage*.

'That makes it your fault, Tim,' I said, trying to remain jovial. 'Because if you'd parked nearer to the ticket machine I wouldn't have had to open the door.'

'All right, Hawks, you win,' said Tim. 'We'll go back for your poxy jacket.'

A fruitless journey though, because on arriving for the second time at the entrance to the *péage*, there was no sign of my jacket.

'Bugger,' I said. 'Someone must have made off with it.'

'You've had that jacket too long anyway,' said Matt. 'You were wearing it fifteen years ago.'

'It's the diary I'm bothered about. There's some after-dinner speaking engagements in it that I haven't got round to copying into my other diary.'

'Never mind,' said Tim. 'Let's just hope whoever finds it turns up and does them for you.'

'It'll probably be funnier,' joked Matt.

'Maybe it fell out of the van on Jean-Claude's drive before we left,' said Tim. 'Why don't you give him a quick call and check?'

Tim had correctly identified another possibility and the call had to be made, however much I hated making phone calls in French. I was at a level in the language where I needed to see who was speaking to me so that I could follow the contours of their mouths as they framed the words, and where I could have the option if necessary of drawing pictures on a piece of paper when things went horribly wrong. Phone calls were scary things.

'Can you do it for me?' I said to Matt. 'You're better at French than me.'

'I know, but I want to see you squirm,' he replied.

Amidst much childish tittering I made the call, immediately struggling to form the correct sentence. I wanted to say that I thought that I might have dropped my jacket somewhere on his driveway – but I couldn't think of the word for jacket and I didn't know the word for driveway. And so Matt got his way. He saw me squirm. Momentarily lifted by the fact that the word for 'jacket' magically popped into my head, I launched into a long sentence in which I attempted to get my meaning across. I'm not sure if I was entirely successful because on its completion there was silence at the end of the line, followed by a slightly pained '*Comment?*' (The polite way in French of saying, 'What in God's name was all that about?') I had another go, but, again, with little apparent success because Jean-Claude countered with a long and speedily delivered sentence, the intonation of which suggested that it might be a question. Shortly afterwards I said my goodbyes and hung up.

'Well?' enquired Tim, whilst Matt, who had recently descended into fits of giggles, looked on. 'Is it there or not?'

'I'm not sure,' I replied. 'But I don't think so.'

'You bloody idiot,' said Matt, once he regained a modicum of composure. 'You screwed up big time.'

'How?'

'Instead of using the word *blouson*, which means "jacket", you used the word *bouchon*, which means "cork". You just asked him if he could look and see if you dropped your cork somewhere outside his house.'

Tim now joined Matt in raucous laughter, causing the van to swerve rather dangerously towards the hard shoulder.

'Then,' continued Matt, 'you asked him if he would call you on your mobile as a matter of urgency if he found your cork lying anywhere around the place – so that we could then turn the van round and go back for it.'

Oh dear. My credibility with the vendor would be in tatters. All future negotiations would be tarnished by his belief that I was a strange and celibate bachelor with an unreasonable and obsessive attachment to corks.

We were just outside Paris when I got the explanation of what had happened to the jacket. I received a call to my mobile from a French woman who explained that she had found the jacket, picked it up, and then found my mobile number in the front of my diary.

'Fancy turning round and going back?' I enquired of Tim, Matt having been released from the van several hours back.

'Don't want to sound selfish,' he replied dryly, 'but I think you'll have to go back for it another time.'

'Fair enough, I suppose. Anyway – I'll be back in a month to sign the papers and formally take over the house.'

'Perhaps this jacket lady will turn out to be the woman for you,' said Tim with a cheeky grin. 'What did she sound like?'

'Well, she had a nice voice,' I said, 'but there didn't seem to be any major reason to suggest a blossoming romance.'

'That'll come,' said Tim. 'I mean, talk about fate drawing you two together. She's all the things you could want in a woman – resourceful, kind, public-spirited, and has a car.'

'Yes,' I said, sceptically. 'I'll let you know.'

5

Cows, Cows and More Cows

'Blimey, how far were you hoping to get in this thing?' asked the man who'd come to tow the van away.

To say that he was eyeing the abandoned white van disparagingly doesn't do justice to the extent to which he'd managed to contort his face.

'The French Pyrenees,' I said, not without shame, whilst furtively looking around me hoping that no one else in the road would overhear.

'Bloody hell!' he exclaimed. 'In that thing you'd have been lucky to get to the end of this road.'

Then he thought for a moment and added, 'Well, you didn't, obviously.'

'No, I didn't.'

Then I gave him a cheque for £70 and he hooked up the front of the disgraced van to some kind of hoist and towed the bloody thing away.

Final bill then: £585.00. A bargain.

★ ★ ★

A few weeks later I was back in France to sign the papers that would make the house mine, all mine. As I sped along the motorway in the hire car, I was fully prepared for the many administrative chores that lay in store for me. I was also ready for potential romance. I knew that I was probably being a ridiculous dreamer, but I couldn't help wondering if there might be something special about to happen between me and 'Jacket Lady'.

Tim was responsible for this. His words had refused to leave me. And I was rather fascinated by the way in which this woman and I had made contact. The romantic in me wanted to be sitting at a dinner table in years to come answering the question about how we'd met. It would probably trigger a round of applause from all present – the finest example of a relationship that was simply meant to be.

We had spoken on the phone a week previously, but a combination of her lack of English and my incompetence in telephone French had made it impossible to fathom whether we had anything in common. All I knew was that she had quite a nice voice. I felt a tingle of nerves as I drove the car into Tarbes and began to follow the muddled directions to her apartment that I'd taken down. On the passenger seat next to me there was a beautiful bouquet of flowers. Well, I'd thought, even if there wasn't a hint of a spark between us, she deserved a big thank-you anyway. She'd 'saved' my leather jacket, after all. And if she was gorgeous? Well, the flowers weren't going to do me any harm.

Jacket Lady lived in a block of flats that looked just like those I remembered from a photograph in my first French textbook at school. They'd probably been 'state of the art' when they'd been built in the 1970s, but they hadn't aged well. I pulled over in the car and tooted my horn, as I had been instructed to do. I picked up the flowers, got out of the car and stood there, watching the exit to the flats in anticipation. Then my heart sank. An elderly lady appeared, grey-haired, perhaps in her late sixties. Surely this couldn't be Jacket Lady? The voice I'd heard on the phone had almost certainly been that of a younger woman than this. Surely I couldn't have got it so wrong.

I sighed with relief when the lady emerged from the doorway and then turned to the left, moving away from me. Good, it wasn't her. I could now get on with the job of fixing my eyes upon the doorway, hoping to be delighted by the imminent emergence of an attractive, sophisticated woman in her mid-thirties. A minute passed. Jacket Lady was certainly taking her time. Perhaps she was sprucing herself up and making herself look even more lovely. Maybe, like me, she had felt that there was something special in the way that we had been drawn together. Did she also suspect that we might have been supposed to meet?

I continued to stare at the doorway, but no one appeared. Suddenly I was startled by a voice coming from my right.

'You are Tony?'

I knew that voice. I'd heard it twice before over the telephone. I spun round to see her standing before me, holding my leather jacket in her left hand. An attractive, sophisticated lady in her mid-thirties? Not at all. This was the same sixty-something woman I had seen moments before. She must have gone to get my jacket from her car before coming to say hello. Terrible news.

'You are Tony?' she repeated.

'Yes,' I replied, trying to conceal my spectacular and foolish disappointment.

'*Votre blouson*,' she said, handing me the jacket.

That voice. So young-sounding. How did she do that? Why did she do that? So unfair. No doubt she had been a fine-looking woman in her day. Unfortunately for me, that day had been February 5th, 1966.

'*Merci*,' I said, shaking her hand and making a mental note to scold Tim for having built up my hopes so high.

Suddenly I became aware of the bouquet of flowers that I was clutching close by my side, and I held them out in front of me.

'*Pour vous*,' I said.

'*Ah merci,*' said the lady with the faintest of smiles, taking the flowers with her free hand. '*Au revoir.*'

And that was it. Immediately she turned and walked back towards the same doorway from which she had materialised minutes before in all her grandmotherly splendour. No invitation to her apartment for tea. No cordial small talk. With the brisk and calculating efficiency of Cold War spies, we'd exchanged items and parted company. The job done, there was no reason to hang around.

I walked back to my car, opened the door and slumped into the seat. Love, it seemed, would have to wait. At least until after lunch.

Lunch found me once again at Malcolm and Anne's. When they'd heard I was coming back to the village, they'd been quick with the invitation. I was grateful to them for their hospitality, and it felt good to have some company to take my mind off the morning's disappointment.

'What are you doing tomorrow?' asked Anne, as she chomped on some charcuterie.

'In the morning we have the last signing session at the *notaire*'s office, which will finally make the house mine.'

'Oh that's a shame – you won't get to do the *transhumance*.'

'*Transhumance*?'

Anne explained that this was an annual event in the pastoral calendar, during which the cattle are moved from the hilly fields that surround the village up to mountainous grazing. This is done so that the lowland pastures can be used for producing hay through the summer months, which can then be fed to the cattle through the winter. I was told that anyone could tag along, and they did so in quite large numbers.

'And what would I do, if I were able to join in?' I enquired. 'I have very little experience with cows.'

Up until this point in my life, all contact with these creatures had been limited to frosty staring matches on country walks (which I always lost), or, back in the days before I'd given up eating meat, surveying small bits of them arriving on my dinner plate. These latter encounters had somehow made up for all the unsatisfactory staring matches, as they acted as comforting proof that I had been the one who'd finally prevailed.

'All we do is follow the cows,' said Anne. 'It's easy.'

'Sounds fun. If I didn't have the other appointment, I definitely would have been up for it.'

This wasn't entirely true. The truth was that to me it seemed like an event that lacked pizzazz. Walking behind cows? It didn't quite do it for me.

'Where are you going to stay tonight?' asked Malcolm.

'At a hotel in the town,' I replied.

'Why don't you stay here?' he continued. 'The loft apartment is empty. It's yours if you want it.'

'Really?'

'Of course, now go and get your stuff.'

Wow. The locals appeared to be taking me to their bosom. Well, the Anglo-Saxon ones, at any rate.

The afternoon saw the first of the many managerial chores that face any overseas home-purchaser. I needed to open a bank account. We forget just how laden our adult lives have become with administrative and bureaucratic baggage. Because we have taken a number of years to acquire our bank accounts, credit cards, insurance policies, driver's licences, national insurance numbers and the rest, we have forgotten just how uninspiring and tedious each individual acquisition happened to be. Now that I had chosen to establish my bureaucratic presence in a new nation state, a veritable plethora of dreary, pompous and largely incomprehensible French paperwork lay in wait for me.

I was blissfully unaware of this as I drove into town and so my mood was still upbeat. Bagnères was big enough to offer a selection of banks, and so it would be important to make the right choice.

Obviously it would be best to find one that could offer favourable interest rates on any lump sums that I may deposit. Furthermore I would require my bank to be understanding, and sympathetic to the different problems faced by the foreigner with a new home. I would need to take care.

I didn't take care though. Far from it. Instead I proceeded to choose my bank on the basis of which one was nearest to the spot where I'd managed to park.

I guess this was a conscious rebellion against the increasingly large section of our media that continually instructs us to be careful with our money. TV and radio 'money' programmes and thousands of column inches in our newspapers and magazines advise us how to invest, avoid tax or move our money about, seemingly unconcerned that our lives are being frittered away beneath the heavy duvet of pecuniary prudence. They constantly tell us to shop around in the financial marketplace, overlooking all the much nicer things we could be doing with our time. Would we prefer to talk to a spotty bloke in glasses from Lloyds TSB about an investment account, or go for a nice stroll in the country? Not that difficult a choice for me. Besides, financial planning is actually so much easier than they make out. Here's all you need to do: earn a bit, spend a bit and stash a bit under the bed. It needn't be any more complicated than that − and that's why the pleasingly adjacent Banque Populaire was good enough for me. It was a bank, it was popular, and it was just over the road.

Having negotiated a series of high-security doors and buzzers, I found myself in an environment more like an office than a bank. French banks have chosen to put their security at the street end of things, so once inside one encounters no bullet-proof screens or grilles through which to address the teller. No, it's nice and familiar − and dead easy to hold the place up, provided that you manage to sneak a gun in under your coat and don't mind the fact that there's no escape. (How irritating to have all that money, and then only be able to open a deposit account with it.)

After a brief chat with the agreeable and very pretty young lady who greeted new arrivals from behind a pristine and shiny desk, I was ushered upstairs where I had a pleasing meeting with the charming, healthily bronzed Monsieur Daressy. He assured me (from behind another shiny and pristine desk) that I'd made the right choice in picking their bank. It felt extremely good to have my rigorous selection process so promptly endorsed. Monsieur Daressy was extremely helpful and filled out all the forms for me, occasionally throwing in the odd word in English, after which he looked up and beamed at me for approval.

Twenty minutes later I emerged from the bank's security system and onto the street, now in possession of a newly opened bank account, numerous pieces of paper that meant little or nothing to me, and a not altogether wholesome attraction to the girl on the front desk.

Emboldened by this success, I decided to call in at the *notaire*'s office, just to check that everything was OK for the following day's meeting.

The *notaire* – the man who had sniggered at Tony the *célibataire* at that preliminary meeting months ago – was not there. His assistant, a lady lacking in the charms of the bank teller, was unable to find anything about the meeting in the *notaire*'s diary. A flurry of phone calls and asking around the office produced no tangible results. No one had any knowledge of an impending meeting and signing.

'*Mais c'est extraordinaire,*' I complained, before being handed the phone to sort it all out for myself.

The first call I made was to my dear friend, the estate agent Monsieur L'Agent, who quickly established that he was totally in the dark about any meeting. So then, rather nervously, I called the vendor Jean-Claude on his work number. The nerves were because I feared that as soon as he heard my voice he would almost certainly be expecting me to launch into a further barrage of enquiries regarding the whereabouts of my cork.

'*Ah, bonjour, Tony,*' he said as he answered the phone, almost with a tremor in his voice.

No doubt to his great relief, I proceeded to ask about what was happening with regard to this signing session. Confused though he may have been as to why I had suddenly dropped all concerns for my cork, he was forthright in his confirmation that everybody knew about the imminent meeting and that he was fully expecting it to go ahead in the morning. All very odd. Very odd indeed.

I guess I spent about another half hour speaking to all the parties involved. The *notaire*'s secretary informed me that one month previously they had told Monsieur L'Agent that they needed him to request more documents from me, something that he had patently not done. Over the phone Monsieur L'Agent then proceeded to assure me that he knew nothing whatsoever about this. I decided to skip the call to Jean-Claude in which he would have told me that everyone knew everything and that the meeting was still on for the morning. It would have been pointless. Passing the buck, Pyrenean-style, was going on here – and it was a futile exercise trying to pin the blame on any party. Guilt was a movable feast, a cog that turned effortlessly as an integral part of a well-oiled cyclical machine. Why mess with it? Instead, I engaged in an hour of negotiations with the *notaire*'s secretary and was able to establish a new procedure that I hoped would eventually lead to me becoming the owner of this bloody house. The plan was that I would send out the missing documents by registered post and give power of attorney to the *notaire* so that the deal could be done in my absence.

'*Ça va?*' I finally asked of the secretary, her head still buried in a mountain of paperwork.

'*Oui, ça va,*' she replied.

Slightly exhausted, I walked from the *notaire*'s offices, not altogether confident that we could rely on a problem-free process from here on in. Just how much longer, I mused uneasily, was my house going to remain not my house?

★ ★ ★

That night, I dined once again with my new hosts Malcolm and Anne. Wine flowed and we chatted some more about my prospects for settling into the village.

'You don't think they'll resent another Brit buying a property?' I asked.

'God no,' said Malcolm. 'They'd sooner have a Brit than a Parisian. And anyway, they'll like you because you speak the lingo.'

'The best thing to do to really get accepted,' said Anne, 'is to throw yourself into village life and participate in every event that takes place.'

'Yes,' said Malcolm. 'You must come to the village lunch the day after tomorrow – it'll give you the chance to meet lots of your new neighbours.'

'That sounds fun,' I said.

'It's a shame you have the signing in the morning,' said Anne.

'Well, actually that's postponed now.'

'Aha!' said Anne, as Malcolm seemed to wince ever so slightly. 'Then that means you can do the *transhumance* after all!'

Ah yes, now it all fell into place. The obvious upside of having failed to make the house purchase for which the trip had been expressly designed was that I would now have the chance to follow a herd of cows up a load of hills.

'Great,' I said, suspecting that Malcolm was suppressing a snigger. 'Is it an early start?'

'No. Seven o'clock,' said Anne with a deadpan delivery that would have made many a comedian proud.

Malcolm charged my glass from a freshly opened bottle of red wine and the three of us got on with the task of becoming more than just neighbours, but friends. It seemed that we shared a comparable predilection for fine French wine, and an equivalent irresponsibility with regard to preparing for long walks up moun-tains behind cows.

The following morning at 6.45am I arose somewhat begrudgingly, disappointed to find that I had what the French call *une gueule de bois* (wooden gob), and what we British call a hangover. The atmosphere was noticeably less vibrant as Malcolm drove us to the farm that was to be our starting point.

'I won't be doing the walk myself,' he said, as his solid diesel car chugged its way up one of the locality's many available steep hills. 'I'm afraid that I've got business in town to attend to.'

He didn't look very afraid. In fact, he looked ever so slightly smug.

'Good luck,' he said as he dropped us off. 'You'll need it – it's a long way.'

'Yes,' I replied. 'Actually, I never asked, but just how far is it?'

'About 37 kilometres,' he said nonchalantly, before driving off sporting a mischievous grin.

I looked across to Anne, who seemed untroubled by this stunning announcement. She was an experienced walker and I guess she could take all this, quite literally, in her stride. But 37 kilometres? Behind cows? With a wooden throat? Not good news.

I was a little anxious as Anne and I began to wander down the muddy lane to the farm that had been delegated *transhumance* starting point. However, if I wasn't relishing the prospect of the long march ahead, it was made distinctly easier to bear because it was a beautiful, crisp, spring day. My anxiety stemmed from the realisation that I was about to meet many of my new neighbours. Today's walking companions might well represent a good proportion of the select few upon whom my future happiness depended. Just how charming could I be with a wooden throat? What if they all took an active dislike to me?

We turned the corner at the bottom of the lane and there they were, standing before a crumbling farmhouse. A gathering of twenty or so, represented by all ages, most of whom were chatting and sipping coffee from small glass tumblers.

'*Bonjour!*' announced Anne, as we drew close to them.

I was immediately approached by a gaggle of beret-adorned

young-farmer types, who shook my hand vigorously before moving off towards a big field full of cows. Two teenage girls lifted themselves up onto tiptoe and kissed me on either cheek, shuffling away immediately afterwards to rejoin their families. People smiled warmly but no one engaged me in conversation, and after a flurry of attention I was suddenly left standing on my own. I looked and felt out of place. Everyone else had a rustic feel about them, and I stank of the city. In my sweatshirt and training shoes, and without a walking stick, I felt like someone who was prepared for a sporting event at a health club, not a bucolic voyage of discovery.

Anne, the only person who had any idea who I was, had become embroiled in a deep conversation with a lady she clearly hadn't seen in ages, and so I wandered into the farmhouse in search of coffee. A lovely elderly lady greeted me, making a huge fuss of how tall I was. She turned out to be the mother of the owner of the cows that we were about to chaperone. Whilst pouring me a wickedly strong coffee, she explained how for her son it would be a difficult day because he had been kicked by a cow two days previously and had broken his foot. As a consequence, he would not be able to take part in the *transhumance* – the first one he had missed for thirty years. Lucky bugger, I thought.

'*Vous n'avez pas de bâton?*' the old lady asked, pointing to my empty right hand.

'*Er, non. C'est nécessaire?*'

What a silly question, of course it was necessary. One of the rules of the countryside is that you never go on a long walk without a walking stick, in spite of the fact that we walk absolutely everywhere else without one, mostly without falling over. Experienced hikers know full well that it is a vital ingredient in making you look the part. Thick socks, hiking boots and overlarge khaki shorts containing a disproportionate number of pockets aren't enough. You have to have a gnarled walking stick.

I tried to protest to the lady that I was happy without a crappy bit of old wood in my hand (a combination of good manners and lack of vocabulary meant that those weren't the exact words I used), but she insisted that a '*bâton*' was found for me, and a team of excited kids was enlisted to search nearby barns for stick potential. Minutes later the kitchen was full of young people thrusting bits of old wood in my direction. This went on for some time and was just beginning to nudge from 'disconcerting' towards 'uncomfortable' when I heard a call from outside announcing imminent departure. I grabbed the nearest stick, thanked the kids (all of whom were now disappointed, except the one whose stick I'd chosen) and rejoined Anne and the others.

The farmers had been busy whilst I'd been enduring my onslaught of wood, and now around thirty sturdy, muscular and impressively long cows were gathered by the farm gates, ready for the long trek to the mountains. A broad-shouldered farmer raised his stick, made a kind of gurgling sound and we all set off. How very noisy it all was. Every kind of cowbell, from tinkly to boomy, seemed to have been attached to the necks of our bovine companions. The result was a somewhat unsettling cacophony, a strange melange of 'concentrated countryside' and free jazz. Ouch! Not the best recipe for those of us with hangovers, but nonetheless my first *transhumance* was under way.

Cows walk surprisingly quickly. You'd think they'd dawdle – carrying all that soon to be dead meat on them – but no, they move along at a fair old lick. I suppose I would do the same if a bloke in a beret were hovering near my backside occasionally whacking me with a stick.

The initial part of the journey led us up and down the tortuous, narrow roads that connect the surrounding villages. We stopped twice and collected more cows from other farms, just as an army might recruit new troops on the long march into battle. Soon it felt like we were a formidable fighting force, the resounding din from our cowbells ready to strike fear into the hearts of our enemy, had we happened to have one.

I also discovered that the walking was never going to be dull, because every twenty paces or so we were required to use some nifty footwork in order to side-step newly deposited obstacles that were a few inches high, soft and slightly steamy in nature. I'm speaking, of course, of cow poo.

Your cow is an extremely unselfconscious creature. Over the centuries, particularly in Western culture, man has gone to great lengths to make the process of his bodily waste disposal a sanitised and uncompromisingly private business. Sophisticated devices are enclosed within cubicles, enabling the user to evacuate the bowels in pleasingly solitary confinement, away from the eyes of the world. Cows, on the other hand, let it drop out of their arses as they walk along. They don't even break stride. Honestly, the word 'uncouth' is too good for them.

After an hour's road trudging we passed another field of cows on our left, but this time we didn't stop and invite them to join us. These cattle belonged to a farmer who was going to keep them in the lowlands for the summer. Suddenly there was much confusion when one of our cows managed to break free from our party and wander in and join the others. Was it, I wondered, going though some kind of mid-life crisis? Had it been longing to start a new life for some time? Perhaps here it had seen a wonderful opportunity and had jumped at it with all four feet. The new life was short-lived, however, as three of our stick-wielding farmers rounded the offender up, each of them giving it an extra whack in order to communicate the error of its ways.

At the other end of this same field I could see that a bull was hard at work. Or, at least, trying to be hard at work. It was attempting to mount a cow, but the sloping field was making it extremely difficult and he kept sliding off. I stopped walking and watched with some interest, as did a few of the younger members of our party, who would soon return to their parents with some awkward questions. The bull kept trying, and the bull kept failing. He was a firm believer in the old 'if at first you don't succeed' adage, and I

noted there was a distinct lack of romance about the whole procedure. No candles, no soft music, no sense of the moment having to
be right. Nature clearly affords the bull more leeway in these
matters than it does to the human male. As a rule, if during inter-
course a man slides off a woman four times consecutively, he is not
generally made welcome for the fifth, sixth and seventh attempts.
(This is an assumption, I hasten to add. I am pleased to say that I
have gathered no empirical evidence on this.)

I guess the truth of the matter is that it's hard to have sex on a
slope. Personally I've always preferred flatter terrain. Probably
because it makes sense to ask only one part of your body to defy
gravity at any time. I found myself thinking that the bull in
question ought to have known this, and should have found himself
a little flat area he could have called his 'place', which he then used
specifically for horizontal mountings.

At a junction we were greeted by a man who was holding
crutches and propping himself up against a small van. It was the
farmer whose cows we were now transporting. It seems that he
wasn't going to use his injury as an excuse to slope off into town
to play boules or go shopping. No, he wanted to be as involved in
this *transhumance* as was humanly possible. He greeted his farmer
colleagues warmly and then directed us all up a steep path into the
woods, before getting back into his van and speeding off – no
doubt ready to meet us at the next bit of road when we emerged
from cross-country terrain.

This part of the walk was noticeably harder and I began to feel
it in my legs. Two and a half hours of hard graft was not proving
to be the best of hangover cures and I was ready for a break. I was
ready for a sit-down. In fact, to be honest, I was ready to stop for
the day. I'd had enough. We were only a fraction of a way through
the 37 kilometres and yet I was feeling it already. I hadn't trained
for this, and I wasn't prepared physically – and certainly not
mentally. Images of comfy chairs dominated my mind, along with
hot baths and luxurious double beds.

Imagine my relief, then, when we came to a clearing and there before us were half a dozen people busily laying out a magnificent spread of bread, wine, meats, cheeses, yoghurts, fruit and cakes, all laid out on picnic tables. It was like a mirage.

'What's this?' I asked Anne, who was looking irritatingly fresh.

'It's lunch,' she replied. 'Tuck in. You've earned it.'

'We all have,' I said, eyes positively bulging at the sight of the culinary treat that was now before us.

A grey-haired man with chiselled, angular features approached me proffering a plastic cup of red wine. I readily accepted, even though it was only 11.30am and, as everybody knows, drinking before midday means that you're only one step away from being an alcoholic. Never mind, the wine hit the mark and I began happily chatting with the wine's procurer.

'I have done this *transhumance* one time before,' said the man in a tone of voice that suggested he might not be about to do it again soon. 'You must enjoy your lunch because the next part is hard and with many hills. You will not stop again for perhaps three and a half hours.'

'Three and a half hours?' I said, rolling my eyes.

'Yes,' he continued, perhaps taking some pleasure from being the bearer of very bad news. 'And even then you will not yet be half of the way to your destination.'

'Christ!' I said. 'Sod that for a game of soldiers.'

'I do not understand. Where are there soldiers?'

'I'm sorry. It's an expression. It means . . . it means . . . it means it's a long way.'

'Ah yes — it is a long way.'

I shuddered at how far it was, and downed my wine with an impolite gulp. As the man began to pour me another one, the aches in my legs started to make me ponder possible escape options. There had to be some way out of this.

'What is your name?' I asked, deciding that this fellow could be a potential accomplice.

'My name is Rene,' he replied. 'And you?'

'I am Tony. Excuse me asking, Rene, but what are you doing after this picnic lunch?'

'I am returning to the village in my car.'

'Would you be able to give me a lift?'

'Of course. But are you not going to finish the *transhumance*?'

'No,' I said firmly, and with enormous conviction. 'I can't be bothered. And anyway, I have a *gueule de bois*.'

'Oh, OK,' said Rene with a shrug that suggested he wasn't overly impressed with me.

I quickly found Anne, made some feeble pretext about 'just realising that I needed to sort some things out in the town' (a transparent excuse not that different to the one her husband had used) and soon I was heading for Rene's saloon car, having watched him, along with some others, clear up the remains of the magnificent picnic. I should have helped them, but I was just too tired, and besides, I had my second cup of red wine to finish and that needed my full attention.

'So, you do not like walking?' said Rene as I jumped in next to him and he started up the car.

'I don't like walking that far. Anyway, I've seen enough bulls exercising for one day,' I said, making rather a crude mime with my arm and clenched fist.

The recently consumed wine had given me the confidence to experiment with some earthy humour. Rene didn't laugh, though, or make a comment. He merely raised an eyebrow.

'I will soon be a neighbour of yours,' I announced, moving on to a more mundane topic.

'Really?'

'Yes. I am buying Jean-Claude's house.'

'Aaaah!' said Rene, taking his eyes off the road for an alarmingly long period of time in order to size me up. 'We heard that there was another Englishman coming to be with us. And so it is you.'

'Yes, it is me.'

Rene said nothing. There was silence, apart from the hum of the diesel engine. The effect of the wine was being replaced by fatigue, and I had no idea where to take the conversation next. The result was that we said nothing further to each other until he dropped me back at Malcolm and Anne's. Rene, it seemed, was not that keen on me. Never mind, I thought. It was inevitable that I wouldn't be a hit with everyone in the village. So what if I hadn't won Rene over? The main thing was that I made myself popular with the people who really mattered.

'So, will you be coming to the annual village lunch tomorrow?' I enquired, getting out of the car.

'Yes, of course,' he said emphatically. 'It is absolutely necessary for me.'

'Why is that?' I asked, preparing to close the car door.

'Because, Tony, I am the mayor of the village.'

6

Food, Wine and Belote

'So, you met Rene then?' said Anne with a wry smile, as we met in the hallway the next day.

To my shame, I'd been fast asleep in the loft apartment when she'd eventually made it back from the *transhumance* the previous night.

'Yes,' I said. 'I wish I'd known that he's the mayor. I might have handled things differently.'

I was only too aware of how important this man could be to me in the coming months. As I understood it, any changes and improvements to my new house would need to be referred to him for permission. It was important he liked me. Moaning about hangovers, shirking on helping him with the clearing up and making poor jokes about bulls shagging might not have been the best way to speed the process.

'How did your business go in town?' asked Anne.

'Business?' I replied with a raised eyebrow. 'Oh, that business. The business that I had in town. Yes, that went very well, thanks.'

I wasn't lying. Sitting in the sun and doing the odd bit of shopping had all gone off surprisingly well. Virtually no hitches other than an irritating bit of cloud between 16.40 and 16.47.

'How was the rest of your day?' I enquired, trying to appear guilt-free.

'Tiring, but fun,' she said, looking a little fatigued.

'Yes, well, it's a long way,' I said, finally clearing up any ambiguity on the matter.

'Today will be long too,' said Anne with a smile.

'Yes, but with less walking.'

Today was the day of the village lunch. In fact, it was more than just the village lunch – it was both the village lunch and the village dinner. Tradition demanded that the village ate together as one on at least one day of the year, and owing to the constraints of farming and life in general, not everyone could make lunch and not everyone could make dinner. The solution was to have two meals on the same day, running consecutively. Furthermore, those who were free to attend both were strongly encouraged to do so. Since I fell into this latter category, this now meant that I was faced with a long day of eating and drinking. I was better prepared for this than I was the 37-kilometre hike.

In terms of being accepted in these parts, I knew that this might be a make-or-break day. A short and somewhat unimpressive exchange with the mayor aside, the previous day hadn't exactly been an overwhelming success with regard to getting to know the villagers. Today was a great opportunity to put that right, given that it was an event specifically designed to bring people together. I for one had every intention of cooperating with that process.

As is often the case for events to which one is looking forward, I was ready to leave much too early, finding myself waiting in my linen suit on Malcolm and Anne's patio. I drifted in and out of reverie, soothed by the greens of the rolling foothills and the distant grey peaks. I felt content. I guess I'd rather have been about to go to the village dinner as part of a couple — Tony and his lovely wife — but that was not to be, and I was happy to pitch up with Malcolm and Anne as the solitary eccentric Englishman, and have the rest make of me what they would.

'You're not going like that, are you?' said Malcolm as he wandered onto the patio in jeans and T-shirt.

'I was going to, yes,' I replied. 'Is it a bit too smart?'

'Well, it's up to you, but as you can see we don't dress up for this.'

Almost on cue, Anne appeared looking neat and tidy, but still distinctly informal.

'I think I'll go and slip into something more comfortable,' I said.

Malcolm and Anne knew the form for these things as well as anyone. Apart from having been to about fifteen in a row, they were also on the village social committee. If I wanted to learn how to become a part of the local community, then I could do worse than have Malcolm and Anne as my teachers. They had done an incredible job. They had made it their business to get to know absolutely everyone in the village, they organised events, and poor old Malcolm, who had left Britain to escape a life of accountancy, had ended up as honorary treasurer of the social committee.

It was only a twenty-minute walk to the village hall, but I was glad I'd ditched the suit. Malcolm and Anne lived halfway up one side of the valley, and our destination was at the top of the other. The inclines were surprisingly steep and I'd broken into a sweat by the time we were making our final approaches. I could see the village hall ahead, a modern building with big glass windows, a disproportionately large edifice for somewhere with just over a hundred people.

'How come we've got a building that big?' I asked. 'Given that the village doesn't even have a shop or a bar.'

'It's just the French system,' said Anne. 'All villages have to have village halls.'

'It started as a bureaucratic thing,' said Malcolm. 'But now it's a tradition, I guess. Ours is especially good though. It's better than the ones in all the surrounding villages.'

As we entered the building there was a little reception committee of three or four men lined up to greet us. They too were
dressed informally but most were wearing neatly ironed collared
shirts, which made them slightly resemble kids who'd been made
to dress smartly by their mums for their birthday parties. At the
head of this group was Rene the mayor. I felt myself gulp. Just how
much had my behaviour offended him the previous day?

I approached him cautiously, and to my immense relief he
greeted me warmly with a vigorous handshake and ushered me on
to several others who did the same. Perhaps he liked jokes about
shagging bulls after all. He even went as far as to pat me on the
back before pointing me in the direction of a huge table full of
bottles, behind which three young ladies stood in anticipation.

'*Apéritif?*' one of them asked.

'*Oui, merci,*' I replied. '*Un Ricard.*'

I'm not quite sure why I ordered a Ricard, it's an aniseed drink
a bit like Greek ouzo and I don't even like it very much, but
everyone around me seemed to have one, so rather spinelessly I
bowed to peer pressure.

I turned, large glass of white poison in my hand, and surveyed
the room. It was short on people since we were evidently some of
the first to arrive. The décor was bordering on non-existent. A red
polished floor glistened, over which two long lines of tables had
been set in preparation for the meal. Behind them was a pair of
huge sliding doors opening onto a patio with the now routine
splendid views of the surrounding beauty. The walls had been left
undecorated – just the unplastered building blocks, grey and rather
austere. Behind the table of drinks there was a large elevated stage,
at the back of which was a huge mural of a Caribbean scene – a
beautiful bay surrounded by palm trees. Later I was to learn that
this was a survivor from the first event that ever took place here,
the wedding of a local couple who'd no doubt booked their
honeymoon in this far-off beauty spot. Now, fifteen years on, it still
survived as the only bit of decoration in the building, no doubt

destined for at least another decade as the village's meagre nod to ornamentation.

Soon there was a flurry of activity accompanying a glut of new arrivals. Just how much the French like kissing now became abundantly clear. Everyone was at it. There was a flurry of 'double pecks' landing on every available cheek – well, every available cheek above the waist. Soon the hall was a noisy place, as friends and neighbours began to catch up with the latest news and gossip. The place bustled. White hair, thinning hair, brunette mops of tousled hair and little girls' pigtails all took their turns in occasionally bobbing above or in between the sea of bodies. It seemed like every hairdo that had ever adorned a hairdresser's window was on show, maybe because this wasn't just a glimpse of a rural community, but a snapshot of one that had undergone a steady settlement by the odd professional, or Parisian, or, more recently, Brit. Each, of course, with their own peculiar approach to styling their locks.

In no time I too was thrust into a whirlwind of introductions, largely orchestrated by Malcolm and Anne, but also by my new friend the mayor, who evidently approved of *transhumance*-avoiding winos. Along with every new name came an explanation of who everyone was, what they did and where they lived, and soon my mind was reeling from all this new information. I was relieved when we were called to the table.

'Where do we sit?' I quickly called out to Malcolm.

'Anywhere you like,' he hastily replied, before being grabbed by a burly man with a broad bushy moustache. 'You'll be all right, won't you?' he said, adding over his shoulder as he was led away to the far end of one of the tables, 'Just sit anywhere.'

'Of course.'

The words momentarily echoed in my head: 'Just sit anywhere.' Suddenly it felt like I was boarding the plane that had brought me here – one of the budget flights that had long since dispensed with anything as passé as a seat number. It's preferable, it seems, to have an initial scrum amongst the passengers who are desperate to have the best choice of the almost identical seats. It also works very well for the sloths like me who amble onto the plane last of all, having relaxed and read during the twenty minutes that it's taken the seat enthusiasts to board. The sloth figure can then choose whose flight to spoil by selecting a victim and sitting next to them, just when they thought they were going to have the entire journey blessed with lots of elbow room and air space. Sometimes you can hear their sigh of disappointment as you lower yourself into the adjacent seat. Oh, the joy of it all.

Just as I was surveying the steadily filling tables and deciding whose elbow room I might hamper here, I felt a tap on my back.

'Hello, I'm Mary,' said a voice, and I turned to see a lady smiling at me. She looked positively Irish, I thought.

'I'm from Ireland,' she continued.

God, I was good. There was something about how white she was. She was Irish white.

'Hello, I'm Tony.'

'Yes, I know. You've met my son.'

'Really?'

'Yes, come and sit over here.'

And with those words, the short-lived dilemma of where to sit was over.

As we sat down, the dark-haired and sixty-something Mary explained in her gentle Irish brogue that she lived for half of the year in the house two down from where I was about to move. She was a widow who now supported herself by playing the piano in a hotel in nearby Lourdes, mostly for Irish pilgrims who liked a bit of a sing-song after a hard day's mass and genuflection.

'I play the piano too,' I said enthusiastically. 'In fact, one of the reasons for buying the house here is so that I can dedicate myself to practising it.'

'Oh I wish you luck with that. My practising days are long gone.'

'You said that I've met your son?'

'Yes, at the Albert Hall in London.'

A couple of years previously I'd been invited to do an opening set of stand-up comedy for the Corrs at their London concert in aid of the Prince's Trust. It had been the largest audience I had ever played to, and I had been most relieved that the audience had found me amusing. Dying a death in front of three thousand people might have been too much for a performer's fragile ego to bear. So whilst the Corrs were doing their bit, I watched from the side of the stage and celebrated my 'success' by drinking some lovely wine. It kept flowing throughout the Corrs' performance and continued to flow freely at the after-show party I happily attended, secretly hoping to meet and end up snogging one of the band's three beautiful sisters. Needless to say, I didn't. Instead I spoke nonsense to a lot of considerably less pretty blokes, one of whom happened to be Mary's son, who it turns out plays guitar in the Corrs backing band.

'I'm afraid I have absolutely no recollection of meeting him,' I said. 'I was far too pissed.'

Mary gave the traditional Irish response to this, and looked impressed.

'Never mind – you'll meet again soon, I'm sure.'

'*Bonjour, monsieur, vous êtes le nouvel Anglais, n'est-ce pas?*'

I looked up to see a lady in her late sixties or early seventies, beaming broadly from ear to ear. I stood up to greet her, which was enough in itself to cause her to shriek with delight. I absolutely towered over her.

'*Je suis Tony,*' I said, looking down on her as politely as I could.

'*Et moi, je suis Odette.*'

Odette chatted away to me merrily, almost as if we were long-lost friends. Malcolm and Anne had told her about me, she said. They'd said I was very nice. Any friend of theirs was a friend of hers, she added. Did I have any children? No? Odette shook her head. She, as she proudly pointed out, was a great grandmother. To a man in his forties who had yet to father a single child, this was an impressive feat. I knew there wasn't much to do in the evenings around here but I hadn't realised that French television was quite so bad.

Then it occurred to me. Maybe this was one of the reasons why I was still single. I had too much to do. People in these parts get married young. Why? Because there's nothing else to do. It simply cannot be that God looks particularly kindly upon French villages and conveniently puts all their soulmates in the same area. No – far more likely that people got married out of boredom. Could it be that I just hadn't been bored enough in my life so far?

I felt a tap on my shoulder and I turned to see a pretty blonde girl with her hands full of empty carafes of wine. One of the waitressing volunteer force.

'*Porc ou poulet?*' she asked.

Pork or chicken? Was this a question about my preference for the main course or the opening gambit of a traditional local word game? Either way, I got the answer wrong.

'*Avez-vous quelque chose sans viande?*'

The girl looked at me like I was utterly mad. Had she heard me correctly? Was I really asking if they had anything without meat?

'*Pardon?*' she said.

'*Avez-vous quelque chose sans viande?*' I repeated.

The girl tipped her head to one side and gave me a moment to demonstrate that I'd been joking. France is not a great place for the non-meat eater. Years before I'd been on holiday here with friends, one of whom was a vegetarian. When we'd asked if they had anything without meat, the waiter had replied, 'Is ham OK?'

'*Porc ou poulet?*' the waitress asked again, this time with a hint of impatience.

I felt the presence of the French couple to my left, and the long table of villagers who stretched beyond them, all of whom seemed now to be eyeing me with suspicion.

I am a man of some considerable principle. A couple of years back, whilst attempting to win the affections of a girl who was a vegetarian, I had renounced meat. My reasons had been two-fold. Firstly, I was sick and tired of the way animals were kept cooped up in a factory environment just so that we could eat cheap meat, and, secondly, I wanted to impress the girl in question. I will leave you to decide which of these two issues contributed most to my decision.

To my credit, long after the girl and I had split up, I continued to shun the meat option, but I was now in a difficult position as I found myself under considerable pressure to opt for either *porc* or *poulet*. How odd did I want my new neighbours to think me? I'd already turned up on my own without a wife or any sign of a woman in tow. What would they think if I now added to that the fact that I didn't eat meat? Surely I'd just get sent to Rheims, or wherever the French equivalent of Coventry is. No, I didn't want that – and besides, hadn't I only the previous day seen just how well the cows were cared for around here? VIP treatment. Personal escorts to mountain pastures. And then there were all those chickens I'd seen outside farm buildings wandering aimlessly about in the roads. These weren't factory chickens, these were happy, proud, fulfilled little creatures, as ready to face their destiny as any living thing could be. A destiny that would involve being eaten by me, in about five minutes' time.

'*Poulet*,' said the deeply principled one, as the young waitress smiled back politely.

Actually it wasn't just chickens who would be at the business end of my newfound philosophy. My hosts provided a menu that made me feel like some kind of born-again carnivore. After a slightly odd starter of peach stuffed with tuna, we were brought Bayonne ham and bread followed by venison stew and potatoes. Forgetting about my previous order for chicken, I assumed that this was the main course and wolfed down two helpings. Then the chicken arrived. Huge portions, again served with potatoes. I was already stuffed, but once again I felt the heavy force of peer pressure and bowed to it immediately. My stomach began to swell. A lettuce salad arrived next, followed by cheese and yet more bread. Then it was the turn of a vast tranche of strawberry tart, to be washed down with coffee and Armagnac. I undid the button at the top of my trousers and sat back in my chair. I needed to rest from what had seemed like some sort of new Olympic event. The Food Marathon or the 1500-metre Gluttony.

Fuelled by the aperitifs, the free-flowing wine and the brandy, many of the villagers were now on their feet, mixing and mingling. I noted with some apprehension that Rene was having a long chat with Jean-Claude. I wanted to go and join them to make sure that the conversation didn't turn to the subject of my predilection for corks, but I was too bloated to move. When it came to socialising I would have to wait for people to come to me. And come to me they did. Soon I was introduced to Roger, a jovial fellow of about fifty with just the most infectious giggle. He swept from person to person, shaking hands, chuckling and generally demonstrating why the French had come up with the word 'bonhomie'. Then there was Serge, a vast ruddy-complexioned man of Roger's age who sported a broad, bulging moustache and who bellowed incomprehensibly at me in an extremely good-humoured manner. His mate Alain (also a big bloke but not so well endowed on the moustache front) came and joined in with him, laughing, joking and generally doing a lot of slapping me on the back. This backslapping was being administered a tad too heavy-handedly and it was beginning to hurt a bit, as well as making me feel slightly nauseous. I didn't let on though, and grinned incessantly.★

'Come and meet André,' said Malcolm, who was looking a little the worse for wear himself. 'He's one of the great village characters.'

I struggled, pensioner-like, from my chair and followed

★It was probably a smarmy grin – a bit like the one Tony Blair does when an interviewer has him in a bit of a corner.

Malcolm, who gave me a brief character sketch of André as we crossed the hall.

'He's about seventy-five and he's lived in the village all his life. The trouble is, he can be quite difficult to understand because he has a strong local accent, and it's made even worse by the fact that he quite often lapses into the Gascon dialect of Occitan.'

'Ah yes,' I said. 'The Gascon dialect of Occitan. My grasp of that is a little rusty, partly because I never really paid too much attention to it at school.'

'It's a kind of hybrid of French, Spanish and Andalucian.'

I knew more about this than I was letting on to Malcolm, having read about it only days before. Occitan had never been officially accorded the status of a distinct language but it was a product of the many centuries before the eventual establishment of Spain and France, when every valley was like a mini-republic with its own patois. André's use of the language proved that he was a descendant of an era when someone who travelled more than twenty miles was considered an adventurer.

'André has never married,' said Malcolm. 'And he's got some great stories of his childhood when the Nazis had occupied the area.'

Malcolm had taken on a new role. He was becoming to me a little like a Greek chorus is to the audience, filling me in on all the significant details that weren't immediately obvious from the action. With regard to André, in only a couple of minutes he had well and truly whetted my appetite. I couldn't wait to meet this old man.

André was not a disappointment. We found him chatting to another elderly man who quickly moved off when we arrived. André was a small, balding man with an open face, grey moustache and unfeasibly white scalp. Malcolm later told me that this was because the only time he removed his beret was when he came to the village events. The rest of the time his monastic bald pate was spared any exposure to the elements or to the rest of the world. But for now, the contrast between sun-soaked deep-tan face and Persil snow-white skull was simply magnificent. It was strange too that I should meet André on the only day of the year when he looked like this. The next time our paths crossed I might struggle to recognise him.

We began chatting and at first his accent seemed impenetrable, but slowly I began to pick out more and more of what he was saying. It was small talk at first, discussing the meal, where I was going to live and how nice it was to have mountains all around us. Then, in something of a stylish non sequitur, I asked him what he remembered of life here under the German invasion. To his credit, André reacted as if this had been the natural topic to move onto after having just covered the loveliness of the mountains. He told me that he had been thirteen when it had all happened but that he could remember it as if it was yesterday. I said that I would love to come round to see him and hear some of these stories and he replied that I was most welcome but that he didn't have any milk in. This rather threw me. I know that I'd kicked off the stylish non sequiturs, but I hadn't expected him to follow suit with such aplomb. Or perhaps I'd misunderstood.

'*Pardon?*' I queried.

'*Je n'ai pas de lait.*'

No, I wasn't mistaken. He was telling me that he didn't have any milk in.

And then it dawned on me. André thought that I wanted to go round to his house right now to hear these stories and he wanted to let me know that we couldn't have coffee because he didn't have all the requisite ingredients in.

'*Non, pas immédiatement,*' I explained. '*Une autre fois.*'

André looked relieved that this could be done at another time. A time when he could have a decent supply of milk in. A time when there wasn't a party going on, which now seemed to be getting into full swing.

'*Une bière, Tony?*' said a voice, accompanied by a hearty slap on the back.

This was clearly the trademark of Alain, who, when I turned round, was standing there holding out a bottle of beer. To be honest, I wasn't sure whether a beer was altogether a good idea. After all, I'd already consumed a good deal of Ricard, red wine and brandy, but Alain had gone to the trouble so it probably would have been rude not to. I took the bottle and was instantly ushered over to a table where cards were being played.

'*C'est belote*,' announced Alain. '*Allez jouer!*'

Now I definitely wasn't sure about this. Learning a new game of cards is hard enough, but when you add the fact that the rules will be explained in a foreign language, you hardly know what any of the cards are called, and you've drunk and eaten yourself into a state where all you're good for is a bit of a lie-down – then it's something best avoided.

'*Non merci*,' I replied.

'*Mais oui!*' insisted Alain, who then slapped me on the back.

It was starting to feel like this backslapping leant more towards coercion than camaraderie. I was manhandled into a chair alongside a gentle white-haired lady and opposite Serge – he of the bulbous moustache. Beside him was Christine, the young waitress who had offered me the Hobson's choice of *porc ou poulet*. After vociferous introductions from Alain I learned that the old lady was Marie, mother of 'bonhomie' Roger, and that Christine was the daughter of the deputy mayor.

'*Bonne chance!*' said Alain, inevitably providing me with a slap on the back as his parting shot.

And I needed it. Things didn't get off to a good start when Christine explained that we were only going to use thirty-two cards. In my addled state I felt that this was unreasonable. Why not use the whole pack? We had them, and they were ours. It seemed silly not to take advantage. However, I showed great restraint and said nothing as Christine continued her short resumé of the rules.

I now discovered that listening to the rules of cards is just like listening to directions. You only concentrate for the beginning bit and then you allow yourself to get distracted by different features of the information provider. Their hair, their mannerisms and, in this case, their eyes. Christine had lovely eyes.

'*Tu as tout compris?*' she asked, when she'd finished.

'*Oui,*' I replied.

This was a downright lie. Of course I hadn't understood everything. I had only the faintest grasp of what had just been said, but Christine didn't need to know that, and neither did anyone else.

They only needed to wait a matter of seconds before they found out, though. I led a high card and everybody immediately said, '*Non, non!*' I led a much lower one and everyone still said, '*Non.*' Confused, I led the seven of hearts, and despite a few tuts, this seemed to be accepted. This clearly wasn't the best of leads, but at least it fell within the parameters of the rules.

The game continued with me doing my best to look plausibly absorbed, but I was not someone who was gaining knowledge with each passing hand. All I could fathom was that we were playing some kind of whist hybrid, seemingly tailored for the express purpose of confusing the English.

One of the requirements of the game was that I had to shout '*Valet tournant!*' every time a jack was turned over. I did this obediently and with a great sense of purpose, totally oblivious to its significance. Occasionally I was urged to take a jack, at which point I had to shout '*Valet prenant!*' Secretly I hoped that the gusto and enthusiasm with which I performed these pronouncements would more than make up for the pig's ear that I was making of everything else.

I'm not sure that it did. We played three games. In the first I was paired with Christine, in the second with Serge and in the third with Marie. I lost all three of them. I hate it when you get a run of bad luck like that.

I felt a slap on my back. Inevitably it was Alain, offering me another beer and asking me if I'd like to come and see his swimming pool. It was an odd request, but he announced that since I was

English I'd certainly be wanting to put a pool in at my house.
Splendidly bold presumption, I thought.

'My . . . swimming pool . . . is . . . very good!' he announced.
'Only two minutes from here. Come!'

And with those words he began lifting me from my chair. He
then led me by the arm out of the village hall. Had I not known
that he lived with his girlfriend, I might have been less relaxed than
I was. 'Relaxed' is of course a euphemism for wobbly on the feet,
and we were both very relaxed. The short walk to his house was
made hazardous by the fact that we had to avoid sober people who
were arriving for the evening leg of this epic feast. No doubt Alain
and I cut impressive figures as we meandered erratically past them
offering up slurred '*bonsoirs*'.

'The new boy seems to be settling in just fine,' they might well
have observed as we crossed.

Alain's pool completely dominated his back garden. There was
barely room for anything else. He extended his arm proudly
towards it, almost as if he was inviting me to dive in fully clothed.
I opted for a compliment instead.

'It's very good,' I said. 'Very good indeed.'

And it was. It was good. Everything about it was good. But if
only I could have thought of something else to add. All the possibilities that sprang to mind would have seemed like I was taking
the piss:

'It's a very nice blue.'

'The water's shimmering nicely in the evening sun.'

'Good shape. Rectangular is good.'

'The filtration system seems to be chugging along nicely.'

'Nice ladder.'

As I looked at Alain's fine blue rectangular pool with its water
shimmering in the evening sun, filtration system chugging along
nicely and its nice ladder, I began to wonder if a pool was something that I should consider. I'd always assumed that owning a
swimming pool would be too much bother. All that business

people have to go through with filters, chlorine, covers and leaf removal. It never seems to me to be outweighed by the enjoyment attained from the actual time they spend swimming in it. But right now, relaxed as I was, I was tempted.

'I think I ought to get one,' I announced drunkenly, as if it was as easy as buying a shirt.

'*Une bonne idée*,' confirmed Alain, before leading me back to the village hall.

There was something of a throng of new people gathered inside the door as we stepped back into the hall. Rene the Mayor welcomed us like newcomers, as did his smartly shirted posse. They seemed to have forgotten that they'd already greeted us thus some hours before. Or maybe they were just on 'greeting auto-pilot'. Suddenly, and with some horror, I realised that I was still only halfway through the day's social proceedings and that I would now be required to consume another meal, even before I'd had time to digest the first. And it wasn't just food with which I'd have to contend – there'd be more drink too.

'*Un apéritif, monsieur?*' asked a volunteer waitress I'd not seen before.

'*Oui, un Ricard*,' I replied.

Well, if a thing's worth doing, it's worth doing properly.

I have to confess to not remembering a great deal about the second gargantuan repast of the day. What I do recall is that whilst my stomach bulged unattractively, Jean-Claude, the owner of the house I was buying, stood up and made a speech saying goodbye to everyone in the village. Towards the end he welcomed me, '*le nouvel Anglais*', and led everyone in a warm round of applause. I think I may have welled up a bit. I felt like grabbing each and every one of them and slobbering and slurring 'I bloody love you' into their ears at too high a volume, just like the street wino that I was getting ever closer to resembling.

I finished the night at a table wedged between Alain and Serge, the latter of whom congratulated me on my drinking performance.

'*Tony, tu bois bien*,' he pointed out graciously.

Then Alain slapped me on the back.

I liked this place.

I had a headache in the morning, and the only thing that made it better was that I wasn't suffering alone. Malcolm and Anne had bad heads too.

We were attempting to expunge our hangovers by engaging in the public-spirited activity of cleaning up the village hall. Just as volunteers from the village had prepared and presented the whole meal, it fell upon good souls like us to dispense with the debris. There were quite a few of us on duty, including the mayor and deputy mayor. It seemed that in this part of the world positions in high places did not excuse you from the menial tasks. Everyone mucked in together. Seemingly the only perk of being mayor was that you got to use the big 'sprayey thing'. I expect there's a technical term for such a contraption, but I don't know what it is. Basically the 'sprayey thing' was a little machine attached to a hosepipe from which a big spray gun emanated. It was with this spray gun that the mayor prowled the village hall, spraying the tanned floor as he went. It fell to us lesser mortals to follow behind with big 'scrapers', pushing the soapy water away. Rene the Mayor conducted the operation with great pride and authority. There almost seemed to be a swagger about him as he waved his spray gun about the place. For a moment I wondered whether, if he was completely honest with himself, this was the thing he enjoyed best about being mayor.

Of course, there was the small point that the floor had never really been dirty enough to warrant the use of the 'sprayey thing' in the first place. A cursory wipe with a couple of mops would have sufficed. But no one had thought it wise to point this out. I mean, why deny your mayor his fun?

'*Voilà!*' he said as he looked down proudly at the fruits of our labour.

A floor that looked pretty identical to how it had before.

'*Très bien!*' I said, a bit like the school creep.

Rene nodded proudly and smiled back at me.

Shortly afterwards we adjourned for a big lunch. About time too.

No point in overdoing it.

Later that day I found myself clambering into my hire car (which hadn't exactly been overused) and heading off to the airport. My stomach seemed to be considerably nearer the steering wheel than it had been a few days earlier, such had been the spirit with which I'd embraced French hospitality. Yes, I had given a good account of myself, and I swelled with both food and pride as I watched the mountains disappear from view in my rear-view mirror. For someone who didn't yet have the keys to his new house, I'd surely made good progress. In fact, it felt like I was already beginning to settle in.

The steady monotony of the motorway reminded me that this was 'back to England' time. Already the last couple of days felt like a dream. How would I get on, I wondered, when I returned as the legal owner of the property?

What would happen to the dream when it became a reality?

7

SOS DIY

Back home in England I began to think that Alain was right. He'd stated quite clearly that I was English, and that this fact alone made it beholden upon me to get a swimming pool. In his own erudite words, it was '*une bonne idée*', and I was aware that arguing with him on this matter was only going to lead to back trouble in the future. So, I started drawing little plans for where a pool might fit on the available land, and I even wrote to my chum Rene the Mayor to discover what was needed in the way of permission.

I was quite delighted with the form I promptly received back from him. It was called a '*Déclaration de travaux exempts de permis de construire*'. This effectively meant that it was a form you filled out which, if approved, gave you permission not to need permission. If this was an indication of what French bureaucracy had in store for me, then installing myself in this house was going to be an arduous task. Filling out the form made me feel like Corporal Jones from *Dad's Army*, who always asked Captain Mainwaring's consent for everything he did.

'Permission not to need permission,' he would have requested.

'Don't be ridiculous, Jones,' would have come the reply.

But Captain Mainwaring wasn't in charge of the French bureaucratic system. The post-war de Gaulle had been most diligent in ensuring that hadn't happened. No, he'd got French bureaucrats to do it, and the 'Permission not to need permission form' may well have been one of their finest achievements.

As it turned out, not getting permission was quite a complicated business. I had to make a sketch of where the pool was going to be on the land, including its dimensions and a cross-section drawing revealing its depth. My mind boggled as to what would have been required had I actually needed their permission. Presumably they would have demanded further information, like birth certificate, blood type and special dietary requirements.

One of the consequences of completing the form and sending it back to the mayor was that I became aware that the swimming pool was now more than just a 'maybe' in answer to friends' questions about whether I was going to get one or not. If my application for not needing permission were successful then it would become a major project for the new home, alongside plonking on the piano keys. But many questions remained unanswered. How much would it cost? Would I use it enough? Would there be a sporty type on a ladder blowing a whistle if I ever got the opportunity to do some petting?

Then there was the guilt factor. I'd already been through it once with regard to buying the house in the first place. How could I justify having so much, when so many people in the world have so little? Bloody conscience – why couldn't it just mind its own business for once? It was assuaged a little after some surfing on the net revealed that the pool would cost me less than half what I'd pay for a fancy four-wheel drive. Now I didn't feel so bad. Self-serving and hedonistic, yes, but not bad.

Not long after this period of form-filling and soul-searching, I received a letter from the *notaire*'s office informing me that the signing had all gone smoothly in my absence and that the house was now mine, all mine. Yes, I thought, but I'll believe that when the keys are in my hand, and not before. Experience was teaching me that in these matters it was prudent to be a sceptic.

Spring had turned to summer by the time I set off to claim my treasure. I hadn't wanted to go alone and I was travelling with Brad, who months before had done such a sterling job in devising a way for us to get my piano into the original white van. The original white van that regrettably was still not fully out of my life. I hadn't realised that it had been my responsibility to let the Department of Transport know that I'd had the van towed away and crushed. An official letter had recently informed me that my failure to do so now made me liable to a hefty fine. Surely, I mused as I wrote out the cheque, this would finally be an end to the saga? Could there be any other ways that this van, deceased as it was, could drain my resources still further? Was I soon to discover that it had gambling debts for which I was responsible?

Brad and I loitered in the aisle of the plane, waiting for our turn to file down the steps and onto the French tarmac of Pau airport. A wave of hot humid air hit us as we stepped out from the plane's pressurised cabin. The mountains, no longer snow-capped, swallowed up the horizon.

'Yes! We're in heaven!' said Brad, pausing on top of the steps that would soon take him down to earth.

'Good, isn't it?' I replied, slightly less euphorically.

I hoped that this trip would make a good break for Brad. He was waiting on a divorce, and although the process thus far had been amicable and he was well set to become good friends with his wife, I still felt he was carrying a burden of sadness and disappointment around with him. It felt great that I could provide succour by offering him the break of a few days' relentlessly lugging furniture and unpacking boxes. It seemed the least I could do.

The drive was hot and humid, but then it was summer in the

south of France, so it wasn't unexpected. We wound down the windows and let the hot air circulate in the car until gradually it cooled as we began to climb and gain altitude. It wasn't long before we were driving through the centre of Bagnères, almost in awe of the towering grey peaks that seemed to have sprung up all around us.

'What's the first job we have to do?' asked Brad, displaying a splendid understanding of the fundamental nature of his trip.

'We have to collect the keys from the *notaire*'s office,' I replied. 'It's just up here on the left.'

Brad waited in the car whilst I climbed the stairs to the *notaire*'s office. I was nervous. I felt sure there'd be some last-minute bureaucratic hitch. But no, five minutes later I emerged from the offices waving the keys triumphantly above my head.

'No problems?' asked Brad, as I got back in the car.

'None at all. The *notaire*'s secretary handed over the keys. I didn't even have to sign for them.'

A cynic might have believed that now all of my money had been successfully divided up amongst all the interested parties, there were no further hitches because nobody really gave a toss any more. But I was far too excited for such a cynical thought to have crossed my mind. I had the keys! The house was mine at long last.

Ten minutes later, after a drive that had seen Brad exude repeated gasps of approval prompted by the surrounding vistas, I was standing at my new front door and poised to turn the key in the lock. This was it! The moment that all the hours of paperwork, meetings, musing, worry, reverie and stress had been leading towards. The moment when for the first time the house well and truly became mine. Brad stood just behind me, poised with his camera, ready to capture the moment on film.

I turned the key but got no response from the lock. I turned it again. Still nothing. Three consecutive attempts produced little more than heavy sighs.

'Here, let me have a go,' said Brad, fully aware that he was better at this kind of thing than me.

I watched in despair as he turned the lock one way, then the other, only to find that the damn thing wouldn't work.

'It's no good,' said Brad. 'The key just won't open the door.'

'Don't call it a key. It's only a key if it has the good grace to open a lock. At the moment it's just an annoying piece of metal.'

'Maybe it's the wrong one. Let's try it in the back door.'

And we did. And we had no luck there either, however many different key-turning techniques or swear words we used.

'Are you sure they've given you the right ones?' said Brad.

'I think so. They're all labelled up as being for this house – and all the keys seem to fit the locks. They just don't open them.'

'I think we might have to break in then,' said Brad.

'Oh I don't like the sound of that,' I complained. 'I haven't gone through all the rigmarole of the French legal system just so that at the end of it all I can do what a squatter could have done in the first place.'

'All right, let's try the garage door,' said Brad, who was clearly feeling far less despondent than I was.

The garage ran the length of the house beneath, like a giant cellar. However, I didn't follow Brad as he set off down the drive because I was in a sulk. I knew what was going to happen. There was obviously a knack to these French locks, and soon we would have to summon the help of a Frenchman, shortly afterwards suffering the indignity of watching as he turned the key and opened the door with a nonchalant ease. I was extremely fed up that I was going to have to suffer this kind of humiliation in only the first few seconds of ownership. It would have been nicer to have let at least half an hour go by.

'Done it!' shouted Brad from below. 'I'm in!'

I ran down to join him. It was true. Genius that he was, he'd managed to get his head round a French lock, and we were in.

'Well done, mate,' I said, trying to pretend that I'd not spent the last few minutes in a childish sulk. 'We can make our way up into the house using the internal staircase that leads up from here.'

Seconds later we emerged in the ground-floor hallway to be met by a dank smell of emptiness. Vacant houses always have this aroma, which lingers until the furniture of the new tenants arrives and magically exorcises it.

We opened the shutters and windows and a flood of light burst into the long open-plan living room where I'd had a drink with Jean-Claude and his family a few months before. It looked very bare now. Bare except for one very important piece of furniture that was already in situ. The piano. Upon moving out Jean-Claude had kindly got his brothers to help him move it up from the garage and into the living room. A gesture that had probably saved me and Brad from a premature acquaintance with the French health system.

'Go and play something,' said Brad. 'A welcoming ditty.'

I lifted the lid and banged out the first tune that came into my head – which happened to be the *Pink Panther* theme. Quite why this melody emerged through my fingertips I do not know, perhaps it was some kind of subconscious homage to the Clouseau-like way we had entered the house. However, through the recently opened windows it also announced to the neighbourhood that someone new had arrived. Someone who knew the *Pink Panther* theme.

'I think a cup of tea is in order,' I declared as the final chord began to fade. 'I'll unpack the kettle.'

As new English settlers, it was important to mark our territory with a good old-fashioned cup of tea. Not to have done so would have been a betrayal of our heritage. It was certainly true that now I was here in France I wanted to absorb the local culture, but two things were non-negotiable. Tea and Marmite. I was not giving either of these up, and the fact that weeks before I'd made sure that the kettle was the most accessible object amongst the pile of stuff now waiting in the garage to be unpacked went some way to prove it.

In anticipation of a splendid brew, I turned on the tap in the kitchen, only to hear a whirr of escaping air, a sound that announced an hour of frustration. Faced with the prospect of days without water, Brad and I vigorously searched the house, garage and garden, meticulously turning on every tap or stopcock we found to see if it would afford us access to this life-giving commodity. But all we got was air. Life-giving, yes, but useless when you want to make tea or wash the muck out from between your toes.

From my mobile, I called Jean-Claude at his new house.

'*Ah bonjour, Tonnee!*' he said, before welcoming me to my new home.

He then proceeded to direct me to a distant corner of the front garden, talking me through each step as I remained on the phone. Soon I found myself being directed to climb under a prickly bush, beneath which was a small manhole cover. I got down onto my hands and knees and began crawling, all the time still conversing on the phone with an enthusiastic Jean-Claude. A car went by a few feet away in the road and I looked up to see Rene the Mayor. He smiled and offered me a cordial wave. The slightly puzzled expression that accompanied his gesture may have reflected a sense of mystery as to why I was choosing to engage in a phone call from beneath a shrub in my front garden. I winced. What if Jean-Claude and Rene had covered the subject of my interest in corks at the village lunch? If so, the mayor would now be able to add 'crawling under shrubs to make phone calls' to an ever-growing list of eccentric behaviour.

I turned the stopcock, which lay beneath the least visible manhole cover in all of France, and heard the reassuring whoosh of the water bursting forth into the pipes. Music to my ears. How on earth I had been expected to find this stopcock without instructions, I do not know. Perhaps Jean-Claude had simply forgotten to leave a note for me. Maybe it had been an initiative test. Perhaps Jean-Claude had injured his back whilst moving my piano and had wanted a gentle revenge. No matter, the kettle soon boiled and two splendid cups of tea were served on the balcony, to two grateful and thirsty Englishmen.

We had arrived.

* * *

For the next couple of days we were completely unable to do what seemed natural. Instead of basking in the summer sun, we got on with the copious chores that awaited our attention inside the house. The tasks we faced were taxing but fun – at least, that's what I kept telling Brad, and to his credit he kept agreeing. It was most impressive that he could unpack boxes and lug furniture about with such joie de vivre, especially at a time when his emotional life was in a state of transient turmoil. From time to time we'd discuss the meaning of love and relationships – usually in the midst of a mind-blowingly menial task. Just as my life had undergone the scrutiny of Tim and Matt as we'd driven all my belongings down here, now it was Brad's turn to be under the microscope. All sorts of questions were raised. What did he want exactly? What were the things that really made him happy? Why had married life become such a struggle?

Of course, there was a bigger question to be asked. Why had I been finding myself embroiled in so many conversations of this nature in recent months? Was it an age thing? Had I reached a point in my life where drifting through was no longer enough, and I wanted answers? Was I sifting through the emotional debris of Brad's marriage so that I could find clues as to whether any kind of relationship could ever really work out for me?

'Do we need kitchen foil?' asked Brad.

It was a question that convincingly punctured the analytical stuff.

Brad had begun a shopping list, but it was far from being your standard 'milk, eggs and bread' kind. This was the scarier sort that involved light bulbs, pillowcases, electric plugs, extension cables, shower curtains, sandpaper and crockery. Oh yes, and kitchen foil. We needed a big store.

'What does *géant* mean?' asked Brad, as we pulled into the vast car park at the conclusion of the half-hour drive.

'Gigantic,' I replied. 'That's why this is just the store we're looking for.'

Well, it was and it wasn't. By and large, I have a love–hate relationship with these places. By and large, I love hating them. You, the shopper, are seduced by the fact that you can get everything you need in the one place, but once you get inside you end up spending hours trying to find the right aisle for what you're seeking, and when you finally get to the checkout, after what seems like hours of ill-tempered trudging, you realise you've forgotten the sugar. You are then faced with the mile and a half walk back to the aisle where the sugar is, by which time someone with a trolley piled as high as Mount Snowdon has usurped your place in the queue. When you reach the checkout girl, you discover that at least four of the items in your trolley haven't been priced correctly, and the girl has to ring a bell and wave your item in the air until a spotty man appears, looks at your item and then buggers off whilst you wait patiently, and everyone behind you looks at you like you've killed more innocent people than Slobodan Milosevic and Saddam Hussein put together.

When you finally pay for your goods, you make the generous gesture of paying in cash so that the people behind are spared further delay, but the checkout girl slows everything up by having the gall to hold each banknote you give her up to the light to check that it's not forged. When this happens to me I think that it's only right and proper to do exactly the same with each item of shopping I've purchased. Extravagantly I reach down for the breakfast cereal and brandish it aloft saying, 'Hey, these Weetabix are counterfeit.' The result is usually one of all round bad feeling.

Fraught, tired and immensely frustrated, you return to your vehicle hoping that it won't be your turn to be the car that gets dented by that driver. That driver, of course, is the elderly one who can't handle manoeuvring in the kind of car park that crams a thousand cars into a space suitable for 257. If lucky (or even if unlucky), you exit the car park as fast as you can, swearing that you'll never visit one of these places again. A promise you keep until the next time that you actually need some shopping.

The experience in Géant was better than expected. Unlike the staff in their British counterparts, the workers here appeared to be motivated by more than a sense of shame. On the contrary, they genuinely seemed to enjoy their work and take pride in the fact that they knew the layout of the store. In fact, they were almost too helpful. I was approached by one of them after Brad and I had temporarily parted company, having given each other separate bits of the shopping list to track down. The kindly female assistant asked if she could help me. I hesitated. The problem was that I didn't know the French word for kitchen foil, so it was actually a situation where I didn't want help, unless she actually had a French/English, English/French dictionary to hand. My fear was that in the time it would take to try and communicate what I was after, I could have traipsed up and down every aisle in the store three times over.

My fear wasn't unfounded. I began by trying to explain to the lady that I was looking for the stuff that you often use to wrap around a fish when you cook it.

'*Ah!*' she said, raising a finger and looking pleased, before leading me to the fish counter.

'*Non,*' I said, and her face fell.

Unfortunately she wasn't crestfallen for long, and soon she was looking at me expectantly again, much like a dog eyes you when it's nosing you a ball in anticipation. So I had another go, this time by trying to mime 'wrapping something over something else'. For some reason, this made the lady lead me to the section that sold string.

'*Non,*' I said, and her face fell.

Another expectant look ensued, though, as she nosed the ball towards me again. This time I became inspired and threw in the world '*métallique*', following it with another poor attempt at the 'wrapping' mime.

This time I was led to cheese graters.

'*Non,*' I said, and her face fell.

At this point I could see Brad clearly visible not that far behind her, successfully having located the light bulb section by a much less painful means. It seemed that speaking no French whatsoever can be a distinct advantage at times. Especially when in France.

Frustrated, I decided to enunciate what I wanted, loud and in English.

'ALUMINIUM FOIL,' I said.

'*Ah!*' she said, before leading me to . . . yes! The aluminium foil! Success at last.

'*Voilà!*' I said with glee.

'*Alu,*' she said.

'Ah, *alu!*' I repeated.

And with that, the tiniest of words, she was gone from my life. Or so I thought. Minutes later I was aware that she was coming back, no doubt trying to 'help' me with my next item. I wasn't having any more of her unhelpful helpfulness. No thanks. I made damn sure of it, and darted behind the tinned vegetables counter when she approached me. I would find the sandpaper on my own. Crouched out of sight and waiting for her to pass, I found myself dreaming wistfully of the elusive, distracted and downright ignorant staff employed by superstores back home in the UK. For the first time I felt I really appreciated how little they had to offer.

Conforama was next on our shopping expedition, a kind of French IKEA but without the crowds. Back in the UK I'd noticed that IKEAN crowds are able to swarm like bees with such vigour that they can sweep you round the warehouse against your will, dragging you past items that may have interested you before dumping you in a more spacious area where you'd buy pillows or candles you didn't really want in order to justify having made the trip in the first place.

Conforama was more peaceful and sedate, and instead of crowds I was greeted by a pretty young sales assistant. Her badge said that her name was Emmanuelle. I suppressed some unwholesome thoughts loosely based around some films from the 1970s, and asked her to direct me to mirrors, wardrobes and chests of drawers. This she duly did, and I made numerous purchases based on the fact that I was knackered, and that her name was Emmanuelle. Brad looked on, eyeing our sales assistant in a manner that might best be described as 'distinctly heterosexual'. As we made our way to the checkout desk he asked me a question which suggested that for the last ten minutes the quality of the goods I was selecting hadn't been at the forefront of his mind.

'What's the French for "arse"?' he enquired.

'I think it's "*cul*",' I replied.

Brad smiled, and so did I. Perhaps it was because we were two forty-something men buying furniture together that we felt the need suddenly to become 'ladsy'. Perhaps it was because we felt that to Emmanuelle we must have seemed like two men setting up home together. Our automatic and unwitting response to this was to demonstrate our heterosexuality by pointing at women in the store and making references to particular aspects of their anatomy. New men we weren't. More in the mould of shameful, seedy adolescents.

In the queue for the checkout I allowed my eyes to fall on a particular feature of the woman who was two ahead of us.

'Nice *cul*,' I said to Brad, at an indiscreet volume.

Like a complete idiot I had assumed that '*cul*' was a great little code word that Brad and I could safely use. I had instinctively avoided saying 'nice arse' for fear of offending anyone. However, I'd made the profoundly unintelligent choice of picking a French word to use as my cipher. Clearly not the best of ideas when one is actually in France at the time. Had I been Homer Simpson, this would have been the right time to emit a loud 'Doh!'

The husband of the lady in question turned round and scowled at me, whilst I smiled meekly and slowly reached down to my trolley, ready, if necessary, to use one of the flat-pack mirrors in self-defence. Brad, my temporarily fifteen-year-old colleague, sniggered like a juvenile.

It was time to go home.

Four words sum up the problem of the flat-pack mirror. No erection, no reflection. I'd bought three 'Matisse' free-standing mirrors, one for each of the bedrooms, and now they needed to be assembled. The instructions were clear, the makers having dispensed with any need for language by plumping for illustrations. The central drawing at the top of the sheet was a sketch of a man in dungarees holding up a spanner, and next to him was an egg timer with the number '15' beneath it. The omens weren't good. I wasn't wearing dungarees, I didn't have a spanner or an egg timer, and to date the only thing I'd managed to build in fifteen minutes of DIY was a raging fury.

However, today was an exception and this time everything fell into place, quite literally. For the first time ever, I was good, I was very good, managing to assemble my mirror in the time it took Brad to do the same in the adjacent bedroom. I then completed the third mirror, before emerging triumphantly onto the landing.

'Brad, I think I've cracked this DIY business at last,' I boasted. 'It's all about going slowly and being methodical.'

'Exactly,' said Brad, who'd built lots of things in his time and who I believed had a master craftsman inside him, struggling to get out.

'I'm going to have a go at one of the clothes rails now,' I said, eagerly.

'Good for you.'

I had fallen into George Foreman/Nigel Mansell/Björn Borg/ Mike Tyson syndrome. Instead of retiring after winning the world title, my ego had driven me onwards in search of even dizzier heights. It was ridiculous – I didn't even need the money, so what was I thinking of? A free-standing mirror is one thing – but a clothes rail is quite another.

I lay the metal jigsaw pieces out on the floor and tried to ignore the fact that the number under the egg timer was 45. I had never attempted anything of this magnitude before and it felt better not to focus on the size of the task in hand. Yes, I knew this was going to be harder, but if I went slowly and methodically there was no reason why this couldn't be as magnificent a success as the two terrific mirrors I had heroically liberated from their packaging, enabling them to stand majestic and free in the bedrooms.

Things began well enough, but as I progressed I found that I wasn't going slowly and methodically, just slowly. One key drawback on the 'methodical' side had been that I'd failed to notice something quite fundamental in the instructions. It was only much later that Brad pointed out that there were two men in dungarees sketched on the top of these instructions, and that trying to do the job alone, not to mention without dungarees, lacked wisdom.

After an hour and fifteen minutes of 'slowly', the clothes rail was in a precarious state of 'two-thirds finishedness'. The final third was the crucial bit. The bit that needed the other 'dungareed' man. I ploughed on alone, trying to balance metal poles whilst attempting to screw in bolts at the same time. Inevitably everything collapsed at the last possible moment, just when I thought I was about to be successful. After the fifth failed attempt at one particularly tricky part of the assembly, I allowed myself to slump onto the wooden floor (I didn't have far to go as I was already in a prostrate position with feet, arse and hands all performing pivotal roles in a highly intricate manoeuvre). I began to beat the floorboards with my fists, letting out a gentle wail as I did so.

'You all right in there?' called Brad from the next bedroom, no doubt well onto his second clothes rail in the time that I'd managed to construct something that resembled debris from a motorcycle accident.

'I'm fine,' I called back, as cheerily as I could. 'Nearly finished. How are you getting on?'

'Done one. Halfway through number two.'

I beat the floor once more.

'You sure you're all right?' came a concerned voice.

'Fine. Just fine.'

★ ★ ★

'Shall we go out tonight?' asked Brad, as we tucked into the delicious home-cooked ratatouille.

I'd volunteered to cook, largely as a means of getting out of finishing my apology for a clothes rail. Quite how Brad had managed to succeed in erecting all three rails without a dungareed assistant I didn't know, and I wasn't about to ask.

'What do you mean, go out?' I replied. 'The bars round here aren't exactly barrel loads of fun.'

I'd noted, with some chagrin, that the French aren't drawn to bars in the same way that the British are attracted to a pub.

'I was wondering if there are any discos around here,' said Brad. 'Maybe we should check out the local talent.'

Hmm. Local talent. How best to put Brad in the picture?

'It's not heavily populated in these parts,' I explained. 'And a lot of the young people go off to the big cities to study – and they don't necessarily come back. And the ones that do, tend to get married.'

'Yeah, but it's Friday night. There must be some local talent,' insisted Brad.

No doubt there were talented musicians, even farmers who showed a great aptitude for handling tractors, but not necessarily talent of the sort to which Brad was alluding. I'd spent a little more time here than Brad and I knew that it being 'Friday night' wasn't necessarily enough.

'What about that disco we saw on the way to Conforama?' persisted Brad.

'We could give it a go, I suppose,' I said with a pronounced lack of enthusiasm, hoping that he might spot this and go off the idea.

'Great!' he said eagerly. 'I've always liked French girls. They're really sexy.'

'And you really think you might find one tonight?'

'Of course. Anything is possible. Only a fool thinks otherwise.'

'Yes. Yes, you're right.'

For all Brad's noble positive thinking, I couldn't help but believe that he had a night of disappointment ahead of him.

8

Pool Hell

It would be quite cool, we thought, to wander nonchalantly into the disco when the party was in full flow and head straight onto the dance floor. We believed we'd got our timing just about right as we arrived at precisely 11.30pm.

'Try and look as young as you can,' I said to Brad as we approached the drab converted warehouse that now housed the club. 'We'll probably be the oldest ones here, barring the owner.'

Brad's eagerness to 'get down and boogie' meant he reached the nightspot's big red door several paces ahead of me.

'That's odd,' he said. 'There's a note here saying something.'

A beat later I caught up with my friend, and I read the sign that had halted his progress.

'That's weird,' I said. 'It says it doesn't open until midnight.'

'Midnight?' queried Brad.

'That's what's written here.'

To us this seemed most odd. We weren't in Paris now. We were in a distinctly rural part of France where the entertainment options appeared to be minimal. Where the hell were all the disco's potential clientele right now? They weren't in the local bar because we'd driven past it on the way here and noted that it was almost empty.

'What shall we do?' I asked, hoping for a two-word answer – 'go home'.

'Find another bar,' said a determined Brad. 'We could have a drink there and then come back.'

And so we decided to look for another bar in Tarbes, the home of Conforama, which was a twenty-minute drive away.

'Perhaps we'll bump into Emmanuelle,' said Brad optimistically.

'Yes, she'd like that,' I replied in sardonic tone.

It was probably her idea of a splendid Friday night – meeting two ageing foreigners whose only faltering conversation would be based around the earlier purchase of some free-standing mirrors and clothes rails. Yes, you could see how, quite quickly, it could get her 'all steamed up'.

Quite what Brad, as someone who spoke no French, was hoping for from tonight I wasn't entirely sure. To score, he would have to rely on looks and animal attraction. Or perhaps enormous amounts of alcohol could ease the path to communication. Either way, I reckoned that the odds were heavily against either of us having any company back at the house that night. Brad, however, remained upbeat.

'I love French women,' he kept saying, almost as if this desire alone would be enough to provide him with one.

A brief drive around Tarbes town centre didn't reveal any inviting hostelries and so we settled for the least gloomy bar from three of the dingiest in south-west France. Alas, drinking in bars just isn't a part of French popular culture, and Brad and I were paying the price for this right now. That was why we got in the mood for partying the night away by downing a couple of beers in the company of a very small number of young people who looked like they'd been tagged by the police, or who would have to report to probation officers first thing in the morning.

We were back at the disco at 12.45am, with considerably diminished expectations. The momentum had gone out of the evening. We had to face it, we were hardly on a roll, and were at an age where we couldn't kick-start the enthusiasm as easily as we'd done twenty years before.

'You still up for this?' I said to Brad, as I pulled in to park.

'Yup. You?'

'Yeah. I guess so.'

I needed to find some enthusiasm from somewhere. Things are more fun if you 'go for it'. I knew that. Yes, it was unlikely that the two of us would find the women of our dreams on this particular night out – but hadn't I always been told that it would happen when I least expected it? Perhaps this was the night for that prophecy to be fulfilled.

'Right, let's go for it!' I said with as much gusto as I could muster.

We pushed open the big red door and walked into the club.

'Oh dear,' said Brad, looking around him.

Instead of being greeted by a throng of young revellers, we were faced by the closest thing to one man and his dog that a nightclub can produce. There were only three other customers – a hippy-looking guy and two girlfriends, who peered up at us as if we'd taken a wrong turning somewhere and believed this to be the Holiday Inn, Toulouse. We sat down on an ugly velvet banquette, trying not to slump. I glanced across at the two girls, just in case something could still happen when I least expected. Neither girl took my fancy, and judging by the way my look was returned, the feeling was emphatically mutual.

'Well, Brad, what do you think?' I said, hoping that he'd be ready to throw in the towel.

'Let's have a drink and see if the place fills up,' he replied doggedly.

'OK, I'll get a round in.'

A drink each and twenty euros later we looked out across the empty dance floor as it paraded itself before us like a cheap temptress. Lights flashed all around it, and the euro-pop blasting from the speakers ensured that at least two-fifths of the clientele weren't remotely tempted to make use of it.

'The barmaid said that the club doesn't really start to get busy until about 3am,' I part-bellowed above the echoey boom, boom, boom of the sound system's bass.

Brad looked at his watch: 1.15am.

'You know what,' Brad called back. 'I reckon that this is the wrong thing for us to be doing out here. If you want nightlife, it's available in London.'

'Precisely. We can see the Pyrenees from my house. It should be a spiritual haven, a veritable antidote to nightspots like this – a place for meditation, reflection, early nights and bright new dawns.'

'I'll drink to that!' said Brad, holding his almost empty whisky and coke aloft.

We downed our drinks, got up and left, safe in the knowledge that in future, as we slept soundly in our beds, we wouldn't be missing out on anything.

God we were getting old.

'So are you any closer to knowing what you want to do about this swimming pool?' asked Brad, as I hung up the phone.

We'd already spent the morning driving around the half dozen swimming pool centres that dotted the surrounding area. It had been a much more difficult business than I'd expected, mainly because I hadn't realised how little I knew about swimming pools. They're more than just holes in the ground with water in them. Oh yes. They come in all different shapes and sizes; they can be made in fibreglass, steel, plastic, polystyrene blocks or concrete; they require pumps, skimmers, filtration systems and floating surface cleaners; some of them need liners, others special paint; and then there's the question of how you get in and out of them – do you build steps or have an old-fashioned swimming ladder? And don't forget that you also have to decide what kind of cover you are going to put over it in the winter. All these questions and more were fired at me by each retailer we visited. I would have struggled in English, but in French I was left feeling utterly flummoxed.

'It's so tough to make a decision,' I said. 'That was Malcolm on the phone just now, and he was suggesting that I go and talk to Paul and Berry for advice.'

'Who are Paul and Berry?'

'They're another English couple, who live the other side of the village.'

'There are more English here? I thought it was just you and Malcolm and Anne.'

'I'm afraid not. Apparently they were away for the weekend of the village lunch so I didn't get to meet them then. Malcolm says they've got a pool and that they should be able to offer some advice I can actually understand.'

'God, more English people!' said Brad, still amazed by the news.

'Yes, I know. I've got mixed feelings about it.'

This spot in the Pyrenees was supposed to have been my discovery, my little part of rustic France. I'd come to terms with the fact that Malcolm and Anne had beaten me to it, but another couple as well? I wasn't Pioneer Tony after all.

As I walked round to Paul and Berry's house, uplifted as ever by the scenic backdrop, I started to reflect on why rural France had become such a draw for the British. I passed the village hall, tacked onto the side of *la mairie* like a bureaucratic afterthought, and I wondered if this building summed it all up. This gave the place a sense of community, and it had been here that newcomers were made welcome by the warmth and neighbourliness of the locals. This seemed to be something that has slipped from our limp British grasps in the last quarter of a century. My generation, to its shame, has somehow overseen this loss, and the result is that the Brits are looking overseas to find a replacement for it.

A tall, fit man in his late fifties greeted me at the door.

'You must be Tony,' he said. 'Good to meet you.'

'Thanks,' I said. 'I'm sorry to drop in on you at such short notice. It's just that I'm getting so confused about pools.'

'I'm not surprised, pools are bloody confusing. Come and meet Berry.'

Paul's wife was lying by the pool, looking in the kind of shape that proved life in the French Pyrenees is good for you.

'Hey, nice pool,' I said, after completion of the formal introductions.

I wasn't just being polite. This had to be one of the most relaxing of locations. The sun was beating down on us as we sipped fresh orange juice by the azure-blue water of the pool, with the Pic du Midi observing our hedonism from a safe distance. Having a swimming pool was making more sense than it ever had before. This was really cool.

'We'll give you the benefit of what we know,' said Berry. 'But we're no experts.'

Paul and Berry didn't need to be experts. They just needed to know more than I did, and they certainly fulfilled that brief. However, after a long discussion about the various methods and materials available for construction, I still found myself as confused as ever. But the worst news was hearing that whichever company I went with, none of them would be able to start work on installing the pool until the following August, such was the demand.

'But that means I'll miss next summer,' I said, almost in the tone of voice of a sulking child.

'Yes, it's awful, isn't it?' said Berry. 'There are just too many people having pools built.'

'Do you reckon I could get some local builders to help me?' I asked.

'Fat chance,' scoffed Paul. 'They're all snowed under with work too. There just aren't enough builders in this region to meet the need.'

'Oh,' I said, realising that my pool project was looking rather dead in the non-existent water.

'I guess you'll just have to be patient,' said Berry.

'Or build it yourself,' said Paul, completely unaware of my recent travails with a clothes rail.

'Er yes. I'm not sure if that would be playing to my strengths though.'

From the kitchen an English voice interrupted us. It sounded familiar. I looked up and, dog-like, cocked my head.

'Who's that?' I asked.

'That's Steve.'

'Steve?'

'It's BBC radio. It's Steve Wright in the afternoon.'

'Wow – you can get that here?'

'The miracle of the internet,' said Paul.

'I love my English radio and TV,' said Berry. 'It keeps me in touch with things. I couldn't live without *Casualty* on a Saturday night. I'm hooked.'

Berry, it seemed, had developed a different approach to living in France. She openly admitted that she missed being close to her family and that the constant effort required with the language was fatiguing. The sound of an English DJ, or time spent with a British soap opera, were things that she'd struggle to do without. For her, technology meant that the country of her roots wasn't so far away and she was happy to live in a kind of cultural hybrid.

'Well, thanks for your time,' I said as I stood up to go.

'I'm sure we weren't much help,' said Paul.

'You were. If nothing else, you've confirmed for me that I have to get a pool.'

'Bring your trunks next time and have a swim,' said Berry.

'I will, thanks.'

The way it was looking, I'd be doing exactly that for years to come.

★ ★ ★

The following day Brad continued with DIY chores around the

house and I set off bright and early to purchase an ever-growing list of tools from the *quincaillerie*. I didn't know it yet but this hardware store was going to become one of my favourite shops in Bagnères. It didn't look much from the road, but once inside I was amazed to discover that the shop stretched out into little anterooms, each of which harboured a different specialist area of bolts, nuts or electrical paraphernalia. The man who ran the place was in his late sixties, and he had an assistant who was younger than him, but only just. I watched them serve the two customers before me and I was quickly convinced that the two of them knew everything about their stock, right the way down to the last nut and bolt.

It occurred to me that these are the kinds of shops that have all but disappeared in England with the onset of the big chains and their knockdown prices. Somehow in France these family-run stores are still able to survive alongside the capitalist giants. For how long, I wonder? I guess they'll only be there for as long as there's a generation who feel like they belong in the shop – and who don't have aspirations for big profits. These retailers tick over – that's all. They're never going to have a big money-spinning year that will enable them to sell up and go and live on a yacht in Monte Carlo. Not that the two men in the shop would have necessarily fitted in particularly well to that environment anyway. That world was of no interest. I bet that all they'd ever wanted to do was work in this *quincaillerie* and do it well, whilst raising a family along the way. This was their lot, and from the expression on their faces, it seemed to be a happy one.

As I headed home, pleased with my new purchases, I was in relaxed mood. I drove slowly. It's something I've always done. Passengers often look at me like there's something wrong with me, or make an irritated remark.

'Put your foot down, Grandad, for Christ's sake.'

I usually oblige, just for an easy life, but it's not something that comes naturally. I prefer to take it nice'n'easy. I'm not sure why, as

I'm not someone who lives my life without taking risks. Perhaps it's just that I can't see the point of hurrying everywhere. One of the great ironies of modern life is that people rush like crazy to get to places where quite often, in their heart of hearts, they don't really want to be. Not me though – I happily flirt with the lower end of the speed limit, however unfashionable it may be.

It wouldn't have been a problem in these parts had I been able to enjoy empty roads on which to dawdle with impunity. Unfortunately I had to share them with others, and they happened to be French Pyrenean drivers. What distinguishes this particular group from many others is their total disregard for braking distance. It is simply a concept they cannot grasp. Why allow a little space between you and the car in front, enabling you to relax and enjoy the drive? Far better to spend the entire journey in a constant state of anxiety by hugging the rear end of the car in front, even if all you're doing is nipping down to the supermarket for a pint of milk.

Just as I was driving through the local town at a sensible speed, a young couple stepped onto a pedestrian crossing in front of me, pushing a baby in a pram. I probably could have kept going, swerving where necessary, but I wasn't entirely sure whether the couple were expecting me to stop, and I had no idea whether they would continue to walk into my line of fire without looking. A split second of indecision followed before I resolved that stopping would be a better option than killing a young family. I quickly applied the brakes and drew the car to a halt at the crossing. However, a quick glance in the mirror immediately revealed that the vehicle behind me had been taken somewhat by surprise by my act of mercy. A bloody great big van was careering towards me, brakes screeching and driver making an excellent fist of looking horrified.

Fortunately the van had good brakes.

Unfortunately this didn't mean that collision was avoided. The van did hit me. Just not as hard as it might have done, that's all.

Thud!*

My head was jolted backwards, but the seat's headrest did its job and whiplash was avoided. For a second I just sat there – emotionless, stunned. A beat later and I was able to feel relief. Relief that I hadn't been injured. This was closely followed by disappointment. All things considered, having a hefty vehicle smash into your rear end isn't the ideal finale to any shopping trip.

Meanwhile, the couple with the pram crossed in front of me, as calm as you like. They looked across to me and managed a nod of thanks. Was that it? Was a cursory and almost desultory nod all I was going to get? I'd just saved their lives for God's sake – had they not realised this? And I'd sacrificed the rear end of my car in the process.

Not having a face to pull that could successfully express these feelings of outrage, I nodded back and the couple moved off, continuing their day seemingly unmoved by the recent collision of van and hatchback. No such luck for me, however. I got out of the car only to find myself confronted by an angry man. He was tall and wiry, and even though he wasn't wearing a beret, he was quintessentially French. I guess he was around forty years old, with a ruddy complexion, pointed nose and features that somehow suggested a penchant for intransigency. He waved his arms and berated me for having stopped. I timidly pointed out that I hadn't wanted to kill three people. This seemed a reasonable enough point of view, but my position had been immeasurably weakened by the fact that I was undoubtedly not French. Worse still, I was English.

Experience had shown me that the whole 'French not getting on with the English' business is nothing but a fallacy promoted by our modern tabloid culture, but every now and again there was a moment when one could almost begin to subscribe to it, and such a moment was upon me.

---

*Bang! or Crash! would do here too. You decide which best conjures up the noise of a large van colliding with a small Ford Ka.

I persisted with my defence, doing my utmost to form the best French sentences at my disposal, perceiving that errors in grammar would do more to harm my argument than any flaws in logic. Slowly, and with each correctly delivered turn of phrase, my Gallic foe calmed down. I pointed out that no one had caused the accident deliberately and that we could discuss rather than accuse, and soon we started to become chatty, almost to the point of being a bit 'pally'.

The best news of all was that close inspection revealed that there had been no noticeable damage to either vehicle. Miraculously my hire car, sturdy customer that it was, had withstood the impact without a scratch, and I was saved from an administrative nightmare involving insurance and car hire companies. This happy discovery enabled the two of us to shake hands warmly and say goodbye, only one notch short of arranging to meet for a drink later in the week. We had proved that European brethren can get on, even after one of them has driven into the back of the other.

I noticed as he drove off, however, that his vehicle was no ordinary van. No. Of course, it was a white van. What was it with me and white vans?

I hoped that I was living a good enough life to make it to heaven, because I reckoned I knew what my welcome at hell would be like.

'Ah, Hawks, there you are. We've arranged to have the soles of your feet beaten before you go to spend the night with the ravenous jackals. It's just a short journey of five hundred miles. Ah – here's the dodgy vehicle that will take you there now. It's a white van. Have a good trip . . .'

'There are a lot of lorries parked in the square, aren't there?' said Brad.

'Yes. I wonder why.'

Brad and I were driving through Bagnères on the way to the mountains where we were planning to take a nice walk. It had been my suggestion. It was a beautiful day so why not take a break from all this furniture assembly, fitting of lights and putting up of shelves? We were flying back to Britain the following day and we needed to be sure that we got ourselves a dose of some healing fresh air.

'It looks like there's been some sort of bike race going on,' said Brad.

The clue had been the scores of men in multi-coloured Lycra and the hundreds of state-of-the-art bikes strapped to vans and jeeps. A logo on one of the vans revealed the identity of the race.

'It's only the Tour de France!' I said.

It was a measure of just how cut off we'd allowed ourselves to become that the most watched sporting event in the world could pass by under our very noses without us knowing anything about it.

'It's a shame we missed that,' said Brad. 'I'd love to have seen the tour come through. Just a bit of it.'

'That's all you would have seen,' I said. 'A bit of it.'

I'd cast my eye over this race the previous year after having been persuaded by a friend to travel over to northern France for the day to watch it from a roadside. This experience had shown me that there may be many stages to the Tour, but for the spectator there are only seven.

1) Set up by roadside three hours before the cyclists are due to arrive and watch an empty road.
2) Eat a packed lunch whilst watching an empty road.
3) Half an hour before the arrival of the cyclists, become assaulted by a caravan of publicity vehicles with blaring loudhailers. Allow yourself to be bombarded by free samples of shampoos, peanuts or sweets, all tossed from the backs of passing vans by bored blonde models.
4) Wait for the brouhaha to die away again so that you can get on with the fascinating business of watching an empty road.

5) Enjoy thirty seconds of immense excitement as a pack of a hundred or so cyclists flashes by you at great speed.
6) Applaud.
7) Watch an empty road for a bit, and then bugger off home.

The Tour de France, rather pleasingly, was becoming France's Wimbledon – that is, a world-famous sporting event that nobody from the host country seems to win. It has been a generation since a Frenchman has triumphed in the tour and, worse still, in recent years it's been dominated by an American. Salt in the wound.

We drove on through Bagnères and left behind the ant-like hustle and bustle of the tour's enormous entourage of back-up teams, promotions people, television crews and journalists. We were heading for more peaceful climes. I dropped the car down into second gear as we began to climb towards the thinner air of the mountains.

This was to be my first proper mountain walk here, presumably the first of many. Up until this moment walking had never been a pursuit that had appealed that much. It wasn't exciting enough and it had no competitive element. Yes, walking is an event in the Olympics but everyone knows full well that it's the worst event in the games by some margin. I mean, that kind of walking isn't really walking anyway. It's nearly running. And what is the point of nearly running? If someone is chasing after you with a red-hot poker intent on inserting it where the sun don't shine then you don't nearly run away from them. I'm sorry, but you run as fast as you can. That's why running as fast as you can is such a tiptop event. Unlike the walking. I believe that in the Olympics the walkers (for want of changing one letter in their name) should have to enter another event as well – called Nearly Swimming.

No, for me, walking had always been an activity for middle-aged people. Maybe that was why I was looking forward to it so much.

Casual walkers (I can't speak for the competitive ones) are extremely friendly. As Brad and I set out on the ninety-minute walk across the side of a Pyrenean foothill towards a pretty lake, each person we passed offered up a jovial '*bonjour*'. Every single person, without fail. It was almost as if the moment they'd left the speed, noise and fluster of the town behind and exchanged it for the freedom of the countryside, their manners had changed.

'*Bonjour!*'

'*Bonjour!*'

'*Bonjour!*'

'*Bonjour!*'

We all said.

Initially Brad and I found this all rather charming and we happily returned each salutation at volume, and with relish. However, as the walk progressed and we were called upon to expend a lot of energy on a long steady climb, we began to resent every '*bonjour*', seeing each one as a waste of valuable oxygen. I started to mumble my '*bonjours*', and then, as I became even more out of breath, I noticed that Brad had come up with a good technique. He simply put his head down and avoided all eye contact with passing walkers. If a '*bonjour*' was still forthcoming from the opposing hiker then he did little more than mumble or grunt. A clever technique, and one I immediately adopted.

The problem was that, although these people were saying '*bonjour*', they didn't really want to stop, chat or pass on any meaningful information. I was reminded of a coastal walk I'd taken once in California where everyone I'd passed had said, 'Hi, how ya doin'?' I wouldn't have minded if they'd paused for a moment to find out how I was actually doing, but no, not the slightest reduction in the speed of their gait, not even a turn of the head to see what my reply might have been.

'Shall we take a short break here? I'm knackered,' I said to Brad.

'OK,' said Brad, without a hint of hesitation.

We were looking out across a stunning vista. Rolling hills, meadows, pastures with grazing sheep and cows, a busy stream and a smattering of barns and farmhouses. The town of Bagnères was visible in the distance, as was the whole region of the Bigorre, in all its bucolic simplicity. We scrambled up to a large rock where we could be '*bonjour*-free' for a while. Here, contented and calm, we sat and marvelled at the peace of it all.

'You see those sheep over there?' said Brad.

'Yes.'

'Well, why do you think there's one lot all sticking together and pointing the same way, and another lot over there, doing exactly the same, but having nothing to do with the first lot?'

It was a good question. Were sheep tribal creatures? There were definitely two distinct gangs on this mountainside.

'I wonder if they ever switch from one group to another?' I mused.

'And do they like each other − or is there an undercurrent of tension between them?' added Brad.

Neither of us had any answers.

We were fast discovering that this is what it's like when 'townies' go for a country walk. For the rest of our outing we found that every ten minutes a question was asked to which neither of us had any answer.

'How long can that buzzard hover there before he gets tired?'

'What kind of animal leaves droppings like that?'

'What altitude do you have to be at for grass not to grow?'

And all the time, the question to ourselves: why didn't we pay more attention in geography at school?

Finally Brad went for a sudden change of subject and delivered the killer question.

'So, did anything Paul and Berry said make you any closer to making a decision about the swimming pool?'

'Well, it's a shame,' I replied. 'But it does look like I'm going to have to be patient and wait until next August.'

'What? You can't wait that long!'

'Well, there's no alternative. What else can I do?'

'Do it yourself. They sell kits.'

'That's what Paul said, but he hadn't seen what a mess I made of the clothes rail. Do we want a swimming pool or a hole with a swamp around it?'

'You could hire in some local builder to do it.'

'There aren't any available. Paul and Berry say that there's a shortage and that they've all got more than enough work already.'

Brad scratched his head. He had a determined look on his face. I'd seen him like this before – in problem-solving mode.

'Maybe the answer,' he said, eventually, 'is for you to fly Ron out to join you. You could do the pool together.'

'Ron?'

'Yes, Ron.'

I looked askance at Brad, but I could see he was serious.

'The same Ron who recommended the white van which made it 500 yards on the epic journey to the south of France?'

'Yes.'

'The same Ron who has been holed up on his boat for the past few months saying he's feeling depressed?'

'Yes. But a trip to France will probably snap him out of it. He's a great builder. He'd be able to mastermind the pool – and do some of the other jobs you need doing.'

'I don't know. I think it might be better just to be patient and wait a year till we can get the pool professionals to do it.'

'Well, you know best.'

I hate that expression, mainly because people only use it when they mean exactly the opposite.

'We'll talk about it on the plane home tomorrow,' I said, closing what was fast becoming a difficult subject.

Brad's enthusiasm for the pool project was colouring his judgement. I'd have him brought back to his senses by the time we landed back in London.

Common sense would prevail.

9

Something in the Woodshed

The next time the plane touched down in Pau airport I knew that I wouldn't be seeing Britain again for months. The to-ing and fro-ing was over. This was it: I was moving to France for the summer. I was saying goodbye to driving on the left, traffic jams and the loud thwack of leather on willow on the cricket greens of our fair villages. It was 'cheerio' to TV soaps and the lurid sensationalism of the tabloid newspapers. I was bidding farewell to Britain and going to live with what some might describe as the beret-clad, garlic-chomping, onion-selling enemy. However, like the big man that I am, I was prepared to set our differences aside. So what if we'd once fought with each other for a hundred years? So what if de Gaulle and Britain hadn't always seen eye to eye? And never mind that some of the French saw us Brits as a nation of shopkeepers who boil everything until the flavour has gone. I didn't mind all that, I was happy to be going to live in France and it felt wonderful. It felt romantic. And it felt a little odd.

Odd, because when I checked in at the airport, my travelling companion was not the beautiful woman of my dreams – my soulmate, friend and lover all rolled into one. No, it was a fifty-six-year-old bearded bloke with a healthy gut and a cigarette hanging from his lips. It was Ron.

Common sense had not prevailed, and as a result Ron and I were going to be living together for the summer. Brad had put together a pretty persuasive argument on the flight back to Britain. How could I pass up the chance to lounge by a pool after my hours of piano practice were complete? Hadn't Ron always done a good job for me? Who else would be free and willing to do a job like this at short notice, and away from family and friends?

Under duress, I'd weakened and called Ron to see if he'd be interested in a daily rate to come and convert the garage into a living space, and start work on constructing a swimming pool.

'What do you think, Ron?' I'd asked. 'Would you be up for it?'

'Yeh, I s'pose so,' he'd said, somehow managing to keep his excitement under control.

I hadn't been as nervous as I might have been about inviting Ron to live with me. Technically he may have been my 'builder' but we'd never really had a relationship like that. Ron had overseen all the knocked-through walls, extensions, lofts and patios of my life, and I'd never had to suffer the torment that seems to engulf others at the moment they let 'the men with hammers' through the front door. 'Bloody builders,' they usually exclaim with a combination of frustration, contempt, resignation and self-pity. 'What a nightmare we're having!'

Not me though. It had always been fun with Ron. He'd turn up with whoever he'd mustered together to help him on the job, and the weeks that followed were invariably filled with cheerful banter. It didn't matter that I was the one who ultimately wrote the cheques, I'd be the butt for as many jokes as anyone else, perhaps more. The job always got done – perhaps not precisely on time or exactly as I'd envisaged, but it was a pain-free experience and that was good enough for me.

Nevertheless, however well you get on with your builder, it's still not normal to get him to move in with you. Certainly not if you're a heterosexual man who is not instantly drawn to beards and bellies. However, because we both have a decent sense of humour, we like our own space, and we were both Piscean men living without a woman in our daily lives, I thought we could make this work.

I must admit, though, that recently I'd noticed a deterioration in Ron's general condition. He'd not had much work lately, mainly because he hadn't picked up the phone and chased it, and he'd spent too much time alone on his boat, slowly letting his self-confidence ebb away. By his own admission, his appetite for building had disappeared and of late he'd tended to perform the role of foreman, preferring to point at work and direct others rather than actually knuckle down and do any hard graft himself. Secretly I hoped that removing him from his boat and dumping him in the Pyrenees might lift his spirits and herald the era of a 'New Ron' – vibrant, cheery and eager to get on with things.

The day of our departure arrived. The airport was packed, and it felt different somehow to my previous trips. At first I was confused as to why, but then I realised. The school holidays had begun and most of those around us were families going on their annual fortnights away. At check-in, instead of being surrounded by the relative calm of the business traveller, Ron and I were subjected to the constant whine of children's questions: 'MUM, WHY DO WE GIVE OUR SUITCASES TO THE LADY?' 'DAD, WHY DID HE WANT TO KNOW WHO PACKED OUR BAGS?' And then there were the weary appeals of exhausted mothers: 'DAMIAN, PLEASE STOP PULLING YOUR SISTER'S HAIR,' topped by the occasional raucous bellow from a short-tempered father: 'DEAN, GET OFF IT RIGHT NOW! IT'S A LUGGAGE TROLLEY NOT A BLOODY DODGEM CAR!'

These people looked dog-tired and it was a pretty good bet that they were all going to return from their two weeks away desperately in need of a holiday. Occasionally a father would look at me with an envious glint in his eye. I'm afraid I had little sympathy. It had been precisely the weary expression that this poor fellow was wearing that had always put me off the idea of starting a family. Why put yourself through the grief?

If Ron and I weren't the original 'odd couple', then we made a splendid second best. From time to time people looked at us with an expression of curiosity, no doubt trying to work out who we were to each other. Just why were we travelling together? Were we relatives? Or work colleagues? Or did they think we were lovers? I quickly encouraged my mind to move on. This last image was one that I wasn't keen to have linger.

We completed the journey quietly, enduring the mayhem of migrating families with good grace and great forbearance. Soon enough we were exposed to the heat and humidity of late July in the south of France, and before long we were driving down the winding narrow road that led to my new home.

'Nice views,' said Ron, who had been in fine spirits for the journey.

'Yes – good, isn't it,' I replied, proudly.

Ahead I could see a small old lady with grey hair, shooing some chickens into an adjacent dilapidated barn. She immediately looked up at the sound of an approaching vehicle. I could now see that this was Marie, the sweet elderly lady with whom I'd played belote on the day of the village dinner. She beamed and waved to me. Well, it was more than a wave, really; it was an instruction to pull over the car and chat. An instruction that I duly followed. I leant out of the window and kissed Marie gently on each cheek. She looked a little taken aback and then I remembered that the etiquette in France was generally to kiss women younger than you, and shake hands with the older ones. Oh well, maybe it fell to me to change all that.

'*Voici mon ami Ron,*' I said, pointing to my passenger.

Marie tried to reach across and shake his hand, but it was too far. Ron nodded meekly and made eye contact with Marie for only the briefest of moments. It reminded me just how painfully shy the man was.

Perhaps it was the two kisses, but Marie definitely had a twinkle in her eye as she fired questions at me. How was I? What was the weather like in London? How long was I here for? She chatted freely, regardless of the fact that all the chickens she'd diligently shooed into the barn were now slowly making their way back out again. She began to rave about how nice my car was but I quickly explained that this was rented and that I would be looking to buy a second-hand one soon. Ah, she said, then I should talk to her son. He would find me one. He repaired cars and often found good second-hand ones for people in the village. I thanked her and said goodbye.

'What was all that about?' asked Ron, who didn't speak a word of French.

'Oh, she was just saying how she's captain of the village volleyball team and that you looked like you'd be a useful addition to the squad. She's expecting you at training tonight.'

'Oh right,' he said, not really taking in what I'd said. 'There was a nice mechanical digger parked round the back of the farmhouse, did you see that? That could be very useful to you if you want to get the hole dug for your pool.'

'Good thinking, Ron.'

I called out to Marie, who was only too pleased to chat further and let more 'shooed' chickens leave the barn again. I learned that the digger belonged to her son Serge. I announced that I'd met him at the village lunch, but Marie put me straight. There were two Serge in the village and her Serge never went to social events. I was delighted to learn, however, that her Serge might be up for digging a big hole for me – he was very busy but it could be fine if I caught him at the right time.

'How did that go?' asked Ron as we drove away.

'Pretty well. The digger belongs to her son. He's captain of the volleyball team. If you play well at training tonight we could be in there.'

'Oh, right.'

We didn't get much further down the road before we were flagged down again, this time by a thin, middle-aged man in a blue peaked cap, sitting aloft in a beaten-up old tractor. I got out of the car and greeted the man, his hardy face ravaged by the sun, before shaking his hand and asking what he wanted. Somehow he seemed to know that I was the new Englishman who had moved to the village, and he was anxious to learn if I wanted to carry on with the same arrangement as the previous owner, Jean-Claude. The question confused me a little. Seeing my bewilderment, the farmer explained that there was a traditional agreement that during the summer he could bring his cows onto the bottom piece of my land to graze. This effectively meant that I wouldn't have to worry about mowing this grass, as the cows would munch it all away for me.

Was I all right with this?

Too right I was. Less work for me, and from time to time I got a herd of cows in my garden.

'*Une bonne idée*,' I said with a big smile.

The farmer, who I took to be as shy as Ron, nodded uncomfortably before starting up his tractor again and disappearing back into his world.

'I've got my own cows!' I announced to Ron, somewhat overstating the case.

'Well done,' said Ron supportively.

Just as the tractor was reaching the brow of the hill behind us, a grey-haired man in blue overalls appeared at the top of the drive to the house that nestled below us. It was 'bonhomie' Roger, the cheerful man I had met briefly at the village lunch and dinner. He was sporting his trademark grin and twinkly eyes.

'Hello, Tony,' he said, shaking my hand. 'Welcome back to France. How long are you here for?'

'A long time,' I replied. 'I am going to be a part of your village now.'

'This is good, you are most welcome.'

Roger's face showed that he meant this. It wasn't just some sycophantic remark that he'd made to pass the time of day. Conversations I'd shared with Anne and Malcolm meant that I knew this man to be genuine. He was one of the stalwarts of village life, working hard behind the scenes for all the village social events, and generally taking neighbourliness to new heights. I was pleased that he seemed to like me.

'I saw from the window in my house,' he said, still beaming broadly, 'that you were speaking with my mother.'

'Your mother?'

'Yes. Up the road. She lives in that house – where you stopped one minute before.'

Of course. I knew this from the village dinner. Marie was Roger's mother. And now I knew that Roger had a brother called Serge. And he had a mechanical digger. Serge probably lived with his mother Marie because he was single. Evidently Roger and his wife had built a new house on the family land, so he now lived next door to his mother and brother. In only a matter of minutes I was beginning to unravel the plot of the village's soap opera.

'Your mother tells me, Roger,' I said, 'that you might be able to find me a second-hand car?'

'But of course. What would you like?'

'An estate car would be good. About ten years old? A Peugeot – or a Renault.' I wanted to ingratiate myself by buying French.

'Don't worry. I will find you one,' he said, not altogether convincingly. 'And if you need help – you must knock on my door.'

With those words Roger disappeared back down his driveway, and Ron and I drove on, hoping to make it to the house this time. Our stomachs were calling for lunch.

'Very friendly round here, isn't it?' said Ron, somewhat amused by all the attention we'd already received even though we'd only been in the village a matter of minutes.

'Certainly is,' I said, smiling broadly.

'Were Roger and that farmer on about volleyball too?'

'No, Ron,' I said. 'They're president and vice-president of the Village Independence Party and they're arranging a march on Paris tomorrow morning.'

'Right.'

Just as we turned the final bend before my house, Irish Mary, who lived next door but one, waved to us from her terrace.

'Shall I stop and say hello?' I asked Ron.

'No, I'm starving. She'll have to wait till after lunch,' said Ron, unaware that he was missing out on the one conversation with the locals that he would have understood.

'Yeh, I'll be happy enough in there,' said Ron, with trademark monotone delivery.

We were busy sorting out where Ron would sleep whilst he was at the house.

'Are you sure?' I said. 'I mean, there's plenty of room inside.'

'Nah, this is probably better. It means that when your friends arrive, I'll be out the way.'

'Only if you're sure.'

'Yeh, I'll be all right in there.'

And so it was, with perhaps an oblique nod towards the Nativity, that Ron moved into the woodshed.

It was a good woodshed, mind you. Better than a stable, anyway. It had electricity, it was dry and it had a decent roof. Once we'd put a bit of carpet down and given the walls a lick of paint it was fit for . . . well, it was fit for Ron. He confirmed that he'd be happy enough in this bolthole, preferring to be out of the way of house guests. Ron liked his own space, but didn't necessarily need a lot of it. Life on a narrow boat had cured him of that indulgence. For him, the woodshed was relatively spacious, and after we'd finished moving in items of furniture it definitely resembled a hut which hardy young travellers would happily rent on a beach in Thailand or Goa. The only real difference was the lack of adjacent sun-soaked beach populated by scantily clad women. But no matter, Ron's imagination was as good as the next man's.

In the coming days we were kept very busy. Ron began tiling the downstairs double garage, the first stage of making it a habitable overspill for when the house was brimming with guests. Meanwhile I drove around the region buying materials and calling in on swimming pool shops, all the time wondering for how long I'd be stuck with the hire car. Was Roger seriously going to find me a second-hand estate car? Genuine though he may be, there had been nothing about his demeanour to suggest that this would be a priority for him. And why should it be? He had a full-time job as an engineer in nearby Tarbes, and he tinkered with cars at the weekend. He'd hardly have much spare time.

One morning as I drove towards his house I decided to drop by and make further enquiries. As I negotiated the steep driveway and neared his garage, I could hear the gentle tinkering of spanner on carburettor. Or screwdriver on alternator. Or similar. Well, you get the gist.

'*Roger? Tu es là?*' I asked, eager to announce a new presence.

An oil-covered man slowly revealed himself on a little trolley from beneath the big Peugeot estate before me. He could have been a diver emerging from the depths of the sea for all the knowledge I had of the world whence he had just come. The World of the Mechanic. An alien, scary world and not one where you'd choose to spend your holidays. Roger proffered his arm, since his hand, as he ably demonstrated with a brief flourish, was too oil-caked for the conventional grasp and shake. I smiled, shook his elbow and enquired as to how he was getting on in the 'finding me a nice ten-year-old estate car' stakes. He threw his head back, rolled his eyes and bent his bottom lip. A possible sign that he hadn't lined up a choice of six for my inspection.

'*Ah, c'est difficile,*' he said, adding a shrug to his vast range of gestures. 'The estate cars are hard to find – but do not worry. I am trying.'

Somehow I doubted that he'd done much vigorous phoning around or scouring of the local ads – or that he was about to do so. He just looked too laid back. Almost unhealthily so. I strongly suspected that his 'finding' an estate car would have had to involve someone driving one round to his place and handing him the keys.

It had been the shrug that Roger had given me when we'd said goodbye that led me to take such drastic action later that same day. It had been a gesture that I took to mean that although he wanted to help, he just wouldn't be able to find the time. That's why I pulled the car over when I spotted a nice little red Peugeot 106 for sale, parked outside a car spares shop. Ron and I had just liberated ourselves from another particularly confusing session with a pool retailer in which we'd endured a long and baffling speech on the differences between sand and chlorine filtration systems. Now I was going to invest time in something else that I knew nothing about.

'I think we should take a look at this car,' I said to Ron. 'It looks in good nick.'

'But I thought you wanted an estate.'

'I do, but Roger assures me that they're difficult to find, and I can't hire forever so maybe I'll have to compromise.'

Soon Ron and I were giving it the once over and Ron bestowed upon it his seal of approval.

'Sounds all right to me,' he said, as the owner jammed down the accelerator pedal. 'I think you've got a nice little runner there.'

The owner of the car appeared to be the proprietor of the shop as well, and I took this to be a very good sign. Provided that he wasn't a crook (and he didn't look like one – no stripy top, mask or sack over the shoulder marked 'swag') then the vehicle surely would have had spare parts showered upon it whenever it had needed them. Indeed, the owner reeled off a list of recently fitted new parts, all of which sounded impressively expensive.

'Sod it,' I said to Ron. 'I'm fed up of driving a hire car. It's a waste of money. If he'll accept a cheque, shall I buy it straight away?'

'Yeh,' said Ron. 'I think it's a good bet.'

I circled the car once more, trying to erase from my mind the fact that it had been Ron who had sanctioned the purchase of the White Van. To be fair, though, he hadn't given it an enthusiastic final appraisal. A 'piece of shit' had been his eloquent judgement upon it, and one that time had all too speedily borne out.

France is an excellent place to keep a pied-à-terre, have tête-à-têtes, use double entendres, arrange a ménage à trois or discover one's joie de vivre and raison d'être. It is also a smashing place to experience déjà vu. And that is precisely what I felt as I drove the red Peugeot away with Ron following behind in the hire car. The road ahead of me could easily have been in a suburb of Croydon and the wheel between my fingers that of a Luton van. Bereft of confidence, I drove on with a growing feeling of trepidation and impending doom. However, the kilometres rolled by and the car motored on, eventually delivering me home – accident and break-down-free, and in fine style. Quite extraordinary.

'There,' I said from the balcony, as I viewed my recent purchase glistening in the midday sun. 'Now I have a house and a car.'

'All you need now is a bird and you've got the set,' said Ron, succinctly evincing his uncomplicated view of the world.

'Yes, I suppose so,' I said. 'But cars and houses are so much easier to find.'

'And cheaper to run.'

I changed the subject. I like to view myself as a 'New Man'* and

---

*Male readers might like to test how much of a 'New Man' they are. In the street, if there is a woman walking towards you to whom you are greatly attracted, then your 'New Man-ness' is measured by the distance you allow her to continue walking past before you turn round to see what she looks like from behind. I'm about a five-yarder. Dock a point if you mumble 'nice cul' under your breath.

this conversation was heading in a direction where maintaining that position would have become increasingly difficult.

With each passing day my French improved. My vocabulary expanded to include the French words for obscure items within the building trade. And if we needed any more aluminium foil, I was well on top of that task too. I was building superficial but nonetheless agreeable relationships with a coterie of shop assistants. The only frustrating thing about the French shopping experience was the number of times I was caught by the midday closing. Exhausted by the three hours of toil between nine and twelve, staff would down tools and head off for a healthy lunch followed by *une sieste*. For someone who didn't necessarily get his act together to jump in the car and go shopping till 10.30am, this gave me a tiny window of opportunity to make my required purchases. If, as usually happened, I failed to make all the stores on time, then I was subjected to a couple of dead hours whilst I had to wait for the dozy gastronomes to open back up again.

Another annoying consequence of this tradition was the way in which my builder took to it. Whilst it would be stretching it to describe Ron as a Francophile, culturally he was at one with the concept of having a lie-down after lunch. For me, he embraced it with far too much relish. His working day seemed to take on an extraordinary shape. The combination of breakfast, mid-morning tea and biscuits, lunch, sleep and mid-afternoon tea didn't seem to leave much time for other things. Like tiling the floor of the garage, for instance.

Work advanced slowly. It seemed that my hope that the mountains would inspire Ron was unfulfilled. Ron would regularly fail to surface following his *sieste*.

'I think I'll just do a half day today,' he'd call from his reclining position within the woodshed.

I would then produce a frustrated sigh. Knowing that Ron would only ever charge me for the hours that he'd actually worked, I had little grounds for complaint. I just wished I could think of a way to motivate him.

Just after we'd first arrived I'd come close to getting him to agree to exercise a little each morning. I'd purchased a cheap bike from the Géant superstore on which I intended to undertake a daily circuit of the village, notwithstanding the precipitous gradients.

'Ron, why don't you walk down to the sawmill and back whilst I do the cycling,' I'd suggested. 'Very healthy.'

The old sawmill was fifteen minutes' walk away, nestled at the bottom of the valley in an idyllic location.

'Yeh, I think I might,' he'd said, once again skilfully concealing his excitement.

On the first morning of this new health regime I set off zealously at 7.30am on the dot. It was a beautiful day. The sun was just rising over the distant peaks, backlighting a narrow strip of wispy clouds. The grass glistened with a hint of dew and the cowbells echoed through the valley. Against this picture-postcard backdrop, a forty-something English bloke struggled up some extraordinarily steep hills on a bottom-of-the-range bike. Sweat poured from his brow as he panted and gasped like an octogenarian lover in the throes of potentially fatal lovemaking. Neither bike nor legs could cope with what was required, and willpower notwithstanding, the Englishman ended up dismounting the bike and opting for the pushing option, so rarely favoured in the Tour de France.

I must have cut an unimpressive figure to the drivers of the occasional cars that sped past me as I wheeled my bike up these punishing hills. The problem was that the Tour du Village involved no normal cycling. It was either gruelling, thigh-busting heaves up hills better suited for mountaineering, or legs akimbo freewheeling down the other side of them. Nothing aerobic about this, but exhausting just the same. A bit of a lose/lose situation.

At the top of one of the steeper of the five slopes which *le tour* included, I met a little old man coming the other way, stick in hand. As I drew closer I recognised him to be André, the delightful elderly gentleman who would have taken me back to his place after the village dinner had it not been for the fact that he hadn't any milk in. I didn't recognise him instantly because the top of his head, which previously had dazzled all comers with its 'Persil whiter-than-whiteness', was now covered with textbook French beret.

'*B'jour,*' said André.

'*Bonjour,*' I replied.

'*Toon v'sage er ruj,*' he seemed to say.

'*Pardon?*'

This was going to be a difficult exchange. André spoke no English and made little compensation for the fact that I was not someone who was well versed in the regional accent or the fusion of French and patois in which he liked to indulge.

'*Toon v'sage er ruj,*' he repeated.

'*Encore, s'il vous plaît. Je n'ai pas compris.*'

'*Toon v'sage er ruj.*'

'*Ah oui!*' I said, feigning comprehension.

This was standard practice for me. Once something had been said three times and I still failed to understand, then I would fake it. It was unsatisfactory for both parties but at least things moved along.

Funnily enough, just after I'd pretended to understand, the real meaning of André's short sentence popped into my head. '*Toon v'sage er ruj*' meant '*Ton visage est rouge*'. My face was red. Of course, given the state of me, how could he not comment on that?

André then pointed to my bike before remarking that it would be much easier if I used a Mobylette.

'*Je fais de la bicyclette pour être en forme,*' I explained.

André's immediate frown suggested that he was some way from embracing this as a valid concept. Cycling for him, it seemed, was not a good way of keeping fit.

'*Moi, j'ai six vaches,*' he said.

André seemed to be suggesting that having six cows was a better way of achieving a peak of fitness than the method I had chosen. He explained that although he was retired, a nice little EU subsidy made keeping the cows worthwhile. There was another reason for keeping them too, he claimed with a defiant smile – because what else would he have to fill his day? The comment acted as something of a reminder as to how our two worlds differed. Over the years I had become very accomplished at leading quite an active life without any recourse to cows. Ideally, I hoped to keep it that way.

Then, for reasons that his accent rendered utterly incomprehensible, André led me the few paces back to his house and beckoned me into his yard. It was like another world, full of farmhouse equipment that appeared to date from the nineteenth century. He began to take me on a tour, pointing out different things whilst all the time shooing away an overenthusiastic dog that was gambolling about his ankles. The reason for the yard tour became apparent when he opened a barn door and showed me his Mobylette, as if it was an exhibition piece. In fact, judging by its age, it might well have been. I nodded approvingly at the contraption and made some trite comment about how '*jolie*' it was. Mobylettes aren't 'pretty', but André didn't mind this. He just seemed to be happy to have someone to show it to. I imagined that a good period of time might have passed since he'd last coaxed any passer-by into a private viewing.

'*Bonne journée!*' he called after me as I began to freewheel down the country lane ahead of me.

'*Merci!*'

'*Bonne journée*' is the French equivalent of 'Have a nice day' but without the smarmy connotations. I'd noted that in France people seemed to say it when they really meant it, unlike in America where it often seems to roll off people's tongues as easily as my builder succumbed to the lure of a siesta in the woodshed.

André bade me farewell and headed off to tend to the six cows that helped fill his days. As I glanced back over my shoulder and saw him become a silhouette against the skyline, I realised that he'd been right. The only satisfactory way to tackle the undulating terrain of the village was on a moped.

I didn't tell Ron this when I got back to the house, though. Instead I did my best to be unfalteringly positive.

'That was fab!' I declared, as I scooted down the short drive to see Ron propped up against the banisters of the balcony, sipping a cup of tea.

'How was your walk?' I asked.

'It was all right, I s'pose,' he replied, with customary lack of gusto. 'I only went halfway, then I came back.'

The conversation ended there. I spent the rest of the morning completely knackered but trying to look full of beans, but when it was time for *la sieste* I was suddenly as keen on the idea as Ron.

'Goodnight, Ron,' I said, as the clock struck one and I headed upstairs to bed.

'Goodnight, Tone,' replied Ron, eyes glinting in anticipation of imminent woodshed repose.

I never 'cycled' around the village again and, as far as I know, Ron never went on another walk.

And all the time the work progressed, but very, very slowly.

10

Mad Wood

Oh dear. Roger wasn't displaying his usual grin. In fact, he looked a little hurt. He'd flagged me down in my new car after I'd returned from an early morning excursion to get fresh bread for Ron's breakfast.

'*Tonny. Qu'est-ce que tu as fait?* You tell me that you want to have an estate car?' he said, looking rather dolefully at my red Peugeot 106.

'Well, I did,' I replied. 'But you seemed to say that they were difficult to find — and I just saw this one and it seemed to be a good deal.'

Roger threw a look at the car as if to suggest that it might fall apart quite soon.

'It is difficult to find an estate car, yes,' he said, 'but you did not give me very long.'

'Sorry, Roger. I thought that you might be too busy.'

Roger shrugged and offered a little smile.

'*Pas un problème,*' he said, before waving me on my way.

As I negotiated the two bends that would return me to my house I began to wonder if I'd been too hasty. Should I have given Roger more time? Perhaps I needed to work harder at losing my impatient city ways. Things happened slower around here, and I would have to get used to that if I didn't want to upset people. With Roger, I reckoned that I'd got away with a frown and shrug, but with others I might not always be that lucky.

'You do realise you're going to have to make a decision on this pool, don't you?' said Ron, one morning over breakfast.

I was painfully aware of this fact. There were just too many ways to build a swimming pool, and too many reasons being offered by each manufacturer for why theirs was the best. Paul and Berry had done their best to help but I remained as confused as ever.

'All right,' I replied. 'We've got one more place that sells them to visit. We'll go there this afternoon and then I'll take an executive decision.'

Ron looked sceptical.

It was a guy of about thirty who approached us and offered to help.

'My name is Fabrice,' he said, demonstrating that he had a smattering of English words.

I warmed to him immediately. He was slim, dark-haired, Gallic to a T, and with a cheeky grin not redolent of your average salesman. He invited us to sit down at his desk in one corner of the pool showroom and announced that he would talk slowly so that I could try and understand. This already put him ahead of his competitors. He took us through various options but he touched on one method of building a pool that seemed to have Ron very interested indeed. This was the method of using polystyrene blocks that you slotted together and then filled with concrete. Fabrice demonstrated how these blocks fitted together by pointing to pictures in a thick brochure. Pictures instead of technical French.

What a joy. We learned that the blocks were extremely light, and what's more they suffered less heat loss than your ordinary concrete block.

'This sounds like your best bet,' said Ron, leaning over to me as Fabrice nipped off to fetch some more pool literature.

'You think so?'

Ron nodded.

I couldn't help suspecting that he had been drawn to this system because polystyrene blocks are considerably lighter than concrete ones. For a moment I looked at Ron and I imagined a Homer Simpson-style bubble appearing above his head containing an image of him standing and drooling over a pile of polystyrene blocks, just as Homer might over a bag of doughnuts, purring, 'Mmm. Polystyrene. No heavy lifting.'

Having agreed on how we should build the shell of the pool, the subject then turned to pumps and filtration. For this Fabrice called over a young lady to help, whom he introduced as Audrey. Ron's eyes lit up and so, I have to admit, did mine. Audrey was a young woman you might have expected to see working in a fashion house or at a perfume counter in a department store. Not in a swimming pool shop. She was immaculately turned out, perhaps a tad too heavily made up, but generally she was quite a stirring sight for two men who had been living together in a remote village with an extremely sparse population of women with Box Office appeal. Audrey explained about various pumps and filter systems and seemed to display an exceptional grasp of her métier.

'Blimey, I wouldn't mind grasping her métier!' I nearly announced. If, seconds ago, Ron had been Homer Simpson, then I was now in danger of becoming Sid James in a *Carry On* film.

Twenty minutes later I was writing out a cheque.

'You just bought the pool off them 'cos you fancied Audrey,' said Ron as we drove home. 'I saw the way you were flirting with her.'

'Not at all,' I protested. 'It was because I liked Fabrice.'

'Rubbish!'

'Look, Audrey's very nice but she's too young for me and knows far too much about chemical pH balances and chlorination systems,' I continued, citing two examples of Audrey's unsuitability, both of which I might have been prepared to overlook in the right circumstances.

'Well, either way that's it,' said Ron. 'You're committed now – you've got yourself a swimming pool.'

If only that had been the case. All I'd purchased was a load of polystyrene blocks, lots of square metres of liner, a pump and a filter. It was hardly a swimming pool yet. Somehow it would all need to be put together. Nervous though I was, I attempted to exude confidence.

'It'll be a piece of piss,' I said.

Not the best choice of words when referring to a swimming pool.

One of the disadvantages of having building work done is that you don't get as much time as you'd like to practise the piano. The opportunities that arose between running errands and generally helping out were inevitably interrupted. Every time I sat down to play, Ron instinctively sensed that this would be an excellent moment to switch tasks and engage in thunderous banging or drilling. Then there was the further obstacle caused by unreasonable and unnecessary guilt. However much I tried to tell myself that I earn my living by being creative, and that piano practice could therefore justifiably be described as 'work', I felt guilty whenever I played during Ron's working hours. It was pathetic, but it felt like I was thoughtlessly leaving 'my man' to toil subserviently in the garage below whilst I decadently dallied with the pianoforte like an aristocratic overlord.

So if work was progressing slowly, piano practice was too.

Things didn't get any better when Kevin and Nic arrived. The moments of peace that the evenings had previously afforded were no longer dotted with sporadic and gentle piano tinkling, but were now filled with playful banter, games of Perudo,* and wine consumption.

Kevin had come back to the house that he'd first seen on our abortive skiing weekend. This time he came with his girlfriend Nic. For a couple of years now he'd been seeing Nic, and they appeared to be getting on just fine. Nic adored the outdoors and, unlike many of the women I know, she preferred a tent to a hotel room, and a long walk to a comfy taxi ride. She loved sport, enjoyed staying healthy and had an admirable tolerance level for some of Kevin's eccentricities.

One of which was wood.

In recent years Kevin had acquired an inexplicable attraction to this substance, filling his home with bits of driftwood that he had picked up on seafront walks during overseas holidays. When most of us fly home, we carry bottles of spirit or gifts in our hand luggage, but not Kevin. He walks down the aisle of the plane nearly taking people's eyes out with oversized and interestingly shaped (in his opinion) lumps of wood. The stewardesses have to change the spiel that they deliver to passengers upon landing: 'Do take care when removing articles from the overhead lockers as items may have moved about during the flight, and that big bit of wood which that bloke brought on board might fall on someone's head.'

Despite the first few days of their stay being uncomfortably hot, Kevin and Nic embarked on several mountain walks. On each occasion they returned with a car full of wood. On every journey back to the house, poor Nic had to endure large branches around her ankles and on her lap. She accused Kevin of being mad, but he would cleverly counter with:

'No I'm not.'

He was a formidable debater.

Within a very short space of time these bits of wood started to appear around the house – on the mantelpiece, on windowsills or

---

*A Peruvian dice game for all the family, but mainly the immature ones.

on top of the bookshelf. Kevin had taken it upon himself to become the interior designer of my new house.

'They're like natural bits of sculpture, don't you think?' he said as we sat down to dinner only three nights into their stay.

'I'd love to see it, Kev,' I replied, 'but to me they're just rather bulky bits of wood. Can we call it a day soon? The house is getting too full of the stuff. We're almost certainly contravening fire regulations.'

'OK,' he replied. 'All future pieces will be for outside.'

Nic rolled her eyes.

By the following weekend Kevin had created a kind of mini-gallery of wooden exhibits in front of the house on the grass verge by the roadside. He had set his pieces in mud, all in a line for passers-by to admire and enjoy. Art for the people. A chance to elevate the spirits of the farmers as they trundled by on their tractors. Undoubtedly viewers of these exhibits would be filled with a sense of wonder ('I wonder why he's done that?'), and this innovative 'wooden art' would challenge and provoke ('What's the idiot gone and cluttered up the verge like that for?').

'What do you think of it? Honestly?' Kevin asked one morning as we set off for a day's outing.

'I think it's terrific that you're in touch with your creative side,' I replied. 'It's just a shame that this has to happen when you're at my place.'

The locals thought I was odd enough as it was. My love of cork, my predilection for making phone calls under bushes and my childish games had seen to that. I could have done without the 'mad wood' thing too.

'But the best part is,' continued Kevin, 'delivery men will have no problem finding your house now. Just say it's the house with the wood.'

In one sense, Kevin's 'exhibition' had been my fault. I had complained that the house didn't have a number. My address was simply my surname and the name of the village. Apparently this sufficed for 'le Postman Patrice'. However, arranging deliveries from builders' merchants had been something of a nightmare as I'd had to go through a long and detailed description of where the house was, often having to draw a little map. Why not just have a number? It was one of those French paradoxes. They love bureaucracy but they don't want to give you a number. And of course if they had deigned to supply me with one, it would have needed to be sufficiently 'official', and I'd have ended up living at number G10976835RYV423.

So Kevin, in his own somewhat annoying way, had provided a solution to this particular problem. In future, when ordering tiles or cement, I'd have no problems.

'Turn left off the main road and mine is the house with the mad wood outside.'

Today's outing was to the jazz festival at Marciac. France loves its festivals and fêtes, and in the month of August there are hundreds of thousands of them. Marciac is one of the better known internationally, particularly among jazz aficionados. This quaint fortified town, founded as far back as the thirteenth century, has a population of only 1200 for most of the year, but when it's festival time 100,000 visitors crop up from nowhere to drop in and lend an ear to what's going down, man.

Today, three of those visitors were going to be Tony, Nic and Wood Boy. We'd booked no tickets for shows as we'd been told that the whole village becomes a centre for jazz musicians who play all day, giving free concerts in the square and at various bars and cafés. When we arrived the place was buzzing with people, most of whom were pretty cool looking. Jazz seems to attract fewer nerds than, say, heavy metal, although long hair still seems to be de rigueur. The streets were lined with stalls selling anything from sculptures to guitar strings. Every open space had been exploited for some commercial purpose, and a children's playground had been transformed into a kind of food hall where marquees and canopies housed at least a dozen makeshift restaurants.

We sat down to a late lunch in the picturesque and historic square with its preserved medieval arcades, to be serenaded by three musicians from Toulouse who blended jazz and flamenco styles with surprising success. My feet were tapping so fast that I was beginning to sweat. Mind you, it was oppressively hot.

'I think a storm is brewing,' said Nic.

Fifteen minutes later her meteorological skills were confirmed as the clouds opened and God, or whoever does this kind of stuff, tipped a massive tank of water all over us. It was torrential, the kind of rain that has people reaching for anything to fend it off – newspapers, briefcases or shopping bags. Just a few seconds exposed to this kind of outburst and one is well and truly drenched.

The poor jazz/flamenco boys quickly packed up their gear and fled. Clearly the show must not go on – not when electrocution is a possibility. These lads never would have got jobs on the *Titanic*. Suddenly laid-back Marciac had been rudely disturbed. The oasis of calm that had seen dudes sitting back and sipping cocktails as the smooth music washed over them was transformed into a frenzy of activity. People were manically running for cover, scrabbling about for umbrellas or squeezing themselves under porches and shop-fronts. Anything to escape the overpowering wrath of the Pyrenean thunderstorm. August, I was soon to discover, is the month of unexpected and dramatic storms. The reason is quite simple: when the hot air from Spain drifts over the mountains, it collides with the cooler moist air of France, and then . . . er . . . well, God gets pissed off and gives us all a sudden storm.*

The running torrents of water in the village streets told us that our day of jazz was over. We had a choice of huddling under a dripping canopy for four hours and then trying to get into an evening concert somewhere, or heading home. Since we were already damp and we were fast becoming wet, the discussion was short and the decision unanimous.

---

*Sorry, this isn't a geography textbook, so that'll have to do.

Five miles out of Marciac, the mountains became visible on the horizon and we were treated to the most amazing natural sound and light show. As dark clouds hung over us, and with a sense of apocalyptic foreboding, we witnessed an unforgettable electric storm. The sky was intermittently illuminated by jagged white bolts flashing from cloud to earth like a dagger plunging into a victim's heart. Seconds after each one of these explosions of light, the boom of a deafening thunderclap caused us physically to shudder. Each event was followed by our own individual exclamation of wonder ('Wow! Did you see that?' being favourite) and we felt privileged to have such a front row seat for this awesome virtuoso display.

'That one seemed pretty close!' said Nic, after we'd all 'wowed' a truly 'wowable' lightning bolt. 'Do you think we could get hit by one?'

'It's possible,' said Kev. 'But we'd need to be very unlucky.'

'What's going on when there's a bolt of lightning?' I asked. 'I mean, what actually causes it? And what is it, exactly?'

There was a long pause as each of us tried to recall what we'd been taught many years before. I hauled my mind back to that drab Tuesday afternoon in 1976 when Mr Baxter had taught us all about thunder and lightning. That Tuesday afternoon when I'd not been concentrating properly because far more interesting things were happening outside the window as the headmaster was frogmarching Sally Renn and Mark Fincham to his office.

'I honestly don't know the physics of what's going on,' said Kevin. 'Awful, isn't it?'

'I know it's electrical,' said Nic.

'All I can remember,' I added, 'is that the lightning comes first, because light travels faster than sound.'

The townies were pooling their information. They would not be ready to lecture on this subject any time soon.

'We must ask someone,' I said. 'We can't have this going on all around us and not know what it is.'

'We'll look it up when we get back,' said Kevin, who was not fully cognisant of the number of reference books there were at the house.★

It was nightfall before we made it home, and we were greeted by good news and bad news.

The good news: the house had not been struck by lightning.

The bad news: neither had any of Kevin's pieces of wood.

Immediately we headed for the balcony, drinks in hand, eager to watch the rest of the electrical performance play itself out across the mountains. Up until now I'd always experienced weather. I'd never seen it before. Because that's what we were doing – we were watching the weather. And great fun it was too.

'It's no wonder ancient civilisations believed in an angry God,' I said. 'Thunder and lightning don't really suggest that He's a benign deity.'

'I guess we all have our off days,' remarked Kevin, not exactly taking the bait for a deep and meaningful conversation.

The next day, God was in a better mood. Whoever had pissed Him off must have apologised because the air was clear, the sky was blue and the sun was out. We decided that it was a beautiful morning for a long, leisurely walk around the village.

'How long does it take?' asked Nic.

'About forty-five minutes if you don't bump into anybody,' I replied. 'But I somehow doubt we'll manage that.'

The old lady at the former sawmill was first. As we walked towards the mill she greeted us with a '*bonjour*' and then immediately told us she was ninety-three. Younger women, I've noticed, tend to be less forthcoming with their age. Presumably there's a point one reaches in life where being old becomes something to boast about. I wonder if I'm there yet?

'Hello, I'm Tony – I'm forty-four.'

It could be a way to disarm people when you first meet them.

★0.

The sawmill lady at ninety-three looked fitter and healthier than many seventy-year-old women I'd seen in Britain. The hardy country life might not involve much yoga but it delivered in other ways, certainly if this woman was anything to go by. The lady was in chatty mood and she told us how this was still actually a working mill, and she even took the time to lead us into the barn in order to turn it on for a few minutes. A series of wooden pulleys and levers kicked into action. There wasn't a hint of modern technology in sight. She told us that they'd had a flood here in 1973 that had destroyed the sawmill, but that they'd worked like dogs to rebuild it. Then, like a bolt from the blue, her husband had died the following year. Suddenly, in the wrinkles and folds of her ninety-three-year-old face, I could see the lines of pain.

'You just don't know what life is going to chuck at you,' said Nic as we climbed the hill on the other side of the valley, tucking her arm into Kevin's and snuggling into his shoulder.

I agreed, and dropped back a couple of paces, allowing the affectionate couple to lead the way.

'It's not fair,' added Nic.

As I walked alone, I had to concede that she had a point.

I was rather pleased when we bumped into André on our walk. I was growing rather fond of him. We saw his diminutive figure as we reached the brow of the hill. He had a stick in his hand and two dogs were running about his ankles. Presumably he had just deposited his six cows in some field somewhere and this had freed him up for chatting, which was something he clearly loved to do. I guess cows, even if you have six of them, don't provide much in the way of interesting conversation. Even I, with my far from fluent French, could do better. I introduced Kevin and Nic and he shook their hands and welcomed them to the village, asking a string of questions about who they were and what they were doing here. He then beckoned us into his yard, much as he had done with me when he'd shown me his Mobylette.

A guided tour followed. The reason for this remains a mystery, but the tour guide was charming and we were afforded a further fascinating glimpse of life without technology. Apart from the Mobylette, everything André showed us appeared to be about a hundred years old and made of wood. (No wonder Kevin looked to be enjoying himself so much.) André had no need for modern gadgetry. He hadn't signed up for the rat race. What did he need to do things at breakneck speed for? He had all day. He had all week. He had all year. André didn't need huge profits. He wasn't planning on buying a new Volvo, and he didn't go on holiday. Holiday? What did he need a holiday for? The word 'stress' wasn't in his vocabulary.

Just as André was opening a barn door and showing us some new farming paraphernalia, Kevin surprised us all with his next remark.

'André,' he said. 'Do you know how lightning works?'

Nic and I looked at each other in surprise. When we'd all discussed the possibility of asking someone about this, we'd thought there'd been tacit understanding that we might run it by a university professor or such-like. Not a semi-retired rural farmer in his late seventies. To his credit, André was not remotely vexed by the question. Instead, he closed the barn door, turned to face us and launched into a short speech.

The truth, he explained, was that no one really knew how lightning worked. He maintained that this was not the only area where humans were deficient in the knowledge department. When people saw mushrooms in the ground, the fungi were always at a reasonable size, and consequently no one could be exactly sure how they grew. No one actually saw them growing. He held that the same theory could be applied to lightning. It was there sure enough, but nobody knew how it worked.

This was quite brilliant. Clearly, just like us, André didn't have a clue about the science behind a lightning bolt, but the great thing was he knew that he didn't need to know. Besides, he was confident in the fact that no one else knew anyway. I was determined to embrace this new approach, at least in the short term. Every time I came across something that baffled me, instead of fretting until I received an explanation, I could relax in the knowledge that 'no one really knows'. Good old André had confirmed something for me that I'd strongly suspected all along. All these scientists, physicists and medics who tell you stuff – they don't really know, you know. Why not? Because 'no one really knows'. Good old André. He was cool. And he had a new follower of 'André-ism' – the philosophy for the twenty-first century.

When we got back to the house I received a phone call from Fabrice, the salesman from the swimming pool shop. He said that he'd just looked at the address on my invoice and noticed a coincidence. His girlfriend's father owned a plot of land in the same village – and they were due to make a visit later that day. Instantly I invited them round for afternoon tea – an offer that seemed to amuse Fabrice, probably because of its Englishness.

'*C'est la maison avec le bois dehors*,' I said.

'*Comment?*' replied a confused Fabrice.

'*Avec le bois fou dehors.*'

'*Ah*,' said Fabrice, clearly still not sure if I was using the right French words.

'There!' said Kevin, as I hung up. 'How useful is that wood?'

'Very,' I replied, noting that Kevin seemed to take pleasure in his art in a different way to many artists.

Kevin and Nic were out on a romantic afternoon walk when Fabrice phoned again for confirmation of where I lived. Presumably he'd thought I'd used the wrong words when I'd talked about 'mad wood'. I confirmed that I had meant what I'd said and enquired as to how long he thought he'd be.

'*Cinq minutes*,' he replied.

Good – this was just enough time for me to tidy up the front of the house, which had become something of a depository for empty tile boxes and general building debris. As I arranged it all into one neat-ish pile, instead of four untidy ones, I felt the need for a wee.

Instead of going in the house, like any normal person, I did something that I guess I must have learned from my father. He was a great one for urinating outside. He saw no reason in flushing water down the pan when a viable alternative was available. French men, I had noted, shared a comparable insouciant attitude to al fresco relief. Over the years I had taken a similar approach and periodically I felt the need for an occasional wee in my own garden, even though a perfectly good toilet was within easy range. It was almost as if I was marking out my territory in some kind of atavistic ritual.

So it was that I opened my zip, popped out my huge and unwieldy member★ and made use of a suitable tree which afforded me the requisite privacy from the road.

Just as I had released the sluices to what was turning out to be a larger pee than expected, a car came over the brow of the hill and began to decelerate as it neared Kevin's wooden exhibits. I panicked, and desperately tried to curtail the flow of urine that was now making an impressive rainbow-like arc to the foot of the tree trunk. The car slowed still further and began to pull into the drive. I recognised Fabrice as the driver but was horrified to note that he wasn't alone. A young woman was in the passenger seat and an older man was in the back. Shit. And I had my tadger out.

This piss just had to be stopped. Emergency bladder muscles were called upon and somehow, drawing more on instinct than anything else, I managed to stem the flow and slowly haul my penis back into my trousers.★

A price had to be paid, however, because the conclusion to proceedings had meant that there was considerable leakage once everything was back inside. I looked down to see a large dark blotch on my beige trousers, and then raised my eye-line again to

---

★I wonder if this sentence means that the book will find its way into the 'fiction' section in bookshops.
★As previous footnote.

see Fabrice emerging from his car. It didn't appear that I was about to make the best of impressions. Fortunately I was wearing a fairly large T-shirt that I was able to untuck and just about pull down over most of the offending blemish. No one would suspect that I was not properly toilet-trained as long as I remained ever so slightly hunched and didn't straighten my torso fully.

Fabrice greeted me warmly and introduced me to his girlfriend Marie-Laure, a beautiful girl with almost child-like rosy cheeks and a lovely smile. For some reason, the older man remained in the car.

'This is my farver,' said Marie-Laure, bravely addressing me in my mother tongue and pointing to the car. 'Can you help him? He is in a wheelchair.'

'Of course.'

Fabrice opened the car's rear door and I shook hands with the man before reaching down and helping to lift the wheelchair out. An easy enough task for me since my unnatural stooping position was leading my body in that direction anyway.

'You are my neighbour!' said Marie-Laure's father. 'My plot of land is exactly opposite your house.'

'It is an amazing coincidence,' I said. 'Of course, I never would have bought the house if I'd known about the neighbours.'

'You must know, Tony,' said Fabrice, 'that we have the planning permission to put a discotheque here. It will be open every night till 4am!'

This kind of playful banter continued over the next hour during which we drank tea (me), coffee (the French men) and cordials (Marie-Laure). We talked about the area and my proposed swimming pool, and we teased each other about our cultural differences. Then Fabrice took the conversation in a new direction.

'Tony, you must come to dinner with me and Marie-Laure soon.'

'That would be lovely,' I replied.

It now occurred to me that something extraordinary had just happened. I'd made my first French friends. Yes, I already had people in the village who I might have begun to describe thus, but that just wasn't the same. I hadn't gone out there and made them myself – they were neighbours. My new chums Fabrice and Marie-Laure had only turned out to be neighbours by default. And provided I could stoop sufficiently well until they left, then the invitation would stand and I would be well on the way to cementing this new friendship.

'I think I saw something move in there,' said Marie-Laure, pointing down to the woodshed.

I hesitated. Oh yes, I hadn't explained about Ron. Oh well, I would have to do it now. So, in my best French, I explained that I had brought a British builder out to France with me and that he was living in the woodshed. There was no reaction from my French friends. They just looked at me silently. It was as if they were waiting for me to have another go at this sentence, this time finding the right words to convey my intended meaning. I repeated my sentence. They smiled. Not without a hint of nervousness. Ron then emerged from the woodshed, post-siesta and in his underpants, blowing his nose indelicately.

'What do you want for dinner tonight?' he called up to me without seeing my visitors, who were gently observing all from behind me. 'I've made some lovely soup.'

'Er . . . right. Yes, soup would be nice,' I called back, somewhat awkwardly, trying to avoid the eye contact of my guests.

'Brill,' said Ron before disappearing through the side gate, the place where I knew he liked to take his own al fresco pees.

I felt an urgent need to get everyone out of the house in order to save them the uncomfortable experience of having to see the almost naked Ron when he returned from relieving himself.

Even at the time I think I knew that I was panicking, probably unreasonably.

'Well,' I said, moving round to Marie-Laure's father, grabbing his wheelchair and starting to lead him off to Fabrice's car. 'It's been lovely seeing you. So, until the next time. *A bientôt!*'

'*Au revoir*,' said my guests as they quickly gathered their things, slightly surprised at the speed with which proceedings had been called to a halt.

'Yes, *au revoir*,' I said, just beginning to realise how badly I'd handled the situation.

Well, it was too late to take a different approach now. I hurried them out of the door and off to their car, keeping up the mood of urgency until I was able to watch them drive off, bemusedly waving goodbye as they went.

I would have to get better at this entertaining thing.

11

Trees, Holes and Pilgrims

I awoke to the sound of cowbells. Not a bad way to start the day, especially for a city boy. When I looked out of the window I could see that the shy farmer's cows were not far from the boundaries of my land.

'They'll be in my garden soon!' I said, even though there was nobody else with me.*

Ron was toiling in the garage and Kevin and Nic were having a lie-in when Mary, the widowed Irish lady I'd met at the village dinner, called round. I'd seen her several times since then, but usually just for a brief neighbourly exchange. Now she had some interesting news.

'You'll probably hear Miles playing the piano at my place in the

---

*Talking to yourself is said to be the first sign of madness. I'm sorry, but I have to question this. What if, before you've done any talking to yourself, you start foaming at the mouth, shouting at passing cars and hopping round Sainsbury's? Do these not count as preliminary signs?

next few days,' she said. 'He's over for the music night. The other boys will be over soon, too.'

'Mary,' I replied, 'why don't you have a cup of coffee and tell me what on earth you're talking about?'

Mary soon had me up to speed. Miles and the 'boys' were her sons, and they were all musicians. They combined coming over to see their mum with visits to the Marciac jazz festival, and last year Malcolm and Anne had seized on the opportunity to exploit their talents by putting on a music night in the village. Local French musicians had joined forces with these Irish guests to create '*une soirée musicale Franco-Irlandaise*'. By all accounts it had been a great success.

'The boys are looking forward to it this year,' said Mary. 'You play piano – will you do a little turn yourself? I know that Malcolm and Anne want you to. They're organising it.'

'Well, I could do,' I replied, 'but I don't want to muscle in on someone else's gig.'

'Heavens, you won't be doing that,' said Mary, sipping on her coffee, sitting back on the settee and relaxing into full 'chatty' mode. 'I'll tell Malcolm and Anne that you'll do it, then. They got me to play last year and no doubt they will this year, too. I don't like doing it because I'm best when I'm just playing to accompany others. That's what I do up at the hotel in Lourdes. Actually you must come up and listen one night very soon – there's a priest who is with the present party of pilgrims who says he wants to meet you. He's read your fridge book, you see.'*

'I'd love to come, Mary,' I said. 'We haven't made any plans for tonight actually. I'll suggest it to the others when they get up.'

'Well, it would be lovely to see you up there, and you must come round for a beer when the boys arrive.'

'Thanks. I will.'

Just as Mary was saying her goodbyes another caller arrived. It was Malcolm – just too late to be the first to give me the news of

---

*Round Ireland With A Fridge. Available from all good bookshops.

the impending music night. He did, however, have some other interesting information.

'I've just been talking to Serge,' he said.

'Moustachioed Serge?'

'No, the other Serge.'

'Ah, Serge II? Brother of Roger the mechanic – the one with the mechanical digger?'

'Yes, him. Well, you know you said you might want him to dig the hole for your pool?'

'Yes.'

'Well, he's just had a job cancelled and he can do it this morning. He says if he doesn't do it now, he won't have any more time for a month.'

'Blimey, this is all a bit sudden. I haven't even had breakfast yet.' Suddenly my hand was forced. Although I'd purchased the poly-styrene blocks and all the additional pool equipment, I still hadn't yet quite come to terms with the concept of digging out a massive great hole in my back garden. I was in denial. Part of me wanted a pool. I loved the idea of improving my fitness by doing lengths before hoisting myself out and lounging poolside, basking in the sun with a cool drink in hand. However, I was also afraid of creat-ing a millstone around my neck – a monster that would constantly need attention, with its filtration systems, pumps and complicated prescription of chemicals. I was worried that every time I left it for a few weeks I would return to find something resembling a stagnant cesspit. Yes, I'd made the purchase but somehow I still hadn't fully committed.

'What shall I tell him?' asked Malcolm.

Damn. I had to make a decision right now. I hated that.

'Er . . . well, can you tell him to pop down and we'll talk the job through and agree a price?'

'Sure.'

I'd bought myself another ten minutes.

★ ★ ★

Ron was just emerging from the woodshed as Serge pulled up in his van and got out. It was strange, but the two men seemed to like each other instantly. I watched from the balcony as they shook hands and engaged for the first time. They had no language in common (Ron had not been spending his ample downtime with his head buried in *Teach Yourself French*) and yet there was much communication taking place. There seemed to be a kind of instant male bonding going on. Perhaps they saw themselves in each other. Serge was younger and slimmer than Ron, but he shared the same characteristics. A durable face with a no-nonsense expression, grubby overalls which are the builder's battle fatigues, and a muscular upper body cultivated by years of heavy lifting rather than gym membership at a poncy sports club. A lot of pointing and gesturing was going on by the time I made it down to join them.

Serge wanted to know who was going to build the pool. I hesitated. I had a feeling that he was going to be surprised by my answer. And he was.

He raised an eyebrow and cocked an ear. He wanted to hear this from me again. I confirmed the facts. We were going to build it ourselves. There now followed an extraordinary display of face-pulling dexterity. I had thought that Roger, his brother, had excelled himself with his performance after I had asked him to find me a nice ten-year-old estate car, but it was nothing compared to what now followed. Serge grimaced, winced, shook his head, closed his eyes, scowled, laughed, threw his head back and nervously ran his fingers through his hair. He simply couldn't believe that we were going to take the job on ourselves, and in the following few minutes he did everything in his power to persuade me to do otherwise. Did we know how difficult these kinds of jobs were? Did we not realise that if we built it ourselves then we wouldn't be covered by the manufacturer's insurance if anything went wrong? (No, I hadn't realised, but I wasn't going to tell Serge that.)

'*Ce n'est pas un problème,*' I said.

Serge threw his head back again, aghast. I told him that I was an eccentric and that I liked adventures. Ron looked on, bemused. Meanwhile, Kevin and Nic slept on upstairs, unaware of the momentous events now unfolding. Serge looked around him, shrugged, and then marched off to inspect the small tree that had afforded us valuable shade from the summer sun. He paced out just how far it was from the edge of the proposed pool, the dimensions of which Ron and I had hastily marked out in the ten frantic minutes before his arrival.

Serge stopped, looked at the tree, stared down at the ground and then turned to me, somehow managing to form yet another new expression. He sighed, shrugged again, and then ran his finger quickly along his throat. The tree, it seemed, would have to go. I tried to defend it, but Serge was adamant that it would be a huge problem if allowed to remain.

'He's right,' said Ron. 'Those roots will eventually destroy the pool's walls.'

This was a blow. It was a nice tree and there was no doubt that it added to the garden. But we were in one of those spaces in time where everything was in fast motion. The kind of decision that needed days of mulling over was required to be taken instantly. I felt some sympathy for world leaders who must be forced into this kind of position on a regular basis, particularly during wartime. I'm not sure it would have suited me.

'Prime Minister Hawks, we have to drop those bombs in the next ten minutes otherwise all will be lost.'

'Errmm, right, er . . . yup, gosh . . . right, yes . . . important stuff, yes . . . um . . . er . . . Look, I'm busy right now with my corn-flakes – I'll have an answer for you when I'm done.'

A few minutes later all was sorted. Serge had quoted a very reasonable price for the job, and he was to come back with his mechanical digger in half an hour. By the end of the day, there would be no tree and a bloody great big hole in the garden. Scary stuff.

Still Kevin and Nic slept on. The lie-in. One of the joys of being on holiday. I'd never come to appreciate this fully, never having held what could be commonly termed a proper job. Apart from the odd day here and there, I'd worked largely from home, relying on self-discipline to kick-start the day's work. I'd rarely made use of my alarm clock, knowing that I would wake up when I was ready. The lie-in was all too available for me and consequently had never become a treat. But Kevin and Nic were enjoying it now, the length of their slumber a sign that they both needed this rest, and that they were relaxing into the new pace that life here demanded.

The same was not true of me on this particular morning. This was the closest thing to stress that life here could engender. Ron soothed my nerves by pouring me a comforting cup of tea in the kitchen. We made a pot of coffee, too, ready to offer to Serge when he returned with his digger. This, as we were soon to discover, was rather naïve of us. Serge was not the 'sit around and have a cup of coffee before you start work' type.

Moments later we heard the distant hum of a large piece of machinery.

'That'll be him,' said Ron.

I poured Serge a cup of coffee and we both moved outside to greet him, only to see the digger turn the corner from the road and head straight down the steep drive. Serge didn't even glance at me or Ron, but simply aimed his speeding contraption directly at the tree and let gravity bolster his speed. The poor tree was then duly and unceremoniously rammed. BANG!

Ron giggled. A nervous kind of giggle.

'Oh well,' he said. 'That's the tree sorted anyway.'

'Bloody hell,' I said in amazement. 'What if I'd changed my mind about the tree in the last twenty minutes?'

'Well, he would have just changed it back again for you.'

I heard a commotion upstairs and looked up to the window to see Kevin and Nic, sleep still in their eyes, staring down at the extraordinary scene below them.

'Tony,' said Nic. 'Someone's knocked your tree over.'

It's always good to have someone around who's on top of what's going on.

'Yes,' I said. 'It does look that way, doesn't it?'

The tree was now at a forty-five degree angle, roots exposed to the sun, with a good proportion of the lawn having been hauled along with it. Serge was oblivious to the adjacent astonishment. He simply reversed his digger – or battering ram as it might be more accurately described – and rammed it straight back into the stricken tree. This successfully reduced its hanging angle by a further twenty degrees.

'Blimey,' said Kevin from the upstairs window. 'He doesn't muck about, does he?'

Serge dismounted his yellow monster and reached inside the cab of his machine. This seemed like a good moment to take over the cup of coffee that I was still holding for him. However, just as I started to move towards him, he spun round from the cab brandishing a huge chainsaw. For a moment it seemed like I was facing a character from a horror movie. I retreated to safety immediately.

'Coffee can wait,' I whispered to Ron.

'Yes, he doesn't seem to be the hot-drink type,' said Ron with a dry smile.

We watched in awe as Serge reduced the tree to manageable-sized pieces of wood, and I could have sworn that I saw Kevin lick his lips. Soon the tree was firewood. I felt guilty. Had we done something environmentally wrong? Would it be OK as long as we planted another? And who adjudicated on these issues anyway? I decided it best to adopt a local approach to the matter, and so I shrugged my biggest shrug and sat down to drink Serge's coffee for him.

Once the tree was history, Serge wasted no time in getting on with excavating the hole. His approach was brutal. He used his machine like a ruthless general might use an army. Any obstacle was removed or destroyed. No prisoners were taken. In, out, in, out, went the huge claw of his mechanical digger, and soon a huge pile of mud was building up on the boundary with my far neighbour.

'You'd better have a word with next door about that,' said Ron. 'It's not exactly going to look pretty by the time Serge has finished.'

'Yes, you're right,' I replied. 'His car's there now. I might pop round in a minute.'

'And what do you want to do about those dead pine trees?'

Oh dear. Another major decision was looming. Two tall trees had died during the previous summer's drought. Dead though they were, they offered valuable privacy from the outside world. Without them, this particular part of my garden – the pool section – would be visible from the village road. Unusually, I became bestowed with a sense of both authority and clarity.

'Let's leave them,' I said. 'We can always cut them down a bit, or remove them completely at a later date.'

'Righto,' said Ron.

I'd only spoken to my neighbour Bruno once before. I'd been told that he was a private man who worked terribly hard running a mountain restaurant, and he had no time or inclination to participate in village events like the dinners or fêtes. When he was lucky enough to get some time off, he liked to spend it with his wife and children. All I'd managed thus far was a short and genial exchange with him when I'd driven past once and had seen him getting into his car. We'd chatted briefly and established a positive neighbourly relationship, and so I was anxious not to upset that now with the creation of the huge and unattractive pile of mud on his borders.

Bruno was organising things in his garage as I walked down his drive to explain. He greeted me warmly and offered up some reassuring small talk about the weather, possibly in deference to my Englishness. He proceeded to quiz me about the pool and when I explained about the imminent mound of soil he said that he had no problem whatsoever with it, and he wished me luck. I thanked him and strolled back to my place, in splendid spirits, largely as a result of this highly successful conversation.

The feeling was short-lived, however, as I was immediately intercepted by Ron who pointed towards the boundary of my land. It looked very exposed somehow. Serge was still spinning around in the cab of his digger, its claw feverishly pounding this way and that.

'There's something missing,' I said.

'Yes,' said a sheepish Ron. 'The pines. I'm afraid Serge took an executive decision.'

'What?'

'Serge seemed to decide they were dead and that they needed to be removed.'

'So he just rammed them?'

'Yes.'

'Without asking?'

'Yes.'

'Why didn't you stop him?'

'What was I supposed to do? Throw myself in front of the digger?'

'Well, kind of, yes.'

'How can you kind of run in the way of a digger?'

'I don't know. You improvise.'

'Yes, you improvise, and you get knocked over by a digger.'

Ron was right, of course. There was nothing he could have done other than wave his arms, which no doubt he had done. I'd already seen that Serge, when in full 'digger mode', was not the sort of chap who pays a good deal of attention to external influences such as arms. Even as we spoke he was decimating further parts of the garden.

'Well, there's nothing we can do,' I offered with yet another shrug. 'Once a tree has been uprooted, that's pretty much the final word on the matter.'

'Yes,' said Ron. 'Especially when it's dead already.'

A fair point, I suppose.

'Some of our privacy has gone,' I announced. 'Our bungling attempts to build a pool will just have to be visible to anyone who drives or walks by.'

'Should be good for village morale.'

The rest of the excavation went off largely without incident. Ron continued to oversee proceedings with an occasional authoritative thumbs-up or pointy gesture, and he and Serge continued to bond in spite of being locked into a world of improvised sign language. At 3pm Serge shook my hand and headed off home, seemingly content with his day of destruction. He was leaving us with a massive hole, two huge mounds of mud and a large pile of ex-trees.

That night Kevin, Nic and I decided to celebrate the miracle of Serge's hole. Where else but with a trip to Lourdes? Up until 1858 Lourdes had been nothing more than a modest town of about 4,000 inhabitants with a castle and a few hostelries catering for mountaineers and those in search of the healing waters at nearby spas. However, all that changed when a fourteen-year-old girl called Bernadette went collecting firewood in a cave. She heard a sound like a gust of wind and saw the ghost of another young girl, surrounded by a shaft of light. People subsequently decided that this was an apparition of the young Virgin Mary. Well, of course it was. Who else could it have been?

Bernadette continued to see this apparition on a fairly regular basis over the next six months, in spite of her parents trying her with a whole host of different breakfast cereals. On her ninth sighting, the apparition lady (or Mary, as we'll call her henceforth) instructed Bernadette to dig a hole in the ground and bathe in it (an instruction you might more commonly expect from a middle-aged male apparition). Mary also instructed Bernadette to tell the local pastor to have a chapel built in honour of her appearances there. The pastor, for some strange reason, was reluctant. Perhaps it was because there had been nothing in his ecclesiastical training telling him to accept building instructions from fourteen-year-old girls with vivid imaginations. Anyway, he accused Bernadette of lying, and demanded proof – which Mary duly provided at the next meeting by telling Bernadette, '*Que soy era Immaculado Conceptiou,*' which means, 'She's not lying, guv, honest.'

Naturally enough this was accepted as concrete proof and in 1862 Bernadette's apparitions were officially declared authentic and Lourdes rapidly became one of the world's leading pilgrimage sites. It has five million visitors every year and it has around 270 hotels, the second greatest number in France – one of which catered for an Irish clientele, with my neighbour Mary tinkling the ivories of an evening.

Jesus is well known for his ministry in Judea in which he preached forgiveness, love and good will to all men. However, few are aware that he secretly hoped one of the future spin-offs of his teachings would be that a small French town in the foothills of the Pyrenees would grow large and profitable, primarily sustained by sales of trinkets of his mum in various virtuous and heavenly poses. The good people of Lourdes have not let him down in this regard. As Kevin, Nic and I drove through the town centre in search of an elusive parking space, we noted that every other building seemed to be a gift shop, full to the brim with cheap souvenirs of the Virgin Mary, surrounded by a vast miscellany of religious iconography. Jesus would have been proud.

And then there are the miracles. Every day sick people are brought to Lourdes in their thousands, largely because many have claimed to have received miracle cures here.

'The biggest miracle of Lourdes seems to me to be that so many people have bought into it,' I said to the others as we left the car and set off on a brief sightseeing tour of the town.

'That's a bit cynical,' said Kevin. 'Don't knock it if it works. Some people end up cured.'

'That's more likely to be them healing themselves by believing they're going to get better rather than as a result of any miracle occurring.'

'What does it matter if they end up getting better?'

'I suppose it doesn't,' I replied, sceptically. 'But there must be a lot of disappointed people who leave here in the same wheelchair they came in. It does look to me as if the primary aim is tourism and profit – over and above any overwhelming drive to do good.'

'You don't know that.'

Kevin was right. I didn't know that. And today we didn't have time to find out. The agenda was clear and simple and time was short: quick sightseeing tour and then off to listen to Mary play in her hotel. The obvious first stop was the extravagant Basilique du Rosaire et de l'Immaculée Conception – the big church which dominates the town. It's very beautiful if you like big, brash Romano-Byzantine and neo-Gothic architecture, and if you don't, it isn't. We wandered silently around its grand environs, and then past the entrance to the Grotte de Massabielle (the site of Bernadette's visions). Up to this day I had never seen so many nuns. They came in all shapes and sizes. The only things they had in common were uncolourful clothing and a pallid complexion. I guess that sunbathing doesn't feature as one of a nun's daily activities. I've certainly never seen a nun in a swimsuit (except in 1985 on the video my mate Geoff showed me – and I don't think she was a real nun anyway).

'Oh Sister Josephine,' I sang, much to Kevin and Nic's surprise, 'what a very funny nun you are.'

'What?' said Nic.

'It's a song. By Jake Thackray. He used to sing it on the telly when I was a kid.'

'Yeah, I remember that,' said Kevin.

'It was about a criminal on the run who disguised himself as a nun to escape capture,' I continued. 'And all the other nuns thought he – or she – was great.'

'That's the one,' said Kevin. 'They don't write songs like they used to.'

'Thanks goodness for that,' said Nic, dryly.

The hotel had big glass doors and we could see into the lounge bar from the street. It looked more crowded and rowdier than I had expected.

'Are you sure this is the right place?' said Nic.

'They don't look like a bunch of pilgrims to me,' said Kevin.

'Nor to me,' I said. 'Although, come to think of it, I've never seen a bunch of pilgrims before, so I wouldn't know what they look like.'

'I can see a piano,' said Nic. 'But there's no lady playing it.'

'I think this is the right place though, so let's go!' I said, uncannily like a commander in a war movie.

We pushed open the doors and moved inside, only to be hit by a wall of sound — and one that was familiar somehow. But from where? Ah, yes! This was the noise that I'd heard nearly every night for a month when, years before, I'd hitchhiked around the circumference of Ireland with a small refrigerator to win a one-hundred-pound bet. Yes, there it was — sporadic shouting, yelps of joy, pockets of singing, loud exclamations of derision, jovial high-pitched banter, the chink of glasses — all laid over a soundtrack of contented chatter. I knew it so well. I just hadn't expected it from pilgrims, that's all.

As soon as we reached the bar we were assaulted by two grey-haired women who announced themselves as being two of five sisters. They didn't share any obvious resemblance other than the fact that they were both impressively sloshed.

'Are you going to sing?' one of them slurred, not to any one of us in particular.

'We'll see,' I replied diplomatically. 'Perhaps we'll get a drink first.'

I swiftly moved off, concerning myself with the business of buying a round of drinks, leaving Kevin and Nic to fend off the overenthusiastic siblings. I looked around me and I could see that these sisters were not the only ones who didn't necessarily associate pilgrimages with abstinence. This was a bar full of people in high spirits, most of whom appeared to be adhering to a policy of getting 'massed' by day and 'pissed' by night. What a good job for these people that Jesus had enjoyed a glass of wine at the last supper. Had Catholicism demanded an alcohol-free existence, I doubt very much if the religion would have gained any foothold at all in the Emerald Isle.

'Ah, Tony, so you came!' It was the voice of Mary. 'Not a bad atmosphere, is it?'

'Very good,' I replied. 'Very good indeed.'

'I'm playing again in a minute,' she continued. 'But before I do that, let me introduce you to the priest. He's a lovely fella and he's hosting tonight's entertainment.'

Mary then disappeared for a few seconds before returning with a man who bore little resemblance to what you might expect from a priest. He looked like a ladies' man, shirt open at the collar, hair carefully coiffured – not your average monsignor at all.

'Ah, you must be Tony!' he announced, accurately enough. 'Are you going to sing?'

'Well, I don't know, I hadn't—'

'Ah, you'll have to sing, so you will.'

'Yes. Well. Maybe.'

'Excuse me, Tony, I have to go and play,' said Mary, as she moved off to the piano.

'Oh dear, Tony, that means I have to go too,' said the priest.

He proceeded to glide across the room, smiling to all and sundry as he went, before picking a microphone off the piano and addressing the audience.

'Welcome back to the entertainment,' he said, as smoothly as any DJ. 'It's time now to welcome Pat, who is going to sing "If You Were The Only Girl In The World".'

Cheers and applause from the assembled throng. After a brief consultation with the elderly and frail Pat, Mary began playing, and soon the singer was bellowing out the tune, with very little regard for the original melody. The drunken sisters sang along and whooped and hollered when it was all over. Another singer followed, and then another, and soon it became apparent that the priest had used the word 'entertainment' in its loosest sense. There was no shortage of volunteer crooners – the songs and the singers just kept on coming. Mary skilfully accompanied whatever the song, and whatever key it needed to be in. Kevin, Nic and I looked on, almost in awe.

'Tony, are you going to give us a song?' asked the priest from the microphone.

I shook my head and pointed to my neck, mouthing the words 'sore throat'. I know, it's terrible – I lied to a priest – but I knew that I didn't want to sing. It had been a long day and all three of us were fading fast. I for one felt exhausted. It was time to go home.

I whispered my thanks to Mary, and we slid off into the night. Back to France. The small piece of Ireland we had just left was going to party for some time yet, that was for sure. I knew what they'd all be saying at some point the following day:

'Forgive me, father, for I got pissed out of me head last night.'

As the car reached the outskirts of the town, we were still feeling a little dazed by the bewildering evening we had just experienced. It was to become stranger still. Upon approaching a large round-about we were flagged down by a cordon of traffic police.

'My goodness,' I said, observing them more closely as we ground to a halt. 'They're wearing very tight trousers.'

'Yes,' said Nic, not looking altogether displeased.

'It's almost as if they've been sprayed on.'

I was to notice more and more in the coming weeks that the French policemen who rode motorbikes all seemed to have a conceited air about them. They strutted around like male models on a catwalk, convinced that their big modelling break was just around the corner and that this police work was only a temporary stopgap.

'What do they want?' asked Kevin.

Soon enough we knew. They wanted our passports, driving licences and all the relevant paperwork connected with Nic and

Kevin's hire car. And they wanted a good old rummage and search in the boot.

'What was that all about?' asked Nic as we drove on, having successfully avoided arrest and internment.

'Oh, I get it!' said Kevin, in a moment of sudden enlightenment. 'It'll be because of the Pope.'

'The Pope wanted to have us searched?' I asked, still in flippant mood.

'No. He's coming to Lourdes next week on an official visit,' explained Kevin. 'This will be the extra security.'

'Right,' I said, assimilating the new information. 'So the police search us as we leave Lourdes?'

'Evidently.'

'So it's just as well we didn't forget to plant all the bombs and set up the gear for the snipers before we left the town. Otherwise they would have had us bang to rights.'

'Yes. Silly, isn't it?' said Nic.

'They spend too long getting into their trousers and not enough time discussing policy.'

The comment went unanswered. We were all tired after a long day. Kevin eventually broke the silence.

'OK, guys. So what's the best thing about Lourdes, do we think?'

Another short silence before I pitched something in.

'Well, it does have excellent wheelchair access.'

Nic and Kevin laughed. Buoyed with confidence I decided to offer up my Lourdes gag – the one I'd come up with some forty minutes earlier.

'What do you call ham that's been to Lourdes?' I said.

'Cured ham?' said a deadpan Kevin.

'Er . . . yes.'

Don't you just hate it when that happens?

12

Sophie

Mary must have had her French windows open. The sound of a piano wafted over to our balcony, leaving me feeling uplifted and yet guilty. No doubt one of Mary's sons was playing, and it was beautiful: a kind of hybrid improvisation of jazz and traditional Irish music. I turned and looked at my piano, with its keys seemingly longing to be caressed by loving fingers. What had happened to my practice regime? Could I ever get back on track?

Kevin was outside stacking Serge's wood debris into a neat little pile, his broad smile confirming my suspicion that he was now officially a 'wood obsessive' (there's no medical term). Nic was doing some yoga stretches on the lawn, not far from the enormous hole that now dominated the garden. Lizards darted across tiles and up walls. The cows, now tantalisingly close to my land, munched grass to the sound of their own tinkling bells, and Ron partook of his seventh cup of tea of the morning (there's no medical term). The birds were singing to the percussive rhythms of the cicadas and crickets. The mountaintops were bathed in the morning sun. There wasn't a cloud in the sky. In short: it was a beautiful day.

A beautiful day for practising the piano. I told myself that the regime would start this morning. One hour on scales, arpeggios and general exercises to strengthen the fingers – then an hour of free-form improvisation. That was it. It was decided. Nothing was going to stop me.

'Want to come with us on a walk, Tony?' called Nic from the lawn.

'Well, I'd love to,' I said, 'but I have other—'

'Oh you've got to!' said Nic. 'Today is our last day, and we haven't been on a walk with you yet.'

'Yes, I know that, but today—'

'Shut up, Tony,' interrupted Kevin. 'You're coming for a walk. End of discussion. Whatever else you had planned will just have to be delayed by a few hours.'

'Oh all right,' I conceded, revealing one of the many reasons why I wasn't a concert pianist.

I did well to resist the initial suggestion of an excursion to the mountains. It probably would have ended up being a longer walk than I would have wanted. For the investment of energy made, the 'long trek' often provided only limited returns of pleasure, sometimes following this pattern:

Trudge, trudge – nice view – trudge, trudge, trudge, trudge – another nice view – trudge, trudge, trudge, trudge, trudge, trudge – aching pain – trudge, trudge – blister – trudge, trudge – aching pain, blister and sense of feeling lost – trudge, trudge, stagger, stagger – mild delirium – stagger, stagger – feelings of bewilderment – stagger, stagger, stumble, fall – St John's Ambulance Brigade.

No, instead I had insisted that the walk should involve an exploration of the immediate locality. For too long all I'd done was look out across the little valley and the lush green pastures that bordered my new house. Closer investigation was overdue. The walk would constitute ambling though my acre of land, past the grazing cows and down to the bottom of the valley where we would meet the stream and follow its course. I figured that this way, the moment I got tired, the 'turning round and heading home' option would always be on the table.

'We may have to climb over a lot of electric fences,' I warned, 'and dodge a few cows, but apart from that it'll be nice and easy.'

The walk was more beautiful than I could have expected, and not just because the stroll along the stream supplied us with glistening running water, brightly coloured dragonflies and shafts of sunlight darting through the overhanging trees like beams of light illuminating a film set. It was also beautiful because of what was said. After about an hour of walking, we took a break to sip some bottled water, each of us balancing on rocks in the stream as its sparkling waters cascaded round our ankles.

'The other day when we went on our trip to the coast,' said Nic, with almost a nervous tremor in her voice, 'well . . . Kevin proposed to me. And I said yes.'

There was a tear in Nic's eye, and I must admit one was starting to form in mine too.

'That's fantastic news!' I said. 'I think a group hug is in order!'

The three of us leant in towards each other, still balancing rather precariously on the small stones we'd carefully selected for our feet. Then we hugged. A big lovely hug. A hug of friendship and love. You know those nice moments that life can bung your way from time to time? Well, this was definitely one of those. It didn't last too long because I slipped off my rock and we all overbalanced, trying not to fall in the stream. The subsequent giggles punctured the rare moment of sentimentality. Rare, because Kevin and I certainly hadn't shared that many up until now. Both of us largely being of the opinion that moments like these ate up valuable time that could be better spent taking the piss out of each other.

'Guys,' I said, just before we resumed our walk, 'I'm proud of you.'

I was also proud that the house had provided the backdrop for this pivotal moment in their personal history.

'You'll be next,' said Nic. 'I expect you'll find yourself a nice French girl out here!'

'Yes,' I said without conviction. 'Perhaps I will.'

The rest of the day had that strange air of impending loss about it – the kind that so often pervades the atmosphere when people are about to leave. Kevin and Nic wandered around gathering up their things and slowly assembling a neat pile of luggage by the front door. The house would seem empty without them and I felt a little sad. There was a short ceremony on the balcony in which Kevin and Nic presented their many gifts to the house, all drawn from a big plastic bag by Nic. I felt like a child at Christmas, one minute genuinely delighted with a gift, the next – pretending to be. It wasn't difficult to recognise who had been behind each present: Nic, the nice ones – Kevin, the crappy ones (mostly made of plastic). Men may be better at walking past shoe shops without stopping, but they're hopeless at buying presents. They're descended from hunter-gatherers, and as a rule, hunter-gatherers tended to spend very little time in gift shops.

'What time are you leaving for the airport?' I asked, as I put down what I thought was my last gift, a nutcracker.

'In about half an hour,' said Kevin. 'Which gives me just enough time to erect your last present.'

Erect a present? Oh dear. I feared the worst, and when Kevin disappeared outside the front of the house my suspicions only deepened. Nic's resigned expression offered further confirmation. Regrettably, 'wood boy' had one more work of art to bestow upon the house as his legacy.

Twenty minutes later we were all standing around it as its creator looked on proudly. Much as he had done with his other work, the artist had taken a large knobbly piece of wood and set it in mud.

'Well, what do you think of my latest creation?' asked Kevin, expectantly.

I looked down at it. 'Creation' seemed too grand a word. 'Aberration' did it just as well.

'I like it,' I said, trying hard to produce a facial expression that backed up this sentiment. 'Another interesting piece.'

I'd tell him what I really thought of it all in a few weeks' time. For now, he may as well enjoy his journey home basking in critical acclaim.

'Well, goodbye, Tony,' said Nic. 'And thanks for everything.'

We all hugged again, and soon their car was climbing the hill and becoming a dot in the distance. I turned round to see Ron surveying the new-look grass verge. He'd not actually been beyond his den, the kitchen or the back garden for several days and therefore he hadn't seen any of Kevin's great works.

'What's all this bollocks?' he enquired.

'I'll explain over a cup of tea.'

Until the next guest arrived, Ron and I were back to being a couple.

That night I had dinner in a small village down in the heart of the Bigorre. I was *chez Fabrice et Marie-Laure* – my new French mates. It had taken me about an hour to drive to their place, which was in the lowland area just north of the Pyrenees. They lived in a quaint farmhouse that they'd renovated over a period of years. I had timed my arrival perfectly – just at the time when the place was nearly finished. Consequently I was able to enjoy a comfortable evening in pleasant surroundings with course after course of delectable food being thrust upon me. As the evening unfolded it became apparent that Fabrice and I had more in common than we'd suspected. He loved music, and he played both guitar and the fool (like me – one better than the other). Both he and Marie-Laure explained that they were devotees of 'Sophrologie'. At first I thought this might be some kind of strange religious cult and I began to prepare possible excuses for an early exit:

'I have to go. Ron becomes hysterical if I'm not back before eleven.'

'I have to go. My knee hurts.'

'I have to go. I notice from the glow outside that my car is on fire.'

Since the excuses weren't that great, I stayed on to hear more and I learnt that Sophrologie was an alternative medical treatment that had been devised by a Colombian neuropsychiatrist called Alfonso Caycedo. Fabrice outlined the finer details but my knowledge of French medical terminology wasn't expansive enough to enable full comprehension. I think I got the gist though. If we can train our minds to see the positive in everything then the health of the body naturally follows.*

Up until now, I had never known that my own philosophy of life, which experience had given me little choice but to embrace, actually had a name. As far as I could make out, I was a Sophrologist, and I said as much.

'*Exactement! Tu es Sophrologiste!*' confirmed Fabrice.

After dinner Fabrice announced that the night was still far from over and that it was now time for us to go to a fête in a nearby town. It was close to midnight, but when we got there the party was in full swing. In the small town square, a vast stage and lighting rig had been erected, and microphones, speakers, drum kit, keyboards and guitars signalled to the large crowd that entertainment was imminent. Beyond the square a funfair announced its presence by brashly blasting out distorted euro-pop through poor quality speakers. The bumper cars were the most popular attraction by far, packed with spotty teenagers intent on ramming their mates.

Fabrice and Marie-Laure led me to a bar that had a large tented area outside, presumably an adjunct for the fête period only. We weren't allowed to pay for the drinks because these were provided 'on the house' by the patron, Jean-Marc, who seemed to be very

---

*This may be a hopeless misinterpretation of Sophrologie, and if it is, then sincere apologies to all Sophrologists everywhere.

good friends with my hosts. Jean-Marc was a no-nonsense, thickset fellow, who, like many of the men in this region, looked like he'd been a rugby player in his day. Fabrice and I seemed slight figures in comparison, rugby not being our game. The concept of holding onto an egg-shaped object whilst several unreasonably large men ran towards you intent on your dismemberment held little attraction. Rugby wasn't the sport for Sophrologists like us.

Jean-Marc asked me if I liked pigeon-hunting. The answer was no, but that seemed rude, so I gave it a '*Je ne sais pas*' to avoid offence. He then announced that he ran the local hunt and that I was welcome as his guest at any time. What little enthusiasm I might have been able to muster was quashed when I learnt that Marie-Laure's father had fallen from a tree during a pigeon hunt, and that was why he was now a wheelchair user. Jean-Marc explained that he had subsequently constructed an elaborate system of pulleys and winches that meant Marie-Laure's father could still be hoisted into the tree to participate in the pastime that he so enjoyed.

Did I really want to go on a pigeon hunt? Well, on an ethical level I wasn't that crazy about the idea of hunting animals for sport, but when you added the distinct possibility of debilitating injury to the mix, then suddenly I became even more principled. Principled, that was, until Fabrice offered to take me fishing in the mountain streams and lakes in the coming months. Apparently the trip would involve an overnight stay in a tent, and a day filled with hours of peaceful and contemplative meditation whilst the fish made up their minds whether to bite on any of the delectable nibbles tantalisingly dangled before them. This sounded like a rare treat and I immediately invented the argument that it's OK to hunt something as long as it doesn't have legs. That seems sound enough, I thought. Not that the French ever needed any such justification. Anything that happens to move and doesn't hold a passport can be hunted and eaten with almost religious fervour.

Fabrice pointed to the stage. I looked up to see that a ten-piece band, all in matching outfits, were readying themselves for their first number. The two female lead singers were good-looking women in skimpy outfits. Tabloid journalists would have described them as 'leggy models'. Compulsory nervous fidgeting behind microphones over, the band launched into their first number – 'We built this city on rock and roll'. The lyrics seemed inappropriate for a small rural French town but the audience either jigged about or nodded approvingly, depending on their age and fitness levels. I asked Fabrice what the population of the town was and he told me that it was close to seven thousand. All this for seven thousand people? It seemed incredible.

'*C'est la saison de la fête!*' said Marie-Laure.

Party season indeed.

'*Tony, tu es marié?*' asked Jean-Marc.

This question about my marital status was no doubt prompted by the way in which I was ogling the girl singers.

'*Non, je suis célibataire,*' I replied, almost ashamedly.

'Ah,' said Fabrice playfully. 'So you are not married to Ron?'

'No, Fabrice, I am not married to Ron.'

'Then Sophie it is! *Sophie est parfait pour toi!*'

'Sophie?'

Fabrice went on to describe their friend Sophie. She sounded lovely. A thirty-year-old teacher who had been single for about six months. Apparently she was beautiful with brown eyes, long auburn hair and a good sense of humour. My expression immediately revealed that I was somewhere between keen and downright desperate, and so Fabrice produced his mobile phone and announced that he would call her. I protested that it was too late since it was after midnight, but I was assured by all that Sophie never went to sleep before 1am.

A long conversation ensued. Sophie and Fabrice were evidently close friends. I soon learned that she was on excellent terms with both Marie-Laure and Jean-Marc, as they each took their turn in chatting with her. Finally Fabrice looked my way and, with a gesture, invited me to take the phone. I was suddenly uneasy. I didn't know this woman and I wasn't sure if my French would pass the 'late-night flirting' test. I felt a knot of nerves in the pit of my stomach, oddly a sensation that was unpleasant and agreeable in equal measure.

'*Tiens, Tony,*' said Fabrice, dangling his phone before me. '*Sophie veut parler avec toi.*'

I wasn't comfortable with this moment. I might have found it less intimidating if there hadn't been three French people looking on eagerly, hanging on my every word. Tentatively, I reached forward and took the phone and slowly lifted it to my ear. I made a point of turning away from the others to try and create at least a semblance of privacy.

'*Bonsoir, Sophie,*' I said, with as much confidence as I could muster.

Silence.

'*Bonsoir, Sophie,*' I repeated.

Silence again. Had the signal disappeared? Had the phone's batteries run down?

No, the answer was more straightforward than that, and it was revealed to me the moment I turned back and saw the faces of my fellow drinkers. Fabrice, Marie-Laure and Jean-Marc were all in the throes of suppressing laughter. The sight of me – phone in hand, confused expression on face – resulted in a raucous eruption of loud cackling. I had been duped. Sophie, lovely though she may have been, didn't actually exist.

'You bastards!' I said, momentarily dispensing with the language of my hosts. 'There isn't a bloody Sophie, is there?'

No reply. No need for a reply. The laughter sufficed. Laughter so infectious that eventually even the butt of the joke couldn't stop himself from joining in.

We left the fête at half past one. The band was still playing and the bumper cars were still full of kids, some as young as eight or nine years old. I marvelled at the lack of an established bedtime for the children. In the England of my youth I would have been packed off hours before.

'Sorry about Sophie,' said Marie-Laure, as the goodbye moment presented itself.

'It's OK,' I said. 'It was actually very funny.'

I guess I also knew that it had been a kind of backhanded compliment. Fabrice and Marie-Laure wouldn't have embarked on such a playful trick if they hadn't considered me their friend. This nearly compensated for the lack of Sophie.

'You must come to eat and drink with us again,' said Marie-Laure. 'Is this something that you would like?'

'Is the Pope Catholic?' I replied playfully, to understandable confusion.

'*Pardon?*'

'It's an expression we use when something is obviously the case. I would very much like to come again.'

'Actually the Pope is coming to Lourdes soon,' said Fabrice.

'Yes. You know, I think he is going to die in Lourdes. He's so old and frail. Wouldn't it be ironic if he died in the place where people go to get themselves miraculously cured?'

I was pleased to note that my new French friends were not offended by my rather distasteful avenue of thought. That's easy-going Sophrologists for you.

'This is a funny idea, Tony, but I do not think he will die there,' said Fabrice.

'I bet you one euro, Fabrice,' I said, 'that the Pope dies when he comes to Lourdes.'

'You are mad,' he replied, 'but I will make the bet. One euro will surely be mine.'

We shook hands. Now we had well and truly bonded.

In the morning I was thrilled. I was thrilled because the cows had finally made it onto my land. Thirteen cows were now happily munching away on my grass. I wandered down to the edge of the temporary electric fence that the farmer had erected in order to keep his cows from further encroachment onto my property. I was happy enough with a bovine presence on the lower reaches of my land, but I wouldn't want to bump into a cow in the kitchen or bathroom. I watched in awe as the cows chomped, swallowed and digested my grass. I was looking at thirteen top quality lawnmowers, dreamily and happily chomping away. It occurred to me that this was almost the cow's entire life being played out before me. There wasn't a great deal more to its existence beyond eating grass. I just hoped they liked the stuff. I remembered that at school I'd made up my mind that I didn't like cabbage. I was struck by the thought of how awful it would be if a young cow developed a similar dislike for a food, and it happened to be grass. Its whole reason for living would be gone, all because of a maverick taste bud or two.

The presence of the cows wasn't the only difference to my immediate environs. Strung up between two electricity pylons in the stretch of road in front of my house was bunting for the village fête. This marked the beginning of a very busy week in the village's social calendar. Tuesday would see the '*deuxième soirée musicale Franco-Irlandaise*', and Saturday and Sunday would be taken up with the village fête. As far as I knew, the fête's festivities would constitute two meals, some lunchtime aperitifs, a photo call for all in the village and a band on Sunday night. The weekend's events would be a breeze compared to the first event, given that all I'd have to do then was consume. On Tuesday night I'd agreed to perform, although I was beginning to regret it now. Initially I'd believed that there could be no better way of ingratiating myself with the locals, but I'd become nervous about it of late. Living with Ron had meant that I hadn't been practising enough, and besides, I had absolutely no idea what songs from my meagre repertoire would go down well.

I stood in my kitchen, on the verge of picking up the phone and making some feeble excuse as to why I couldn't perform on Tuesday, when the phone beat me to it. It rang.

It was Brad in London.

'I want to come out there again,' he said. 'I miss the place. If you let me stay I'll help Ron build the swimming pool.'

How could I refuse?

'When do you want to come?' I asked.

'There's a flight available tomorrow afternoon. Is it OK if I get that?'

'No problem. You'll be just in time for the music night they're having in the village hall. I was going to play something but I'm seriously thinking of pulling out.'

'Don't do that – let's do something together,' said Brad, who was evidently in buoyant mood. 'I'll bring my guitar and we'll play some songs together. It'll be like the old days.'

'But what about rehearsing?'

'We'll rehearse when I get there.'

'After I've picked you up at the airport and driven you back here, that'll only give us about half an hour.'

'It's OK. We'll rehearse in the car.'

'I'm not sure if that's altogether within the law.'

'Nonsense. You steer the car. I'll play guitar in the back. We both sing. I bet there's nothing in the French Highway Code that says you can't do that.'

Brad and I had always played pretty good music together. When we'd first met as understudies in *Lennon* we'd spent night after night jamming together, and we'd gained the nickname 'The Muzak Brothers' from the rest of the cast, presumably because ours was a predominantly melodic repertoire. Now, fifteen years later, we were about to make a comeback.

'Brad's coming out again,' I said to Ron, who was in the kitchen frying some bacon for his breakfast.

It had been the smell that had woken me up. He shouldn't have been frying bacon and he knew it. Ron was taking tablets for his high blood pressure and he knew this kind of food wasn't good for him.

'He says he's going to come and help you build the pool,' I added.

Ron's face lit up.

'That's good,' he said, not managing words to match the delight of the expression. 'I like Brad.'

Suddenly it all fell into place. I knew now why Ron's periods of hard work had been so sporadic. I understood why breakfast, lunch and the *sieste* had become the most important parts of the day. It was because he didn't like working alone. When I'd first met him, Ron had always worked with an Irishman called Mick, who also happened to be his best friend. Ron hadn't been the same man since Mick had fallen in love, got married and gone to live in Tasmania. I mean, Tasmania of all places? Mick couldn't have found anywhere further away.

Although Ron pretended to like his own company and played the role of the loner with considerable aplomb, I reckoned that he was happiest when there were other people around. After all, this was when he could display his quick dry wit and sometimes cruel sense of humour. Brad's imminent arrival caused an immediate lift in the mood of my friend, builder and housemate. After breakfast he even started to whistle.

'Who can that be?' asked Ron, interrupting a rendition of 'Walking On Sunshine' in response to the sudden and loud knock on the front door.

'I've no idea. We're not expecting any deliveries today, are we?'

'Nope.'

'Perhaps the neighbours have come round to protest about the smell of bacon.'

I made my way to the door and opened it to find Rene the Mayor standing there. He shook my hand, asked me how I was, and then pointed to Kevin's wood exhibits on the grass verge. Oh no, I thought, could it be that he was an admirer of Kevin's work and that he wanted to buy some? Surely rural life couldn't warp artistic taste to such a degree?

'Tony, I am sorry but you will have to move this wood that is before your house,' he said, precisely.

Rene went on to explain that vehicles needed to use this bit of verge to pass each other if they came head to head outside my house.

'I am sorry,' he repeated.

'Please, Rene, don't be sorry,' I said, in all sincerity.

What a lucky break this was. I could now get rid of Kevin's extremely poor quality artistic creations and blame it on the mayor. No need to cause Kevin offence.*

'What was all that about?' asked Ron as he attempted to wedge some thinly cut French bread into the toaster.

'The mayor has asked me to move Kevin's wood.'

Ron burst into laughter. It was more than a fit of giggles. These were big laughs. Expressions of joy. For perhaps the first time since we'd got to the house, Ron appeared to be happy.

I attempted to take advantage.

'Do you want to make a start on the tiling down below?' I asked.

I was being more direct than usual. Normally I had to work hard to select the delicate blend of words that might persuade Ron to vacate the kitchen and slouch off towards the workplace.

'Righto,' said Ron, almost with a spring in his step.

I should have invited Brad over earlier.

Ron remained in splendid form throughout the day and into the evening.

'What shall I cook tonight?' he said, after he had completed the closest thing to a day's work that he'd put in for some time.

Ron's enthusiasm for cooking our evening meal was something that had been slowly building over the past week or so. Previously a self-confessed devotee of the instant meal, since coming to

---

*At least until he reads this.

France he'd broken free from these shackles and become eager to cook whenever possible. In the supermarket, when we shopped together (I tried to keep this to a minimum, for image reasons), Ron seemed strangely drawn to courgettes.

'Do we need that many?' I'd ask, upon viewing the basket brimming with the green vegetable.

'Oh, you can never have too many courgettes.'

But he was wrong – you can. And we did, most of the time. For at least half the average week, one of the kitchen cupboards was rendered completely inaccessible by a huge pile of them.

Ron also bucked the current trend against frying things. In fact, he chose the frying option for pretty much everything he cooked. It was almost as if he'd arrived at the theory that as long as the dish contained courgettes, then it was healthy. Yes, the courgette was healthy, but it was also compulsory. Just as a devout Jew might insist on kosher food, Ron's conscience demanded the fried courgette. Every man needs his religion.

'So, what shall I cook?' repeated Ron.

'Oh, anything you fancy,' I said, knowing what was coming.

It was a fine evening. The sun set over the house as we finally sat down and dined on the balcony. We looked out across the valley.

'Not much movement at the crossroads tonight,' said Ron.

'No. Very little action. But I guess rush hour is over.'

This had become a kind of game. Halfway up the other side of the hill, two single-track roads met. This was the 'crossroads'. Ron would spend hours looking out dreamily in its direction, and when I was with him, I couldn't help but join in with this vaguely meditative pastime. A car passing, the odd pedestrian, a farmer rounding up his sheep in adjacent pastures or the movements of the solitary horse in the adjoining field – these all became topics for discussion as the weary sun slowly retreated beyond the horizon and tucked itself up for the night. It may have been inane, or even utterly pointless, but these lethargic dialogues went some way to affirm the stress-free nature of our existence here.

On this night, though, the conversation went beyond the usual comment on the passing of a Renault van or the swooping of a bird of prey. No, tonight we talked about life. Ron recounted stories of his youthful adventures and of the many scrapes and brushes with danger that he'd survived. He'd lived a full life, but something had gone wrong somewhere, and he made no attempt to disguise the fact. The problem was that he had no enthusiasm for the future. I asked questions, I dug deep. What did Ron want? Did he have a plan for how to head towards it?

'I don't really know,' he said with a shrug.

'Well, I don't think that's so unusual,' I replied. 'None of us really know what we want. We just think we do. But it helps to have a goal or target of some kind. However simple. For instance, it needn't go much beyond a desire to approach the next day full of a passion and enthusiasm for every task in hand.'

Ron looked at me, a little puzzled. Perhaps he suspected that this was all some ploy on my part in order to get a better day's tiling out of him. Or perhaps it was simply because what I'd said was puzzling. Nothing more, nothing less. My sentence, like life itself, was puzzling.

'I keep having this recurring dream,' he said, switching subjects rather.

'Really? Perhaps there is some clue there. What is it?'

'It's to do with my car. Every night I have a dream that involves me leaving my car somewhere, only to find that it's not there when I come back. It happens over and over again.'

'It must mean something.'

'Yes, but what?'

It was a difficult question. What did it mean? What is happening in our subconscious mind? Are there messages there for us, and if so, do we have the skills to interpret them? And what happens if we get it wrong?

'Perhaps it just means that you're crap at remembering where you've left your car.'

'Great. Thanks, Tony,' said Ron with a laugh. 'How much do I owe you?'

'That'll be fifty euros, please.'

'I'll pay you tomorrow. That's it for tonight, I'm off to bed.'

And with those words Ron slid off in the direction of the woodshed.

13

Une Soirée Musicale

'So. You're the fella that went round Ireland with a fridge?'

'That's me.'

'You big eejit.'

We were sitting on Mary's balcony and I was talking to Nigel, an Irishman – one of the four who had arrived the previous night, all somehow crammed into Mary's limited accommodation. I sipped my coffee, glowing a little from the fact that the bizarre journey I had made in Ireland years before continued to bring me recognition and approval.

'Which number son are you, Nigel?' I enquired.

'I'm not actually Mary's son,' he replied. 'I'm the only one here who isn't, though. Paul, Miles and Daniel are.'

The three men all looked over, raised their coffee cups ever so slightly and nodded in confirmation. These guys were a much quieter crowd than I had expected. When Mary had mentioned that her sons were arriving, I'd anticipated a noisy, drunken rabble. A bunch of Irish musicians – on holiday? Wouldn't you?

'Who was playing the piano yesterday?' I enquired.

'Oh, that was me,' said Miles.

'It was beautiful.'

'Thanks.'

On completion of our short exchange, his eyes darted back to the rim of his coffee cup.

'Are you all set for tonight's gig then?' I asked.

'Hardly,' said Nigel, who seemed to be the spokesperson for the group. 'We'll rehearse a little this afternoon, but basically we're just going to have to busk it.'

Brad and I were in the same position. Tonight's concert certainly had the potential to be of a shambolic nature.

'Cakes anyone?' said Mary, emerging from the kitchen with a tray brimming with assorted goodies.

Mary definitely had a spring in her step and an extra zing about her. The mother in her had been instantly revived by the arrival of her offspring. She could now care for, organise and occasionally gently chastise her boys, and it was clearly invigorating her.

I had to leave this pleasant coffee morning one cake earlier than I'd like to have done, because time was pressing and the other half of the British musical duo needed collecting from the airport.

'I'll see you guys tonight,' I said.

'Yes. And maybe we could have a bit of a jam towards the end of the night?' said Nigel.

'Yes, maybe we could,' I replied, a little nervously.

The idea of jamming with some professional musicians appealed. But it also had the potential to highlight just how little piano practice I'd been doing of late.

I kept thinking that the car was going to break down, but it just continued chugging along. As I sped along the motorway at a steady 120kph, I wanted to congratulate the vehicle on what a fine job it was doing for me. It started every morning on command,

and it got me to and from town, trouble free. Two reasons prevented me from vocalising my gratitude:

I didn't want to tempt fate.

I didn't want to get in the habit of talking to cars.

Nevertheless, I was beginning to feel confident that the 'Curse of the White Van' was finally behind me. Perhaps I was in danger of becoming a little too complacent.

On the return leg from the airport Brad and I provided fellow motorway users with light entertainment. As they overtook us, they looked into our car with amazement, perhaps because music rehearsals don't usually take place in speeding saloon cars. One woman in particular seemed to become fascinated and she allowed her four-by-four to cruise parallel for quite a while whilst she tried to fathom what was going on in our car. In an age when everything is getting smaller and smaller, it must have appeared most odd to her that my in-car entertainment system was a bloke in the back seat playing the guitar. I wanted to wind down the window and shout, 'You should see what it's like when I'm listening to classical!' but I was singing harmonies at the time, so it just wasn't possible.

This eccentric and possibly quite dangerous rehearsal had been forced upon us by the constraints of time. Although Brad and I had a repertoire of 'songs around the campfire' material, there was a big difference between that kind of impromptu beer-induced sing-song, and being introduced as an act who would serenade a seated, expectant and sober audience. Emergency rehearsal was crucial.

'I have a bit of a confession to make, Brad,' I said, in a short break between songs.

'Oh,' said Brad, a little concerned. 'And that is?'

'Your name. I'm afraid you have a stage name now.'

'What do you mean?'

'Well, Malcolm phoned me this morning and told me that they're printing up a programme for tonight's event. He wanted to know your surname.'

'And?'

'Well, I just couldn't resist giving you a new name.'

'Why?'

'Not sure. I just couldn't help it.'

'And so what is it?'

'Brad Titman.'

'Brad Titman?'

'Yes, Brad Titman.'

'Brad Titman? That's pathetic.'

'Yes, I suppose it is.'

The problem had been one of timing. The mischievous concept had popped into my head the moment that Malcolm had asked the question. Why not come up with a rude surname for Brad, the significance of which would be lost on the French audience? The problem was that Brad Titman had been the first name that popped into my head, and it just wasn't a very good effort.

'So I'm Brad Titman whenever I'm over here, am I?'

'I'm afraid so.'

Brad sighed and went back to strumming.

We'd only been back at the house five minutes when Malcolm and Anne called round. They looked a little flustered, as well they might. I looked out onto my driveway and noted that their car was full of amplifiers, microphone stands and musical instruments, all of which they'd managed to borrow for the evening from various sources in the locality. As in the previous year, the responsibility for coordinating proceedings had fallen heavily on their capable shoulders.

It seemed to me that Malcolm and Anne were the textbook English settlers in France. I guess like many others before them it had all started when they'd sat in their kitchen in suburban England and discussed the sums. If they sold their house, could they afford to buy in France and still have enough to live on, provided they could muster a moderate stream of income from somewhere once in situ? For them it all added up, and they'd joyfully kissed goodbye to the British rat race, blissfully exchanging nine-to-five stress-laden jobs for stunning views, mountain walks and a daily dose of good red wine. I'd asked Malcolm once what they both missed most about living in England.

'Going down the local for a pint,' Malcolm had replied. 'I miss the pub, especially in the winter. The French just don't go out in that way. They get together with the family or at big festivals or events – but they don't go in for the casual drink and a chat in a bar of an evening.'

'But you're happy here?'

'Oh blissfully, but we've had to work hard.'

And by that I guess he meant that they'd done everything they could to immerse themselves in the local culture. Malcolm and Anne, as English settlers, were probably better villagers than most of the people who were born here. They both sat on the village social committee, and Malcolm was treasurer. They'd mastered the language (Anne with a stunning English accent) and they considered most in the village to be their close friends. They'd done well because they had become part of a culture that wasn't 'theirs'. Not an easy trick to pull off.

'Can you and Brad do fifteen minutes at the start of the second half?' asked Anne, shortly after turning down a cup of tea because time wouldn't permit it.

'Sure,' I replied, as Brad looked on with some anxiety.

'See you later then,' said Malcolm. 'We have to go and get your meal ready now.'

In return for displaying their talents, the musicians were to get a meal and as much as they could drink for the evening. I liked this concept of the musos playing for food and booze. Somehow it seemed 'spiritually correct'. In this system everyone gets paid the same – unless you are particularly good, in which case you might get an extra burger.

Brad and I felt a little like teenagers as Ron dropped us off at the village hall. All he needed to say as we got out of the car with our guitars was: 'Now, don't drink too much and don't be late,' and the image would have been complete.

'Are you sure you don't want to come, Uncle Ron?' asked Brad.

'Yeh, I'm all right,' he replied, a little uncomfortably.

'Well, if you feel like it, pop back later,' I said. 'Just drop by and stand at the back. No one will mind.'

'Yeh, could do, I suppose. Have a good night. See ya.'

And Ron drove off.

'Will he come?' asked Brad.

'Not a chance,' I replied. 'Ron loves music, but he's not a social animal and tonight won't be his thing because there'll be people there.'

'We hope.'

Suddenly Brad let out an agonised yelp. 'God! What's that?'

'What?'

'That smell! Oh God, is that you?'

Have you ever had to suffer that horrible moment when you realise that you've broken wind seconds before without it really registering? Have you ever had to cope with the fact that, for some strange anatomical reason, the emerging gases turn out to be rather more potent than is socially acceptable? Well, I was having one of those moments right now.

'Er yes, I'm afraid it is me,' I said, wafting my hand before me in a futile attempt to remedy the situation. 'I'm sorry.'

'Uggh. That's awful.'

'Yes, it is, isn't it?'

No point in denying the bloody obvious. Little to be gained from countering with: 'Oh I don't think it's that bad – only a seven out of ten for unpleasantness.'

'You know what that is, don't you?' said Brad.

'No.'

'That's a Courgette Fart.'

Of course, Brad had hit the nail on the head. That's exactly what it was. My body simply couldn't cope any longer with the sheer weight of courgettes that it was being asked to process, and the unwelcome result had been this recent arrival – the Courgette Fart. The stomach may be an intricate and sophisticated mechanism but it clearly has its limitations, and my recent diet had ably managed to expose them.

'Are you nervous about our gig?' asked Brad, providing another possible reason for why I'd joined the world ranks of air polluters.

'I don't think so,' I replied. 'Only a little apprehensive, that's all.'

'Well, whatever, let's get inside,' said Brad, leading us both away from the contaminated area. 'And try not to break any more wind in there. You may find you lose friends rather quickly.'

Inside the village hall we found that it had been magically transformed into a kind of jazz club. The walls had been softened with drapes and the lights had been dimmed, candles on every table providing a supplementary and yet mellow source of illumination. The 'stage area', where the assortment of microphones and musical instruments signalled a promise of things to come, was halfway along the far wall, on ground level. The huge raised stage had been shunned. The village social committee had quite correctly decided that placing the musicians on this elevated platform would have separated them too much from their audience. It also meant that they wouldn't be performing in front of the vast mural of the Caribbean beach scene that would have required them to play reggae or calypso all night.

'The organisers have excelled themselves,' I said to Brad, who nodded in agreement.

'All we need now is an audience,' he said.

'And some food. I'm starving.'

A small area had been set aside in the corner of the hall for the purposes of the musicians' pre-concert dining. We looked over to see that the Irish boys were tucking into the nosh with gusto, along with a few others I didn't recognise.

'Come on. Let's go eat,' I said.

'Righto,' said Brad. 'But can I suggest you steer clear of the courgettes?'

'Fair point.'

We were immediately greeted by the delightful Christine – the young lady who had taught me how to play the card game belote at the village dinner all those months before. As she ushered us to the table she told us that her tasks for the evening involved wait-ressing for the meal that we were about to eat, and then filming the concert on her dad's video camera. The young people in this village had to be versatile.

I found myself on the end of a long table seated next to a man called Michel, who seemed delighted to be beside someone on whom he could practise his slightly rusty English. With a cheeky smile he offered a series of short soundbites that initially did little to establish a relationship of great depth: 'How is the Queen?' or 'Ah yes – you is Tony – like Tony Blair.' His curly bouncy haircut resembled the one favoured by Kevin Keegan in the 1970s, just one of several things about him which led me to believe that he wasn't a local farmer. His clothes were stylish and well presented, and his hands bore no traces of the hard skin and deeply ingrained dirt that usually defined those of the manual worker. The long thumbnail on his right hand also revealed to the astute observer that he was almost certainly a guitarist who played with a picking style. The only other alternative I could think of was that he'd been in the process of cutting his nails earlier in the day when he'd been interrupted by a visiting gypsy woman who'd advised him against completing the job or else a curse would fall upon his family.

'Do you play guitar?' I enquired.

'Yes I do,' he replied, holding up his thumb, in a gesture that cleared up any lingering doubts on the gypsy theory.

Michel poured me a red wine and lapsed into French, finally enabling a meaningful exchange to develop between us. He began to tell me how he had moved to the village from Nantes, an area in France where he'd built a following as a songwriter and racon-teur. He returned there regularly for tours and recording sessions, but village life in the Pyrenees provided him with the home where he could nurture his creativity. I began to wonder if this made him a little like a kind of French version of me. One notable difference was that he'd chosen to live here with his wife rather than his builder.

By the end of the meal, which had been pleasingly free of courgettes, the first smatterings of audience were starting to make their way into the village hall. The sight of them brought home the reality of an imminent performance for which we weren't properly prepared. I felt a ripple of nerves sweep through my body, and a slight rumbling in the tummy. This was followed by an unpleasant moment in which I realised what the obvious bodily corollary of this was going to be. Something that was unlikely to endear me to my new friend Michel. I had to move, and quickly, so I jumped to my feet and announced that I was going to the toilet, quite possibly at a volume that normally would have merited a statement of greater profundity.

I began to make my way across to the toilets, happy in the knowledge that an embarrassing incident had been averted. Then I heard a female voice behind me.

'*Bonjour, Tonny!*'

I spun round to see two diminutive septuagenarian ladies looking up at me. It was Odette and Marie, two of the lovely older women I'd first met on village dinner night. By the twinkle in their eyes I could see that they wanted to chat.

Was it true that I was going to perform tonight with my friend?

What were we going to sing?

Would I be singing a song in French?

And then quite suddenly all the questions stopped and their faces displayed a mixture of pain and shock. I knew what had happened. The worst.

I am not proud of what I did next. Not knowing the French for 'He who smelt it dealt it', I made an excuse about having to go and tune a guitar, and moved off with a fleetness of foot that bordered on downright evil. I just left them. I left them wondering who was to blame for the disagreeable odours that were currently engulfing them. Not being ladies in the fresh flush of youth, they both probably had their fair share of medical conditions and would therefore reasonably assume that the other was responsible. They wouldn't for a moment suspect the young, dashing Englishman who was soon to serenade them.

I didn't look back. I couldn't. Once you've chosen your required act of cowardice, never weaken.

Malcolm and Michel kicked off the evening's presentation with an amusing little skit in which Michel spoke deliberately wooden English that was then translated into deliberately wooden French by Malcolm. They were playing to a packed house of about 150 people, drawn from not just our village, but from many of the surrounding ones too. I could see many familiar faces – André, Serge, Alain, Odette, Roger, Marie, Rene the Mayor, Leon the Deputy Mayor, my neighbour Pierre, a host of characters whose names I'd not yet properly committed to memory – and Fabrice and Marie-Laure, my new pals who had driven up here specially.

'I'm starting to get nervous now,' I said to Brad.

'In that case, I'm just going over here,' he said, moving to a safe distance.

I shrugged and continued to watch Malcolm and Michel on stage. Somehow they seemed to represent the 'new' rural France. An Englishman and an outsider from Nantes, performing before the descendants of people who had belonged in these mountains for generations. This was the positive spin on the 'new' rural France. The communities were integrating – they were learning from, and enjoying, each other. This was a fine balance that could easily be upset. Fortunately we all knew it.

'Ladies and gentlemen,' said Michel, 'please welcome from Dublin – Nigel, Paul and Miles.'

The three men must have made quite an impression with their performance the previous year because they walked on stage to a huge reception. Paul and Miles smiled almost self-consciously, whilst Nigel looked more at ease. He picked up a cool-looking jazzy guitar and took his place behind the microphone.

'*Bonsoir – nous allons commencer,*' he said with a delightfully Irish accent, '*avec une belle chanson qui s'appelle – "C'est Si Bon".*'

The audience cheered. The French are often berated for being difficult to win over if you don't speak their language, but the fact is that they don't demand a great deal from you linguistically in order to be on your side. A poorly constructed sentence can often be enough to prompt an extremely friendly response. However, speak no French at all and nine times out of ten they'll derive satisfaction from making things difficult for you.

Paul smoothly slipped a bass guitar over his shoulder and Miles lowered himself onto the stool behind the electric piano. Then all three did what jazz musicians do better than anyone else – they indulged in a few seconds of 'warming up'. Totally independently of each other they flirted with their instruments, their hands darting over keys or strings in harmonious disorder. They seemed more at ease than they'd looked since I'd met them. Even though they hadn't started playing for real yet, their accomplished dexterity was already apparent and it was enabling them to exude a confidence previously not evident. Their fingers were talking.

'I think they're going to be good,' said Brad, who had carelessly allowed himself to drift back close enough to me to be in dangerous air space.

'Yes, I think you may be right.'

And he was.

Miles's tasteful keyboard playing blended with Paul's thoughtful bass, whilst Nigel led them from the front with a slick, bluesy guitar sound. Then, at the end of his first solo, Nigel sang. He had a wonderfully smooth jazzy voice that was both laid-back and melodic, precise yet uninhibited. It was cool. No question. In fact, the whole band embodied the very thing for which the 1960s had invented the word. We could have been in Ronnie Scott's jazz club in Soho but for the sight of André sitting three tables back in his beret and torn jacket, along with others dotted about the room who looked like they'd just stepped off tractors.

The first verse of '*C'est Si Bon*' was a triumph and the audience showed it by clapping before the song was even halfway through. However, they were going to like it even more very soon, because Nigel had a trump card up his sleeve. Just after the boys had completed the musical turnaround at the end of the first verse, Nigel began to do something quite extraordinary. He sang the second verse in French. What a coup (if I may appropriately borrow a French word). The spectators could scarcely contain themselves. Not only had these boys come all the way from Ireland to play top quality jazz music in a free concert, but now they were singing in French! The audience exploded with sundry noises of approbation.

'Tony, do you know any songs in French?' said an anxious-looking Brad, during the semi-ovation that followed completion of the song.

'Only a couple of lines from "*Sur Le Pont d'Avignon*".'

'I'm not sure if that will be good enough.'

'Mmm. I feared as much.'

Seconds later Brad was speedily shuffling away from me, and a few moments after that the family on a nearby table began to look at each other accusingly. Terrible thing, nerves.

Following an amazing half-hour set from the Irish boys, it was the turn of the French. Michel did four songs, two that were well known and a couple he'd written himself. He was an assured and accomplished performer with a fine voice and easy guitar-picking style. I particularly liked the song he'd written many years ago for his wife Christine. '*T'es Petite, T'es Grande, T'es Belle, Toi*' (You – you're small, you're big, you're beautiful). I looked to see if I could find her face in the audience. I didn't know what she looked like, but I reckoned I'd be able to spot her as being the only one who was really glowing.

After the jazzy complexity of the Irish boys' opening set, which had drawn on songs from the Great American Songbook, I was struck by the marked contrast of the 'French song'. Sophisticated chords and subtle melodies didn't seem to be in the forefront of the creative minds of the French songwriters. They preferred the strength of a bold transition from minor to major, and then back again. I bet that during their song-writing sessions there weren't many discussions about whether chord progressions were 'too obvious'. Obvious was good, obvious was strong, obvious was catchy. And anyway, it was the words that were important. The French song told a story or expressed an opinion. What mattered was that you knew what the song was about. I guess that's why the British have never really been fans of French songs. We don't understand them.

Mary closed the first half even though she'd wanted to get out of playing.

'I'll leave it to you fellas,' she'd said. 'You know how to play properly.'

Lacking in confidence though she may have been, her ten-minute set was a big success. She led the whole room in a spirited sing-song, thumping out the chords on the piano whilst Miles shifted onto the nearby drum kit and proved his versatility by banging out an upbeat rhythmic accompaniment. With an almighty rendition of what I recognised as 'Those Were The Days' but which almost everyone else knew as a French song, the first half drew to a close. A first half that had been close to perfect.

Brad and I spent the interval outside, around the back of the hall. The light hadn't completely faded and we finished our frantic last-minute rehearsals as the distant peaks gently surrendered to the advancing darkness. I was suffering from doubts about our choice of songs, but Brad had regained his confidence and was steadfast.

'Let's stick to what we're good at,' he said.

I thought for a moment.

'Drinking and watching?' I replied.

'Come on. Don't be so negative. We're going to knock 'em dead.'

'I do hope so.'

Brad and I continued with our musical equivalent of last-minute cramming for an exam until we were called back in by Malcolm and told to stand by the side of the stage.

We obeyed the instructions in silence. As Malcolm moved towards the microphone, we knew that our time on stage was imminent. I don't know why I felt so uneasy. In my professional career I'd faced larger, noisier and more cynical audiences than this on a fairly regular basis. But all of a sudden, and for the first time, the stakes here seemed high. If Brad and I did well then I would have made a shortcut to acceptance with many in the village, but get it wrong, and then not only would I lose credibility with those I'd already met, but I may well have an uphill struggle with the rest.

'*Mesdames et messieurs*,' announced Malcolm, '*le deuxième acte de la soirée commencera maintenant avec Tony Hawks et Brad Titman.*'

And then my nerves vanished. The sound of my friend being announced by a daft name reminded me just how silly it was to be uptight about this. Yes, it mattered – but by the same token, it didn't matter either. Probably in the grand scheme of things, nothing really matters, but certainly the fifteen-minute set by Tony Hawks and Brad Titman in a small village in France didn't merit any further anxiety.

'Let's enjoy this, Titman!' I whispered to Brad through a suppressed giggle.

Brad turned and nodded and I felt a little like the escape officer addressing a fellow prisoner upon entering the tunnel for our break-out attempt. We had our fake passports, civilian clothing, the tunnel was clear, and all we had to do now was give it our best shot.

We walked onto the stage to a warm round of applause and Brad hit the first chord. E minor. I joined in, and we quickly established a funky rhythm. This caused a ripple of excitement through the audience. A couple of high-pitched whoops wafted up into the rafters of the hall's high ceiling. I took a deep breath and belted out the first line.

'Well, you can tell by the way I use my walk, I'm a woman's man
– no time to talk . . .'

More whoops and hollers. I caught Brad's eye and gave him a
look, as if to say, 'Yup, we're on our way.'

The old Bee Gees song 'Stayin' Alive' had been a little favourite
of ours, a song that we'd found surprisingly easy to convert into an
arrangement for two guitars and two voices. When we'd first learnt
it Brad had worked very hard at the high-pitched harmony line,
and as he leaned into the microphone to deliver it to this new
French audience I noticed that he was grinning like an excited
child.

The Muzak Brothers were back. We were on a performance
high. However else the simple dynamic of the performer/audience
relationship may be confused, abused and perverted by money,
managers, agents and ego, the simplicity of it can return in a
magical instant. And it was happening right now. The real thrill of
the performance comes from a positive exchange of energy –
ephemeral and often elusive, invisible and unquantifiable, but a
natural tonic, a kind of organic battery charge.

Yes! The Muzak Brothers were back.

The end of the song may not have prompted the same audience
response as the one that had greeted the Irish boys in the first half,
but we weren't far off. We were holding our own, and as a consequence I now felt confident enough to test myself still further. I
like to think that over the past fifteen years I'd developed an easy
style of delivery when on stage addressing an audience. But what
would it be like when attempting it in another language? Well, I
was about to find out.

I found myself introducing Brad and explaining that he'd been
at his office desk in London that very morning and now he was
here in the mountains singing for them. The audience applauded
his efforts and Brad smiled. An innocent, naïve smile. And then it
occurred to me.

He had absolutely no idea what I'd just said.

I shared this thought with the audience and they laughed. Brad smiled again. An even more innocent, naïve smile, tinged with a hint of bewilderment. I became mischievous and told the audience that it didn't matter what I said about Brad, he wouldn't understand. There were more chuckles at this, and so I took it as a green light to indulge my whimsy. Brad, I explained to the audience, had started out in life as a small-time burglar who had spent long periods in a string of different prisons. Later he had carried out two contract killings but had successfully blamed them both on innocent men who were now serving sentences in his place. I glanced across at my chum who was grinning inanely.

'What are you doing, you bastard?' he enquired, through clenched teeth.

I smiled back at him, feeling the faintest hint of the all-consuming power of a dictator. What should I say next? I had complete control over Brad's entire history. Tempting though it may have been to continue exploiting the easy laughs provided by the blank canvas of Brad's uninformed face, I elected not to milk it any further and I launched into the opening riff of our next song.

'*Et maintenant – une chanson de Stevie Wonder – "Superstition",*' I announced.

And Brad Titman, the double murderer, joined in – none the wiser.

It turned out to be quite a night. After Brad and I had successfully concluded our five songs, Michel performed some pretty French duets with a mate of his, and the Irish boys played another set, including some traditional Irish music, which went down a storm. The culmination of the night was a huge jam session, a long stint of which I spent tinkling the ivories. Miles was an accomplished drummer as well as a brilliant pianist and once he discovered that I played keyboards, he urged me to take over from him, freeing him up for percussive duties. Initially I'd protested to the others.

'I can't follow Miles – he's so much better than me.'

'Ah, just shut up and play.'

Maybe it was the drink (the beers were now flowing thick and fast, and the musicians were well on the way to drinking any profit that the night's bar takings might have produced), or maybe it was just the high of playing with such fabulous musicians, but quite unexpectedly I played the piano better than I can remember having played it before. The small amount of practice that I had got around to bore fruit, and I found myself exploring the keyboard with a dexterity and a creativity that completely took me by surprise. For at least half an hour I felt like a pianist. What could I achieve if I actually began to do what I'd set out to do? Could this be the kick-start I needed to make full use of the Piano in the Pyrenees?

At around 2.30am I took a break from jamming with the boys and I sat at a table at the far end of the room. For the first time in the evening I was truly relaxed.

'You played very well this evening,' said a voice.

I looked up from my beer and saw an attractive woman, probably close to my age, smiling warmly at me.

'Thank you,' I replied.

'Where are you from?'

'I am from London,' I said, noting her pretty eyes for the first time. 'My name is Tony – what's yours?'

'Monique,' she replied, broadening her smile still further.

A 'getting to know each other' conversation followed. My eyes and instincts had already told me that Monique was an elegant and attractive woman but soon I had information to complement that. She was currently living in a neighbouring village, having moved to the area from Belgium many years ago with her former husband. As far as I could make out, there was no new man in her life, something that seemed to be backed up by the amount of time she was able to set aside for chatting to me at 2.30 in the morning.

'Tony! Tony! We need you on piano,' came a call from Nigel on the stage. 'Miles is going back on the drums.'

Damn. I wanted to stay longer where I was. Monique and I seemed to have made some kind of connection.

'OK!' I called back to the stage, rising from the table.

'Well, goodbye, Tony,' said Monique. 'It was nice to meet you.'

'Yes, it was nice to meet you too.'

I shook her hand. Quite why I chose to be so extraordinarily English at this point of the night, I cannot fully explain. Here I was in a country where they jumped at any excuse to kiss each other, and all I'd managed was a formal shake of the hand after an evening of music and alcohol.

'But did you get her number?' asked Brad, after Monique had disappeared with a wave twenty minutes later at the conclusion of our twelve-minute version of Bill Withers' 'Lovely Day'.

'No, I didn't.'

'Schoolboy error, Hawks.'

'Yes, it was rather, wasn't it?'

Brad didn't respond, allowing himself instead to be seamlessly swept into the latest piece of musical improvisation, a vaguely bossa-nova version of 'Hit The Road Jack'.

We finally packed up playing at 4 o'clock in the morning. Most of the smattering of ne'er-do-wells who were left in the village hall had attempted to play some instrument or other, however badly or drunkenly. When Malcolm's old school chum and house guest Louise hit the drums in a kind of inebriated manic fury, we knew it was time to call it a night. Over the years I have noticed this irritating drawback to the drums. Somehow they call out to people with no musical ability, saying, 'Play me, play me! This is the one instrument you can play!'

After Malcolm had wrested the drumsticks from the latest victim of this delusion, we all headed for the door.

'*Bonne nuit* all,' I said in my best Franglais.

'Goodnight and well played,' said Nigel, politely holding the door open for me and Brad. As we made our way out, I heard Nigel lean across to Brad and whisper, 'By the way – helluva surname you've got there!'

I smiled, but then immediately reproached myself for not having taken Monique's number.

Opportunities like the one I'd just missed didn't come thick and fast in this part of the world.

14

Polka

Inspired by that magical musical evening, I practised on my piano much harder in the days that followed, concentrating particularly on building up the strength in my left hand. This was necessary because the right hand was naturally exercised in the course of my routine improvisations, whilst the left one mostly played chords that demanded less work from the fingers. So when a busy boogie-woogie or rock'n'roll accompaniment was required, this weakness became hopelessly exposed. Sometimes after only a minute of playing this kind of stuff it felt like my left hand was falling off, such was the shooting pain that built up in my wrist.

Many years back, during another period in my life when I'd resolved to improve my piano playing, I'd taken it upon myself to increase the strength in my left hand by using a wrist strengthener, effectively a kind of spring that you had to squeeze between the fingers and palm of the hand. I soon realised that I could use this little gadget pretty much anywhere, especially if I carried the thing with me in my trouser pocket. I only did this once in public, though, following an embarrassing and misinterpreted practice session on the London Underground when I happened to be sitting in front of a couple of rather pretty Scandinavian girls.

Fortunately, there were no such hitches with my Pyrenean practice schedule. I offended hardly anyone, apart from maybe Brad and Ron, who may have become tired of my endless attempts to master the piano solo from 'My Baby Just Cares For Me' or the fast bit from Stevie Wonder's 'Sir Duke'.

Still, I'm sure they recognised that it was all in the name of art. I hope that they had the insight to regard practice as a noble struggle. Few of us get good at anything without having to practice, and for the few lucky ones for whom excellence comes without effort, they miss out on the glow that follows a success achieved through arduous endeavour. It's a universal truth that we just don't appreciate things that come too easy.

That's why I was really going to enjoy my swimming pool, if it ever got finished.

When Rene the Mayor called round, Ron and Brad had just emerged from extensive 'poolside' discussions. From the safety of the interior of the house I had furtively observed them engage in a lengthy period of frantic measuring, head scratching and desperate hypothesising. Too many sentences began with the words 'What if?' for me to feel entirely comfortable with how things were progressing. I watched as small wooden stakes were hammered into the floor of 'Serge's hole', followed by the unravelling of string which was then passed round the stakes. And there it was – clear for any secret observer to see – the shape of my new pool. It was a four-sided figure in which both pairs of opposite sides were parallel and of the same length, with the opposite angles equal. Unfortunately, not all four angles were the same.

In other words, my pool was going to be parallelogram-shaped.

As he approached the house Rene merely glanced in the direction of the dismay that surrounded Serge's hole before popping his head through the open French windows. He called out to me, asking if I would be coming to the village fête dinner on Saturday.

'*Naturellement*,' I replied.

'*Combien de personnes?*'

'*Deux. Moi et Brad.*'

Ron would never come to an event with so many people around. In fact, apart from a bit of 'banger' racing and the occasional day of clay-pigeon shooting, Ron was still shunning all social activities.

'*Bon*,' said Rene, ticking something off in his crumpled notebook.

He looked back down at the vast gaping hole in my garden and saw two men, one scratching his head and the other trying in vain to pull a stake out of the ground. I don't know why, but this sight prompted him to ask me when I thought the swimming pool might be finished. I tried to cobble together the French equivalent of 'It'll all be over by Christmas', and whatever I said Rene seemed to understand. He smiled and raised his eyebrows.

'*Bonne chance!*' he said, before turning and marching briskly back to his car.

I was relieved that he hadn't asked me to which of the remaining Christmases in the current decade I had been referring.

Later that morning the phone rang. This was something of an event in itself. I hadn't passed on the number to many people, partly because I was cherishing the release from the world of 'constant contact' that London life seemed to necessitate.

'Hi, Tony, it's Malcolm,' came the voice from the end of the line. Bizarrely enough, it was a line so close that Malcolm could have almost dispensed with it and just gone outside and bellowed to me. I probably would have heard his voice echoing through the foothills.

'What are you doing tomorrow night?' he enquired.

'Nothing,' I replied, without any need to check my diary.

Life here, rather pleasingly, was anything but a social whirl.

'Well, you've been invited to a party in another village. Actually, I think you might be being fixed up. You are still single, aren't you?'

'Yes, I am. Ron has failed to win my hand in marriage.'

'Er . . . quite. Well . . . er . . . Laura is having a party and she wants you to go. She's the English friend of a lady called Monique who I think you met at the music night.'

'Yes. I remember her,' I said, managing a hint of understatement.

'You and Brad are invited. Fancy it?'

'I do. I haven't been to many parties since I've been here.'

'Yes, well, you're not in Soho now.'

How right he was.

Party night arrived after another day's intensive work (by our standards anyway) on the process of pool construction. Brad and I were tired, but we were both excited by the prospect of a first social event outside our own patch. I was particularly intrigued by the thought that I was being 'set up' with someone – someone who when I'd last seen her had seemed very attractive indeed.

'Big night for you, mate,' said Brad, as the drive took us through the soothing landscapes of the Baronnies – rolling foothills peppered with quaint villages, some of which were even large enough to have a shop and a bar.

'Oh, I wouldn't say that,' I said, trying to play things down.

'How much further?' asked Brad, not unlike a bored child on a family outing.

'I reckon another ten minutes and we'll be there,' I replied as we rounded yet another bend on what was fast becoming the snakiest journey of the decade.

I'd underestimated. It was half an hour before we were pulling into the drive of Laura and James's. Their house was the kind you see photographed in house and garden magazines. It was an old farmhouse perched on the side of a hill, and it was complemented by a glistening glass conservatory that looked out over an imposing Pyrenean peak.

I knocked on the door. A woman in her mid-sixties appeared and addressed me brusquely.

'Not this door!' she said crisply. 'This is the back door. The front door is there.'

She pointed to another entrance, about five yards to our left.

'Oh sorry,' I said, fully expecting to be invited in, regardless of my foolish error on the door front.

The door, however, closed in our faces.

'Charming,' said Brad, as we slowly filed down to the correct door.

We had just met Laura. I wasn't intimidated by her, even though she was tall, austere and had a fairly fearsome manner.

'Come in!' she commanded, as she opened the front door to us.

'Thanks,' I said. 'Lovely house.'

'Yes, it is.'

And it was. Brad and I conceded it with a string of approving nods. Old and new had been combined tastefully: venerable fireplace alongside steel spotlight, wooden beams jutting out from low ceilings and a tasteful pair of art deco sofas.

'I'm afraid Monique is late,' said Laura. 'But then she always is. Even though she was not born in these parts, she has adopted Bigourdian timekeeping with relish.'

Laura then led me and Brad into the conservatory and introduced us to her husband James, who didn't get up from the armchair into which he had well and truly sunk. Balding, wrinkled and tired-looking, James nodded to us rather than shaking hands and sent Laura off to bring us some drinks. He then proceeded to tell the two of us about his life, regardless of the fact that neither of us had asked any questions about it.

'Of course, we're Thatcher exiles,' he said proudly. 'We came to set up home in France when Mrs T won her second term in 1983. We couldn't stand the woman.'

They weren't alone. Dear old Margaret must have been responsible for quite an exodus of old lefties who couldn't face any more of her divisive social policies. Not everyone split as soon as Laura and James, but a fair exodus had certainly followed. The French ministry of the interior estimates the number of British people owning property in France at over 600,000. This is no longer the preserve of a privileged few. Brits from all walks of life are upping anchor and experimenting with '*la vie française*'. The odd thing is that it's happening at a time when Britain is hugely successful. Never mind that the UK is now the fourth largest economy in the world, growing numbers of people don't want to live there any more. It goes to show that success ought to be measured in more than just economic terms. Certainly I'd prefer to live in a country that didn't necessarily have a lot of skyscrapers, but which performed well on the 'number of people smiling' scale.

Monique was smiling when she eventually arrived. It was a nice smile, and one that seemed to be particularly directed at me. She was looking elegant and attractive and she certainly didn't have the air of someone who'd just come out in a hurry. She wore a pretty flowing white dress and a flowery top that allowed more than a glimpse of well-proportioned cleavage.

Brad and Laura tactfully gave us some space and sat down with James in the conservatory, who readily launched into another unprompted anecdote about his first ever trip to this region.

'Do you like to dance?' asked Monique, as we chatted by the fireplace.

'Yes, but I'm not particularly good,' I replied. 'However, I make up for that with enthusiasm.'

'Good. In that case you will dance the polka with me tonight.'

I looked around the living room, noting that it was crowded with furniture, ornaments and sculptures.

'Won't we cause a lot of breakages?' I asked.

'We will not dance here!' laughed Monique. 'The party is not here at Laura's. It is at a chateau owned by a Canadian man. We will go there in a minute. There will be a live band and we will dance.'

★ ★ ★

'Well?' enquired Brad with a cheeky grin as we followed Laura and Monique's car en route to the chateau.

'Well what?'

'Monique. What do you reckon?'

'Well, there's nothing wrong. Nothing wrong at all. And we had a nice chat about our favourite books and films and stuff, but . . .'

'No fireworks?'

'Not yet, certainly, but I think she's a little shy. Maybe she'll relax more after I polka.'

'What?' said a stunned Brad, hearing 'poke her', not 'polka'. 'Aren't you being a bit presumptuous?'

'No, we've already booked it in.'

'What do you mean?'

'We'll do it on the dance floor when the moment's right.'

'I've got to hand it to you, Tony. You don't muck about.'

The chateau was modest in size and was nestled in a beautiful forest setting. The Canadian owner ran it as a hotel and this party was largely for his guests, who mostly seemed to be 'hippy' types. For some reason there were quite a lot of Dutch men with long hair and Dutch women with crew cuts, all looking like they'd come straight from some kind of protest march. 'Would you like a drink?' I asked Monique, as we stood in the chateau courtyard where an outside bar had been erected.

'I am driving, but I suppose I can have one beer,' she said. 'But wait! We must drink later and dance now. I can hear that the band are playing a polka, and we must dance.'

'OK,' I said resignedly as Monique led me by the hand to the barn from where the music was emanating. (This, it seemed, was an authentic barn dance.)

Inside, a trio of young musicians was playing French songs that had little appeal other than providing the requisite rhythms for various dances. Four or five couples were dancing – proper dancing, not just jigging about in front of each other. I'd been brought up on the jigging about stuff. That's what you did when you went to a club or disco. You only got hold of someone and danced together if there was romantic interest, and it had always seemed a shame to me that dancing close with someone meant there were sexual implications. My early youthful trips to France had taught me that things were different here. People dance for the dancing, swapping partners and spinning each other about with an almost naïve sense of fun. It was as a result of seeing this that I'd taken it upon myself to go to classes when I got back to England to learn some of the steps and the moves.

'The polka is just like a fast waltz, right?' I asked Monique, as we stood on the edge of the area designated for dancing.

'Yes, but do you mind if I lead?' she asked.

'What do you mean?'

'Well, I do a lot of dancing in a club where there aren't enough men. So I take the man's role, and I lead.'

'OK. That should be fine. Since I don't really know what I'm doing anyway, it might be better if you took control.'

We stepped onto the dance floor and soon I was being whisked round the floor at speed. In less than a minute I was beginning to gasp for breath, such was the frantic pace of the music. Monique spun me one way, then the next – as I battled hard not to trample her feet with mine.

'What is that face you are pulling?' said Monique, as she spun me round on yet another hasty circuit of the generously sized dance-floor. 'Are you in pain?'

'No, I am concentrating,' I replied.

'Ah, so this is your polka face.'

Was this a witty remark or had Monique just made a joke by accident? I hoped it wasn't the former since I was some years away from making a joke like that in French.

'Do you want to dance again?' Monique asked as the song ended.

'Er . . . I'd love to, but maybe we should chat a little,' I said, doing my best not to pant like an exhausted dog.

'OK. But we have to dance again soon.'

'Yes,' I said, wondering if I should make up a leg injury in order to get me out of it.

We stood by the dance floor and watched as the evening became increasingly bizarre. Traditional Scottish dancing had begun, and it was being called by a Dutchman, whilst the French trio provided the musical accompaniment. An odd, but truly European evening. Brad launched himself into the Scottish dancing with a vigour and eagerness that probably surprised even himself. Monique and I chatted but the conversation trickled rather than flowed. Perhaps it was the language difference, or the noise of the band, but the fireworks to which Brad had referred earlier remained firmly in a sealed box and watched over by a couple of responsible adults.

I felt that there was, however, enough reason to see Monique again. She was an attractive woman who seemed to like me, and what's more she made splendid accidental jokes. Better still, she lived quite near.

'Shall we meet again soon?' I enquired, as the band started to pack up their gear and the guests began a round of goodbyes.

'Perhaps,' she said cagily, 'but I'm not sure what it is that we would do.'

'Well, you live in a village not far from me,' I said. 'I could pop round for tea one afternoon, if you like?'

'Oh, Tony,' she replied, almost frowning, 'but I'm not sure that it would be correct for me to meet you like this, with you unchaperoned.'

I smiled. Another joke from Monique. She was beginning to warm up. However, a look at her face revealed that she was deadly serious. It seemed that she was caught in some kind of time warp and believed that the two of us were characters from a Jane Austen novel.

'Right,' I said, more than a little taken aback. 'Well, how about you come round for tea at my place one afternoon? We won't be alone because Brad will be there, and so will Ron the builder.'

'I am not sure about this,' she said with a shake of the head. 'Perhaps I should know you better before I visit your house.'

'Right,' I said, trying to disguise my sigh and growing frustration. 'Are you sure you want us to meet again?'

'Oh yes, I'm sure,' she replied. 'It would be nice.'

'Well, in that case, what about this as an idea? Since you like to lead when dancing a polka, why don't you lead when it comes to deciding when and how we meet next?'

Another shake of the head.

'No, Tony, I do not think that this would be right.'

Monique wasn't exactly leaving that many options open.

She seemed to be one or all of three things: incredibly mixed up, extraordinarily old-fashioned and amazingly naïve. I looked at her. She wasn't giving anything away. Her polka face.

'Listen,' I said, 'it's late and we're both tired from the dancing. Let's talk again soon.'

'Oh,' she said, seemingly surprised that I was bringing this rather uninspired conversation to a conclusion. 'You are going to go now?'

'Yes,' I said, even more confused by her apparent disappointment. 'I think I need to rescue Brad. A Dutchman appears to be dancing with him rather too eagerly and he looks a little uncomfortable.'

'OK, Tony, goodnight.'

'Goodnight.'

As Monique turned to leave, I began to wonder what had just happened here. Had I misunderstood the French way of doing things? Or was Monique, as I suspected, a little more complicated than I would have preferred. Should I call her again? The answer, I decided, was no. The trouble was that, although I had all the time in the world, somehow I didn't have time for all this.

A few mornings later, I was woken by the sound of a huge lorry manoeuvring in the area where Kevin's wood sculpture had once stood. I looked out of the window and saw pictures that matched the sounds, prompting me to run downstairs and out onto the balcony.

'Ron!' I called in the general direction of the woodshed, almost in panic. 'The concrete has arrived!'

There was a beat, no doubt whilst Ron came to terms with who he was, where he was and what he was doing. These things established, he was ready to respond.

'Shit!' he said. 'I'd better get my trousers on.'

All three of us had to get our trousers on. We'd forgotten about this delivery and it marked a crucial stage in the swimming pool's construction. The concrete base was going to be laid on top of the ballast and the steel mesh that we'd put down in the last few days.

'Get your wellies on!' shouted Ron. 'And get ready for the hardest morning's work that you've done in a long time.'

I winced. I'd been helping Ron and Brad with the labour but I can't pretend I'd been working anywhere near as hard as them. There'd been days when I'd wanted to, but they hadn't let me. The problem was that whenever I volunteered to do something, they explained that I would only get in the way. Given just how much work there was to do in the construction of this pool, it was difficult to take this remark in a positive light.

I wondered how often this had been said to first-rate workers on building sites. I remembered the stunning scene in the film *Witness* when the Amish community toiled tirelessly together to build a huge barn in just a couple of days. I couldn't recall seeing one desolate figure sitting around on a nearby bench, occasionally offering assistance only to be stopped by a raised hand:

'It's all right – you'll only get in the way.'

The problem was that Brad and Ron had become a team. They just didn't need someone like me hanging round them with endless questions, and with the potential to hit the wrong nail into the wrong hole at the wrong time, topping it all by using the wrong tool. Unlike me, Brad was a practical man and a quick learner, so it was never long before he was carrying out a task as speedily and as efficiently as his foreman. Brad brought out the best in Ron, too, mainly because he enjoyed the work so much and demonstrated an almost child-like zeal in each task he took on. Around Brad, Ron's urge to 'go and have a bit of a lie-down' diminished by about 40 per cent. There were even moments when one could see a hint of enthusiasm, although it rarely developed much beyond a twinkle in the eye.

Much as I longed to get my hands dirty and become one of the workers, I remained a reluctant executive who was called upon to place orders with the builders' merchants, liaise with the pool manufacturers and, most important of all, translate from the pool's instruction manual. When it came to physical work, I was only really called upon to assist with mindless tasks.

Mindless tasks like spreading glutinous concrete around the bottom of a large hole in the ground.

'What do I do?' I asked Ron.

I was trying to look nonchalant as I wheeled my wheelbarrow down to the pool. My adrenalin was pumping. At the bottom of my drive, at the edge of 'Serge's hole', there was one of those big concrete lorries that have those swirly things on the back. I could remember seeing these strange contraptions as a kid, but I never imagined that I would ever be at such close quarters with one, let alone be on the receiving end of what lay within.

'Your job is to be in the bottom of the pool with the wheel-barrow,' said Ron. 'All you do is stick it underneath the chute that comes out of the back of the lorry and the driver will open the sluice and let the concrete spill down and fill up your barrow. Then you walk it up the other end and dump it on the ground.'

It sounded straightforward enough and I felt momentarily confident. It didn't last long. When I arrived at the required spot with my empty wheelbarrow, I looked up to the driver who was poised and waiting to release the first dollop of his enormous load. He was a strong man in bright green dungarees and with a huge moustache, one end of which he was twiddling between his fingers. Our eyes met for the first time. Immediately I was aware that he knew. He knew that I wasn't a labourer. He knew that my clean clothes, my rigidity, my hesitancy and my general aura of anxiety meant that I was a concrete virgin. And if you're worth your salt as a concrete deliverer, what do you do with concrete virgins? You fill their wheelbarrows to the very brim, that's what you do.

I could have managed perfectly well with a three-quarters-full barrow, but as the last dollop plopped out of the chute and into my replete vessel, I could feel the muscles in my arms tense. Shifting this barrow was going to be tough. I bent from the knees and hoisted the wheelbarrow upwards, breathing out as I did so, much like a weightlifter completing the first stage of a lift. The moustachioed driver looked on with a keen interest, along with Brad and Ron. They were all clearly disappointed that this first part of my wheelbarrow manoeuvre had been a success. They weren't to be disappointed for long. The moment I attempted to turn the barrow in order to move off, it began to tip. I fought hard to keep it upright, and soon every muscle in my arms and legs was straining to its limit. To no avail. The weight of the concrete proved too much, and over the barrow went, spilling concrete over my legs and wellies.

'Dammit!' I exclaimed. 'Sorry, everyone!'

I looked up to see Ron and Brad laughing heartily and the concrete delivery man smirking. He had reason to smirk. He had done well, after all.

'There's a knack to it,' said Ron, as he wheeled his wheelbarrow into receiving position.

Seconds later he was wheeling his barrow off in the direction of the other end of the pool where he would tip it and leave it to be levelled off by the attendant Brad. The 'knack', it seemed, involved being stronger than me, knowing how much to tip the barrow when starting to move off and, most importantly of all – not having a full barrow to deal with. There was no question that smirking delivery man had not filled Ron's barrow as full as mine. He had done this deliberately, I was sure of it. He recognised Ron as being one of his gang, and not a namby-pamby white-collar type as he clearly perceived me to be. He was making it easier for Ron, just so that he could have a good old smirk at my expense.

Fortunately he didn't continue with his mischievous ways and the next few loads that he gave me were smaller and more manageable. However, the moment that I started to look confident and at ease with my work, he would splodge out an extra large portion of concrete onto my barrow, humbling me once more as I struggled and wobbled with indignity.

'*Bâtard!*' I said under my breath in my best French.

'What does that mean?' asked a smiling Brad, who had overheard it.

'It's French for someone who's born just outside a Cornish village.'

'Which one?'

'Wedlock.'

'Oh, I see.'

15

All Change

The next day I elected to hire a van, having decided that the 300 euros I'd been quoted to have the pool's polystyrene blocks delivered seemed a little excessive. The cost was closer to 50 euros if I collected the blocks myself by hiring a van from a place that offered a bargain 'half-day rental'.

'Is it wise to hire a van?' asked Brad.

'What do you mean?'

'Well, have you thought about the curse?' said Ron.

'What curse?'

'Well,' said Brad, 'Ron and I were discussing your journey down here the other night, and we decided that you're definitely a victim of the "Curse of the White Van".'

'Nonsense.'

'You are,' insisted Ron. 'And you'd be a fool to hire a van.'

The two men, I could tell from their smirks, were enjoying winding me up.

'Look, it'll be fine,' I said.

'I don't know how you can go near another white van,' said Ron.

'Superstitious nonsense,' I said. 'Anyway, it'll be all right. I'll ask for a blue one, or something.'

The lady at the hire shop thought I was a little odd, colour not being something normal people sought to specify when renting a commercial vehicle. However, she assured me over the phone that they had several green vans and one would be available. Pleasingly, there seemed to be no extra cost.

However, when I arrived at the van-hire reception, a different lady told me that they only had white vans and that the green ones were already being used. I protested that another lady had told me over the phone that green ones were available, whilst a young couple eyed me with suspicion. The lady behind the desk asked me why the colour mattered and I struggled to find a reply. It wasn't that I couldn't find the French words, I was just hopelessly short on logic. But why had one lady told me there'd be green vans a-plenty when half an hour later it was clear that this was not the case?

I guess it had been my fault for being a slow learner. I was only now beginning to grasp that in this part of the world when people said things, they were often motivated by a desire to please rather than any great urge to deliver a reliable statement backed by solid facts. My Anglo-Saxon Protestant yearnings for efficiency, facts and frankness were always going to be thwarted.

I went ahead with the hire, though. There was no such thing as the curse and I damn well knew it. The only reason Ron and Brad had come up with the concept in the first place was that our lives at the house had become so gratifyingly uncluttered by other stuff. Clearly, the 'Curse of the White Van' had been the product of a conversation that had taken place while the two men had stared out at the crossroads across the valley one evening.

When I got to the swimming-pool showroom, Fabrice was on great form.

'*Ah, c'est Monsieur Tonny!*' he exclaimed, in mock awe. 'How are you? How are things going with Sophie?'

'Shut up, Fabrice.'

But he didn't shut up. He was in cheeky mood, and made continuous jokes (about half of which I understood) as he helped me pack the polystyrene blocks into the back of my new van. It still felt a little absurd to build a swimming pool out of polystyrene, but my reasons were sound enough. Fabrice had been the jolliest, brightest and friendliest salesman I'd spoken to, and, for me, this put his product ahead of the others. Anyway, Fabrice was my friend now, so even if the pool did end up being a disaster, at least the bloke who had sold it to me would be able to come round and lament along with me.

An hour later I was back at the house. Ron and Brad were busy bending steel rods in preparation for the polystyrene blocks that would slot over them. The two men were wet through, the summer heat making manual labour more of a strain than usual. They mocked me for doing the cushy driving job, and teased me about how I always managed to dodge the heavy work. I was struck by how well Ron and Brad were getting along. After all, they made an unlikely pairing – Ron, fifty-six, a lifetime in the building trade, and Brad, forty-one, an actor/musician who in recent years had set up his own project-management company. There was no reason on earth why they should get on particularly, but get on they did, their playful banter invariably rendering me the butt of the joke.

'You'll never get that van back by twelve-thirty, you tart,' said Ron, disparagingly.

'I will if I leave right now,' I replied.

I was keen to get the van back before lunch because, if I did so, I could get away with the cost of only a morning's hire.

'You reckon?'

'Yes, I reckon.'

It would involve me driving a tad faster than was my wont, but there was still plenty of time to make the 12.30 deadline.

Unfortunately I hadn't counted on the midday traffic. By having a two-hour lunch break, during which most employees liked to get back home, the locals had created the absurdity of four rush hours a day. The midday version I was currently experiencing wasn't that bad, but nonetheless it could still create enough delay to force me into shelling out for the full day's hire.

I dealt with the situation by beginning to drive like a local. Braking distance was a luxury I could no longer afford. In spite of every delay becoming a frustration, and every second lost a blow, it was still looking like I'd make the 12.30 deadline. This continued to be the case until I decided to accelerate through an amber traffic light just as it was changing to red.

As I waited at the next set of lights, a man in a helmet appeared at my window and instructed me to pull over just the other side of the lights. This, I quickly deduced, was a motorcyclist, but not one of the ordinary kind – this was a policeman. My heart sank. The deadline would certainly now be missed, and what's more I was in trouble.

There were two police motorcyclists waiting for me as I got out of the van and made my way towards them on the grass verge. They were immaculately turned out, wearing LA shades, shiny leather boots, neatly pressed shirts and pristine white trousers. In fact, just like the policemen in Lourdes, their trousers were so snug that they resembled tights more than trousers. I got the distinct impression that the policemen in question were extremely proud of how they looked in their uniforms. It was bizarre, but for a moment it felt like I was walking towards 'performers' from a porn movie, rather than two officers of the law. Rather frightened by this thought, I stopped in my tracks. Seeing me stationary, Policeman One swaggered towards me, blurting rapid-fire French at me with each imposing stride. I'm not exactly certain what he said but it was something along the lines of:

'You have been stopped by two of the sexiest men in the city. As men in cute uniforms it falls upon us to inform you that you have just jumped a red light.'

I tried feebly to get myself out of the situation. Adopting a ridiculously placatory tone I explained that it might have been more dangerous if I'd slammed on the brakes in order to stop in time. Another burst of high-speed French followed, which was quite probably:

'Teen idols and Greek God-like figures like myself and my colleague have been specially trained to recognise when a vehicle is travelling too fast in a town centre. It was precisely because you were doing just such a thing that we had to dismount from our fabulously cool motorbikes and display our perfectly toned legs to the general public in the course of booking you and administering a fine.'

Policeman Two then produced a mountain of paperwork which he piled up on the leather seat of his glistening motorbike. I was summoned over to him and a prolonged and tedious interrogation began, during which I had to produce every piece of documentation relating to me, short of bank statements and recent shopping bills. The whole process took fifteen minutes and, despite presenting myself as a picture of contrition, I didn't manage to escape the fine: 90 euros. And all because I was rushing in a pathetic and unsuccessful attempt to save myself 30 euros.

It had all been my fault, of course, but by the time I'd got back to the house, I was able to reallocate the blame.

'That "Curse of the White Van",' I said dolefully, 'it's a . . . it's a . . .'

It was no good, I just couldn't find the word.

'A curse?' suggested Ron.

'Yes, that's it. It's a curse.'

And Brad nodded sympathetically.

By Saturday night, Brad and I were ready to party. We'd had a tough week working on the pool and we were very much looking forward to the village fête up at *la mairie*.

The village fête wasn't really a fête at all. Not in the British sense of the word, anyway. There would be no bunting, apple-dunking facilities or bearded men pulling pints of real ale whilst recounting tales of the unremarkable. Maybe hundreds of years ago our village had experimented with similar concepts until someone had had the wisdom to say, 'Why don't we cut all this crap and just have a bloody good slap-up meal?' Because that's all our fête turned out to be – a similar affair to the village lunch and dinner I had attended, only bigger. This one was open to guests from outside the village, and it was to take place on the large terrace at the rear of *la mairie*, where we would all have the pleasure of dining under the stars.

Thinking it uncool to arrive at 8pm on the dot, Brad and I wandered in at 8.25pm, only to find that we were the first there. Well, almost. The solitary figure of André was standing expectantly alongside the makeshift bar, glass of Ricard in hand.

'*Bonsoir*,' he said, cheerfully.

'*Bonsoir*,' I replied.

'*Bonsoir*,' said Brad, offering up one quarter of his entire French vocabulary.

André took Brad's fluent delivery to mean that he spoke French as well as I did, and he proceeded to hold forth on the visit of the Pope to Lourdes, which was taking place in the morning. Didn't *le pape* look old and frail? Wasn't he brave to keep making these pilgrimages? Brad nodded furiously, which seemed to satisfy André, although I felt he must have had more than an inkling that Brad hadn't understood a word of what he'd said. I resisted the temptation to assert my belief that the Pope would die either in the morning or mid-afternoon, just in case André wasn't a fully paid-up sophrologist.

The rest of the guests seemed to show up all at once, just before 9pm. It seemed that the '8pm' on the invitation was the equivalent of 'doors open' for a rock gig. Only extreme nerds or the chief fire officer actually turned up at that time. (Oh yes – and me, Brad and André.)

All the familiar village faces were there, including my technical advisers.

'So, how are you getting on with that pool?' asked Paul, waving a large Ricard in front of him.

'Well, it's coming on. Slowly. I've gone for polystyrene blocks.'

'Polystyrene?' said Berry, looking shocked. 'Blimey.'

'I don't know much about that,' said Paul. 'You must tell me all about that method.'

I was spared the embarrassment of passing on my limited knowledge on the subject as Paul and Berry were tapped on the shoulders and immediately whisked away into the whirligig of village social life. I took a moment to look round the hall, and I noticed that there were a lot of teenagers. I guess it was Saturday night and this was the only village fête for miles around, so this function provided a welcome alternative to sitting around in a bar in the local town. There was something rather heartening about seeing representatives from such a broad spectrum of ages all out together in common cause. Regrettably, my life in Britain only afforded me such glimpses when I was a guest at weddings or queuing at the post office.

As ever there was no seating plan, so when Mayor Rene gave the nod, everyone quickly found a spot on one of the three long lines of tables. I ended up happily wedged between André and Odette, who entertained me with stories of the village half a century before when *la mairie* had been a school they had both attended. They were now well into their seventies, but for a moment I was able to picture them as young kids, running around a post-war village that had only recently been liberated from the shackles of German occupation. André launched into a tale about these times, but he was interrupted by loud singing from the young contingent on the next table. They sang their little hearts out. I asked Odette whether it was a tradition and she explained that it was because they were drinking too much alcohol, too quickly. She didn't seem to wholly approve. She needed, I thought, to walk round the centre of a British town at 11.30pm on a Friday or Saturday night to realise just how angelic these teenagers were.

The copious amounts of food that we would be required to eat began with various starters, before Alain and Roger appeared to a huge cheer with three absolutely enormous basins of paella. Apparently, Alain had volunteered to prepare the main meal for all 150 diners. (And to think that I panic at the thought of cooking a meal for any more than four.) Alain's efforts, albeit completed with a team of helpers, were nothing less than heroic, and he was formally thanked by Rene after we'd completed what seemed like the seventh course of our gargantuan meal.

'So, Tony, when will we see you here in the village with a nice girl?'

I looked up to see the smiling face of Roger. The cheeky nature of both his grin and his question suggested that I had been forgiven for buying the Peugeot 106.

'I don't know, Roger,' I replied. 'Soon, I hope. I'm working hard at finding a nice French girl.'

'*Non!*' said Roger firmly. 'You must bring *une petite Anglaise.*'

'But I thought a French girl would be nice.'

'It would be nice, certainly. But you must bring *une petite Anglaise.*'

Roger was adamant, and I couldn't understand why. I'd always thought that the French were keen on promoting their home-grown produce.

'I will do my best,' I promised. 'And when I find her, I promise to present her for your approval.'

Roger laughed. 'I like this idea,' he said. 'You need *une petite Anglaise* to go with the rest of your family.'

'The rest of my family?'

'Yes. The family at your house.'

'You mean Ron and Brad? They're not family.'

'I think that they are. They are the family you have chosen,' said Roger, providing me with a slap on the back, the weight of which would have made Alain proud.

What an interesting concept. I'd always heard people say that you choose your friends but you can't choose your family. Perhaps the trick is to produce friends that become family. Short of marrying Brad, Ron, Nic and Kev, perhaps I'd got as close as I could to doing just that. The house had seen to it.

Just like the young people, I drank too much that night. I hadn't intended to, nor did I want to, it was just that the wine kept flowing. The volunteer waiters and waitresses simply plonked another bottle in front of us just as soon as we'd polished off the previous one. Being British, my formative years had seen me nurtured in a drinking culture where you kept going until someone told you to stop. At the absurdly early time of 11 o'clock on a Friday or Saturday night, an unsightly man would usually appear and bellow at you:

'Come on! Finish off your drinks now PLEASE! We've all got homes to go to!'

It had taken me a long time to get used to places where you were welcome as long as you wanted to stay there, and despite lots of practice I still wasn't one of the leading exponents of self-regulation. Some days it might be fair to call me a 'mountaineer drinker'. I drink it because it's there.

'Brad, Roger thinks that I should find an English girl,' I offered up at probably too much volume as we walked home beneath the stars.

'Interesting,' he replied. 'Maybe he's right. Shame, though. French girls are very sexy.'

'Yes, and there are more of them where we are now – in France.'

'Good point. You've got to play the numbers game, I suppose.'

'How about you?' I asked. 'What are you looking for in a woman?'

'I don't know, Tony,' he replied reflectively. 'I guess I'm just not ready.'

'I am,' I said. 'I just don't think we're going to bump into any women between here and my house.'

'No, I don't think so either.'

And do you know? We were both right.

'Where are you going?' asked Ron.

He was tucking into a cooked breakfast on the terrace as the sun rose over the distant rolling hills, nudging its way ever closer to the mountains.

'Church,' I replied impassively.

'Church? Since when did you get religion?'

'I didn't. It's just that they've rigged up a screen in the village church and they're broadcasting the Pope live from Lourdes.'

'What do you want to see the Pope for?'

'I've got my reasons.'

Brad decided to come with me, mainly, he said, because he fancied the walk. It was a measure of how well I'd settled in to this village that I knew exactly who lived in every house we passed along the way. We began by ambling past Bruno, my immediate neighbour, then Irish Mary, before we pressed onwards up the hill past the lovely home of Edouard and Sylvaine, a couple who'd moved down from Paris. Next it was Roger − advocate of *la petite Anglaise*, Serge the hole-digger, and then, at the top of the hill, their mother Marie. We made a left and started to drop down into the valley, a route that took us past Michel, Malcolm and Anne, Odette, and Alain, before we finally arrived at the little church. The very little church.

'Right, let's go in,' I said.

'Are you sure, Tony? It'll probably go on a bit.'

'I'm sure. I want to see the Pope.'

'Since when were you so keen on the Pope?'

'Since the wager with Fabrice. I have a one-euro bet with him that the Pope will die today. In Lourdes.'

'You're joking!'

'I'm not. That's why I'm here.'

Brad began to laugh. 'You are unbelievable sometimes. But he's very old, so I suppose it could happen.'

Of course it could happen, I reasoned. If there is a God – and the Pope certainly seemed to be of that opinion from what I'd gleaned from a lot of his statements – then I'd noted that every now and again He seemed to demonstrate something of a penchant for cruel irony. One example of this was the Lisbon earthquake of 1775 that killed 90,000 people, one third of the city's population. God managed to arrange for this to happen on All Saints' Day, exactly when the churches were full of people who were busy worshipping Him. I reckoned that He was due another such act of grievous mischief, and allowing the Pontiff to snuff it in the very place where pilgrims flocked for miracle cures fitted the bill perfectly.

'Let's go in and see what happens,' I said, leading Brad up to the wooden church door.

Every village in this area, regardless of how small it was, had *une petite église* to service the devout. If the attendance at our church was anything to go by, then the 'devout' were mainly the elderly. The turnout to see *le pape* on the large screen was not huge, and hardly warranted the efforts the village committee had made to set it up.

Brad and I sat down on the same pew as Odette and two back from André, who acknowledged us with a nod. We began to watch proceedings 'live' from Lourdes on the screen that had been erected in front of the altar. The French commentator waxed lyrical, seemingly undeterred by the fact that there was nothing to see yet other than a vast crowd waiting in anticipation. We were waiting in anticipation too. Were we going to see history being made? Or were we going to sit through a doddery old man making an uninspiring speech, delivered in French with a heavy Polish accent?

There was a ripple of excitement amongst the dozen or so of the congregation when the Pope finally appeared on our screen.

'God, he looks ill,' said Brad.

'Yes. But is he ill enough?' I replied.

'I don't think so.'

Brad was good. He could spot a man who wasn't about to die when he saw one. Despite his frailty and his need to be operated by aides who at times resembled puppeteers, John Paul soldiered on courageously and completed his discourse without collapsing.

'He put in a good effort, I felt,' said Brad, as we filed out of the church.

'I think he could have done better,' I replied. 'That whole failing-to-keel-over thing was a disappointment.'

'Where are we going now?' asked Brad.

'*La mairie.*'

'Why?'

'Free aperitifs followed by the annual village photo.'

This was another tradition of which these people had every reason to be proud. Each year, primarily by using the bribe of free aperitifs to ensure a big attendance, a photograph was taken of the village populace on the steps of *la mairie*. As we were cajoled into position by the photographer (who turned out to be Christine, the deputy mayor's daughter), I wondered how many villages in England could manage to pull such a stunt.

I was wedged between Roger and André, smiling rather too enthusiastically as Christine clicked away with relish. It seemed to me to be a great shame that she herself wouldn't be in the picture and I called out something to this effect. She dismissed me with a giggle and a wave. Presumably she was one of the many women who don't like being in photos. Before long, though, the rest of us would be in a framed photo behind the bar in the village hall – a splendid record of a tiny moment in history.

'So, you owe Fabrice one euro,' said Brad.

We were getting out of breath as we climbed the steep hill that took us back to our side of the village.

'Yes, well, I guess I can live with that. I didn't really need to win a euro that much.'

I felt relieved that my rather morbid hopes had not been

fulfilled. The Pope may not have been my hero but certainly a lot of other people seemed quite keen on him. A vast crowd had turned up to see him, and they'd given him a tremendous ovation even though he'd done no singing or dancing, and probably hadn't even turned up for the sound check.

'And if he had pegged it,' said Brad, 'just think of all those puppeteers who would have been made unemployed.'

'You're right. And it wouldn't have been fair on the Pope either. You wouldn't want to die with that many people watching.'

'No. How many people watching you die would be about right, then?'

'Ooh, five or six would be about right, I reckon.'

Our absurd conversation about death continued all the way home. Quite why we lingered on the subject for so long, I do not know. Perhaps it was because at some subconscious level we sensed that we needed to cover this subject in order to prepare ourselves for a bereavement that was about to take place further away than Lourdes. Further away from Lourdes, and yet much closer to home.

I didn't get up until 11 o'clock the following morning. The excesses of the 'Concrete Day' and the village fête had obviously caught up with me. I pulled on my shorts and wandered downstairs, ready to apologise to Ron and Brad for whom I'd promised to provide some extremely unskilled labour.

The two men were seated at the dining table. I knew instantly that something was wrong. The mood was sombre. No one said a word. No jibes about my tardy arrival, no banter about the day ahead. Instead, silence.

I looked at Ron. As ever, his face revealed little. He did grimace a little and nod in the direction of Brad. I looked over to see my friend pale, drained and with bloodshot eyes.

'What's wrong?' I asked.

Brad tried to say something, but he just couldn't seem to make a sound. It was as if his wringing hands were willing him to speak and yet the words were caught in his throat. I looked to Ron for elucidation, but he just waited, allowing Brad the time he needed to squeeze the words out.

'My mum died last night,' said Brad, eventually.

I'm not sure if my jaw physically dropped, but it certainly felt like it did. It was my turn now to be lost for words. What do you say in a situation like this? How do you comfort someone at a time when they are patently uncomfortable? Every sentence that formed in my head seemed wrong. What had Ron said, I wondered? How had he handled this when he'd been told the news?

'That's terrible,' I said, rather pathetically. 'What happened? She hadn't been ill or anything, had she?'

'No. She died peacefully in her sleep.'

There was another long silence which Ron and I seemed to know instinctively not to fill.

'It's just such a shock,' continued Brad. 'Seventy-six seems so young. Her mother lived to ninety-two and her grandmother to ninety-three. I never saw it coming this early.'

I looked at my friend. He had an emptiness about him. But then what did I expect? If this news felt like a body blow to me, then how did it feel to Brad? I got to my feet, trying to muster some positive energy.

'I'll organise some flights home,' I said.

With those words I left the room. Perhaps I should have stayed longer, but I felt that Brad needed to be silent, and yet not completely alone. Somehow I knew that Ron was going to be a better man for the job than I was. And for once, he looked up for it.

One of the frustrations of life is that however much time we spend planning our futures, we are always potentially just a moment away from a piece of news that can shatter everything. We have but a brittle hold on our own lives, let alone those of others.

'Jeez, I might be dead tomorrow.'

It had been a phrase I'd often heard uttered during my travels in Ireland some years before. It was true that very often the provider of these words was about to order a twelfth successive alcoholic beverage, and that the consumption of this next drink might indeed make 'being dead tomorrow' a distinct probability. However, there was a profound wisdom behind it. Is it not the case that we live our lives largely in denial of our own mortality? We may indeed 'be dead tomorrow' or perhaps halfway through next week, but we don't like to consider the prospect. We just don't know when we are going to pass away. Even the greatest minds on the planet are ignorant of when their moment of extinction might come. It's a mystery. However, when the moment of truth does arrive and we are able to look back over our lives, there's one thing we can be sure that we won't be saying:

'You know, my biggest regret is that I didn't worry a bit more. I had so many opportunities to be more uptight about things and I just didn't take them. Oh, how I wish I had.'

This was the general theme of the conversation as Brad and I waited in the airport terminal. After hearing the sad news I'd booked us both on the first available flight back to London. Ron was going to stay on and try to complete the work that we'd started, although I suspected that without company, and without Brad particularly, his work rate would decline considerably.

'How do you feel?' I asked Brad, as he sipped his coffee.

'It changes every few minutes,' he replied. 'Sometimes I feel strong and then suddenly I feel so alone. Irish Mary summed it up when she popped over to say goodbye. "The world changes when your mum dies," she said. And she was right.'

We boarded the plane with a solemnity that belied the nature of the summer that had just passed. But the summer was over. With each passing day it had begun to feel like autumn was looming, and this bereavement somehow made the onset of winter seem more imminent.

'Ron was amazing,' said Brad, looking down on tiny buildings and miniature vehicles, evidence of people below going about their daily business.

'What do you mean?'

'I told Ron what had happened a good couple of hours before you got up. We sat there, drinking tea and smoking his fags. He seemed to know when to ask questions and when to be quiet. At one point he sat in silence opposite me for twenty minutes, while my mind came to terms with the fact that I'd just joined the "loss of a parent club".'

I still longed to know how Ron had handled things when he'd first come upon the traumatised Brad. Had he coped much better than me?

'What did Ron do when you told him?' I asked.

'It was weird. When I struggled to get the words out, he laughed at first. Then, when he saw that something was wrong, he sat down and waited till I was ready. And when I finally spat it out – "My mum died last night" – he found five words that somehow seemed to do the trick.'

'And they were?'

'"Best put the kettle on."'

Ron himself flew back a week later. By his own admission he'd done virtually nothing during that time.

'You only need to sort me out for a couple of half-days,' he said when we met up and I settled up what I owed him.

My project in France seemed to have ground to a halt. For a while the house felt further south than ever. The family that had once happily occupied it had broken up, and the piano rested untouched beneath a thin layer of concrete dust.

16

Home Alone

It was late October before I set foot back in the house. I'd had to spend some time in England securing some income, since my life in France only offered an expensive outlet for it. I made damn sure I visited my mother, too.

'Does the house feel like it's yours yet?' she'd asked, as we'd chatted over tea and biscuits.

'Yes. It's really beginning to feel like I belong.'

'Well, don't belong too much. Or I won't get to see you any more.'

There was a light rain gently cascading down as I pulled the car into the drive and got out to admire the view.

'Mmm, that's good,' I said to myself.

I drew in a deep breath. London was only a matter of hours behind me and yet it seemed a pleasingly long way away. I approached the front door, aware that something felt different about the place. It wasn't just the cooler air, the silence that replaced the constant sound of jabbering crickets, or the autumnal reds and yellows of the leaves on the trees. Something else appeared not as I'd left it back in August, and I stood looking about me trying to fathom what it was. Then I saw it. The big green dumper bin. The big green dumper bin with my name on it. It was printed in big capital letters across its breadth.

TONY HAWKS

Now I felt like I belonged more than I ever had before. What better confirmation could one wish for? I had a green dumper bin inscribed with my name. Surely a sign that I had arrived in this society. I may not have been on the village committee, but clearly now it was only a question of time. My 'bin status' meant that I was finally more than just the Englishman who had bought the house in between Pierre and Bruno. I really belonged now, and I had a bespoke green dumper bin to prove it.

When I opened the front door, still glowing from the welcome of the bin, I could smell that musty aroma again – the one that descends like a cloud over a property that's been vacated for more than seven days. This time I was walking into the house alone. The purpose of my trip was twofold. In my bag was a screenplay that I thought I'd finished earlier in the year but which now required a further rewrite, according to the producers. The house seemed like just the spot to do it. This could be more than a place to practise the piano, it could be an ideal location to work.

I wandered onto the balcony and surveyed the rolling hills beyond. They were about to be enveloped by swooping dark clouds. It wasn't a nice day, and yet the view was fascinating. That was one of the things I liked about this place. You could really see the weather, not just feel it.

I knew that the coming days were to be a real test for what this house meant to me. How would I cope living here alone? Up until now I'd always had the company of friends. Now there was just me and the distant echo of the cowbells. Would it be too quiet? Would I go stir crazy?

The answer was not long in coming. Barely after I'd unpacked my bags I got my first caller. It was Michel saying that he'd seen my car outside and wanting to know if I would come and have dinner with him and his wife Christine in a couple of nights' time. Half an hour after that Malcolm and Anne dropped in, followed shortly afterwards by Irish Mary. Rene the Mayor waved jovially from his car, and Pierre and I chatted over the fence. It all felt pretty uplifting. It was just a shame I didn't have anybody to share it with. This time, not even Ron.

I still had a long night ahead of me. I had no television for company, just the endless babble of French radio. No problem – there was the piano. Here was a perfect opportunity to practise. I sat down. I put my hands over the keys. But nope. I just wasn't in the mood to play.

Never mind. I could do some work. I got out my laptop and laid it on the table in front of me. I looked at my screenplay. Nope. I was in the wrong frame of mind for that, too. It was no good. There was nothing for it but to go out. I paced the balcony considering my options. Since a trip to the theatre, cinema multiplex or jazz club wasn't really on, I opted for what has been the solace of the solitary male for centuries. A beer in a bar. And I knew exactly what bar it was going to be.

I'd driven past the Bar des Sports on numerous occasions, and each time I had been impressed by the number of authentic-looking Frenchmen contained therein. At least 50 per cent wore berets, and the rest looked like extras from a film by Marcel Pagnol. This seemed to me to be where Bagnère's bachelors hung out to discuss the day's events and, perhaps towards the end of the evening, allow themselves the odd maudlin reflection on how love had passed them by. I hoped that I wouldn't fit in too readily.

I parked the car and approached the entrance to the busy bar with some apprehension. Tonight was going to be the first time I would enter it instead of just peering inside inquisitively. As I pushed open the bar's glass door it felt like everyone present was dying to see who it was that was coming in. There seemed to be a strange enquiring twinkle in their eyes. They were looking at me in the same way that dogs look at people, with an odd mixture of hope and bewilderment. Heads weren't turning as such, but I was conscious that at every table, eyes were straining in their sockets, anxious to see the stranger but without making any noticeable head movement. The noise level quickly dipped from raucous to hushed.

I tried not to be self-conscious as I moved slowly to the bar, feeling a little like the bad guy in a scene from a Western. The square room was dotted with about eight tables and dominated by a large staircase at the back with a sign hanging over it pointing down to *les toilettes*. Further along the bar were men in grubby work clothes drinking brightly coloured spirits. Their drinks looked lethal. The barman, who was strong, greasy-haired and deeply tanned, cocked his head in preparation for my order.

'*Une bière, s'il vous plait*,' I said.

The barman nodded and the murmurs increased in volume. It was almost as if each group at every table was discussing my choice of drink:

'Did you hear that?'

'He's gone for a beer.'

'I'd expected as much.'

'What's wrong with our wine?'

The barman passed me my beer with a nod and I turned to see where I could sit. As I did so, I was confronted by a sea of staring faces, all quickly darting their eyes away in the vain hope of keeping up the pretence that I was of no interest. I sat at the only empty table in the place, took out my screenplay and began reading. Or rather, pretending to read. I was too fascinated by everything that was going on all around me to focus properly. And then it occurred to me how odd the music was. I don't know why I hadn't noticed it before because it was loud enough, but I guess my senses were preoccupied with absorbing the new environment. Weirdly, it was marching brass band music, and it seemed distinctly Germanic. It was music that wouldn't have been out of place in a bar full of men in lederhosen. I strained my ears for the sound of an accordion somewhere in the musical mix, but there was nothing. This was all very un-French. I started to wonder if I'd walked in on the Bigourdian division of the 'Third Reich Appreciation Society'.

Suddenly a hush similar to the one that had greeted me upon my arrival descended over the room as a large bearded man emerged from the toilets downstairs and walked slowly to the bar. As he did so, the barman turned around, picked up a cassette and proceeded to change the music. French accordion now replaced the Germanic marching band and everything reverted to what you might expect in a French bar.

What had just happened? I ruminated on the various possibilities as I slowly made headway through my beer. Was this man so important that he demanded theme music whenever he moved anywhere? No, that couldn't be. I decided that it must have been that he suffered from a form of constipation meaning he could only go if his toilet visits were accompanied by the sounds of a loud Tyrolean marching band. The proprietor of this joint certainly took care of his regulars. (Or not so regulars, in this case.)

Just as I was deciding whether to stay for a second beer, or call it a night before I was inducted into some strange cult, I was approached by one of the men who had been standing at the bar and indulging in the spirit-drinking session.

'You? You are English?' he demanded.

'Yes, I am.'

'*Ah bon*. Do you want to buy a house? I have a house to sell in Montauban. You buy it?'

'I have a house here already, thank you.'

The man shrugged and moved off, and rejoined his pals wearing a kind of 'well, I tried, didn't I?' expression. I wondered how long it would take him to sell his property if this was his sole method of marketing it. Waiting till someone English came into the bar and then confronting them brusquely might save on agent's commission, certainly, but it might require more than a healthy dollop of good luck too.

Deciding that this might not necessarily be the place to make new and lasting friendships, I took a final swig of my beer and started to move towards the door. I was stopped by a firm hand on my shoulder, and I turned round to see an unambiguously drunk man before me, finger raised in anticipation of delivering something of great import.

'*Moi, j'suis couvreur,*' he said. '*Vous avez b'soin d'un couvreur chez vous?*'

This translates as:'Me, I'm a roofer. Do you need a roofer at your gaff?'

I tried to think of a way of letting him down gently.

'*Non, merci,*' I said, just before I closed the door to the bar behind me.

OK, so I failed on the 'letting him down gently' front.

As I drove home I began to worry whether I could ever fully assimilate myself into this society. OK, perhaps the Bar des Sports hadn't been the best choice that I could have made for the evening, but the truth was that there weren't that many options. Most of the other places I'd regularly driven past had always been empty by 9pm. And what if I did manage to make the acquaintance of a few of the locals? What would we talk about? I wasn't great on chatting about crop rotation, pigeon shooting, or the best way to slaughter a pig.

Perhaps that was why Roger had been so insistent that I should find myself *une petite Anglaise.* Maybe I'd have to call him 'wise old Roger' from now on.

In the morning the house performed well in its new role as 'workplace'. By setting up my laptop close to the window, lifting my head offered me a glimpse of the mountains, and so whenever the creative muse drifted beyond reach, I was able to look out of the window and receive an inspirational tonic from the beauty that lay on the horizon.

The cooler weather and the absence of Ron meant that *une sieste* was no longer a temptation after lunch. Instead I decided I would take some exercise. In fact, in preparation for the arrival of my own swimming pool (surely to be completed some time in the next decade), I chose the option of a dip in the local baths. By and large I have noticed that French towns are well served with sporting facilities, and Bagnères-de-Bigorre is no exception. Every time I drove into town I passed the big municipal swimming pool on my left-hand side, and today was the day when I would profit from the healthy exercise that it offered within.

I am used to swimming pools being places where notices abound telling you what not to do, usually in a needlessly authoritarian manner. I can remember having been to pools in Britain and been confronted with an array of officious signs:

NO DIVING
NO RUNNING
NO BOMBING
NO DUCKING
NO PETTING

The only one missing is the one that says:

NO ENJOYING YOURSELVES.

Having changed into my swimming shorts and passed under the compulsory shower (always an irritation that, as it denies you the treat of your plunge into the pool being your first taste of the refreshing water), I made my way over to the deep end and started to contemplate whether I should dive in or not. I couldn't see any NO DIVING signs, and even if there was one around somewhere I could claim that I hadn't understood it if I was soundly admonished by the humourless and bored lifeguard. (Lifeguards are like this the world over. It's mandatory.)

Just as I was about to arch my body into a beautiful dive, a piercing whistle penetrated the atmosphere and I looked up to see two lifeguard types rushing towards me as if I was some kind of terrorist.

'*Non! Non! Non, non, non, non!*' one of them shouted.

A confused conversation followed in which I tried to figure out what on earth I could be doing to cause such excitement. There was a lot of animated pointing going on, firstly at my swimming shorts and then at their own swimwear. They were wearing those ridiculously skimpy tight trunks traditionally worn by men on beaches who believe they are irresistible to women, and who try to chat up every female they see. The pointing continued but I still couldn't understand what message these two men were trying to communicate. Did they want me to swap costumes with them? Were these men representatives of an offshoot of the Bigourdian Third Reich Appreciation Society explaining another of their rituals? Or had everyone gone slightly mad in this part of the world since I'd last been over?

'*Il est interdit!*' said the taller of the two men, pointing to my surf shorts.

Interdit meant 'forbidden'. Surely they couldn't be telling me that my choice of swimwear was illegal. We weren't in some kind of rogue police state overseen by an eccentric dictator – we were in Bagnères-de-Bigorre. Surely it wasn't compulsory for male swimmers to wear the obscene skimpy trunks being modelled by the two men before me?

'*Il faut les changer,*' said the second man.

But it was true. They were actually insisting that unless I changed there would be no swim for me. For some reason (which escapes me to this day), in the swimming pool in Bagnères you have to wear skimpy trunks. Nothing else is permitted. No disgusting swimming shorts like the ones I was wearing – never mind that they'd been specifically made for swimming. This was the rule and the French like their rules, and they are extremely good at making sure they're observed. There is no French translation for the sentence: 'Well, you're here now, you may as well have a swim – but don't forget to wear the right trunks next time.'

Unbelievably, I had to leave the pool. In fact, I was chaperoned out like some kind of criminal. My offence had been to wear a swimsuit that didn't reveal my tackle to the small children who were dotted around the pool. I'd been well out of order. It was clear that if I wanted to swim here I would have to go out and purchase some skimpy pervy trunks, the likes of which would possibly be considered too risqué for public pools in England. Oh well – *vive la différence.*

Rather chastened by this experience, I returned home and opted for a form of exercise less likely to cause such controversy. A walk around the village. It was something I'd meant to do a lot more than I had, and despite the fact that it sounded like a rather lazy Sunday afternoon activity, the gradients involved made it a legitimate aerobic exercise, provided you kept up a decent pace.

The trouble was, as I soon discovered, your ability to keep up a 'decent pace' is directly proportionate to how many people you know in the village. Yes, it may have been a weekday afternoon, but for a lot of the villagers work takes place in the fields that surround their houses, so there was a constant danger of 'decent-pace disruption' for the keen aerobic walker like me.

The first interruption came from Alain, the man who in some ways I could hold responsible for the large hole that now filled my garden.

'But you are English! You must have a pool!' he'd said all those months ago, slapping me firmly on the back as he'd done so.

I hadn't seen Alain as much as I would have liked, the problem being that he lived the other side of the village and this meant that our paths didn't cross enough. Although we lived half a mile from each other, I tended only to see him at village events, because when he returned home from work or trips to the shops he took the right fork down the hill away from my house, and consequently we never got the opportunity to flag each other down and stop and chat.

Alain was loading stuff into the boot of his car as I reached his house, slightly out of breath from the long climb that had preceded it.

'Ah, Tony! How are you?' he said, before marching up to me, shaking my hand and providing me with the now trademark slap on the back.

I explained that all was well with me and that I was over here alone on a trip to get some writing done.

'You know that you are always welcome to spend time with us – always,' he said with a big grin. 'Now, about your swimming pool. Last week I saw that it is not yet finished. Why is this?'

'Problems with workers.'

'That is because you were using English.'

'There was no one available here.'

'Tssk.'

Alain threw his head back as if to suggest that this was no excuse. Even though it was. As excuses go, it was about as good as they get. His boot now fully packed, Alain jumped into his car and bade me goodbye with a twirly hand gesture out of the window.

I walked on past *la mairie* until I found myself approaching André's house. Since the rhythm of my aerobic workout had already been broken, I was rather hoping that I'd bump into the man who had rapidly become my favourite elderly French farmer. (He wasn't up against a whole heap of opposition.) As I passed his exhibition piece of a yard, bustling as ever with babbling geese, clucking hens and barking dogs, I looked in to see if I could locate the man himself. There was no sign of him until a face appeared at one of the windows in the L-shaped building that bordered the yard. I could see his familiar face chewing on a piece of bread. He lifted a finger and beckoned me towards him. I felt a little buzz of excitement because it was looking like I was going to be invited into his home. I'd heard that André still lived much as his forefathers had done, making only a cursory nod to the innovations of the current generation. It seemed that any moment I was going to have a glimpse of what French rural life might have been like three-quarters of a century ago.

'*Bonjour, Tony,*' he said, as he appeared at his door. '*Entre!*'

I walked into another world. Despite his house being substantial in size, André only lived in two rooms – his bedroom, and the one I was now in. I guess a modern-day estate agent would call it a kitchen/diner, but it was more of a kitchen/living room. It was dark and extremely bare. There were no tiles on the floor, just cold concrete. The crumbly walls were dimly lit by the inadequate shafts of light that fought their way through the insubstantial and grubby window. A table and chairs filled the centre of the room, surrounded by an old wood-burning stove, an antique wooden sideboard and an ancient fridge on which was perched an old black and white TV. The aerial that was balanced on top of it was a prototype that resembled a deer's antlers. It was tied to hooks on the low ceiling by two pieces of string. (André told me later that he'd done this because he'd grown tired of it falling off as he walked past.)

André offered me a Ricard and apologised for the fact that he was finishing off his chicken stew. I watched him chatter away as he dipped his bread into his bachelor fare. His strong accent and occasional lapse into Occitan meant that I was grasping only about 75 per cent of what he said, but this was a distinct improvement on what I'd been able to grasp when I'd spoken with him earlier in the year. My ear was clearly beginning to adapt and attune itself to the alien sounds of the region. I asked André if the chicken he was now eating was one of his own.

'*Bien sûr. Naturellement,*' he replied.

That must be tough, I thought. Eating something you've been living with. Most meat-eaters console themselves with the fact that they're consuming a creature that they wouldn't recognise. I wonder what percentage of us would be vegetarians if we had to kill and eat the very animal that we'd been feeding and nurturing for months.

André chatted with the fervour of a man who clearly lived alone, wandering as he did from one subject to another with eager abandon. He told me how he'd been born in the village in 1927 and how he'd spent his formative years coping with a country under German occupation. He revealed a deeper side to his personality as he reflected on the futility of war and the senseless loss of young lives. We discussed how he had his bread delivered three times a week and how he'd left the area on only a few occasions − once for an operation (Toulouse), and once just over the border into Spain for a village outing (organised by Malcolm and Anne). He'd never been to Paris and he had no desire so to do. I decided to enquire as to whether he'd ever been married.

'*Non*,' he replied, '*je n'ai jamais trouvé mon âme soeur.*'

I liked this expression − *âme soeur* − which translates literally as soul sister. André was telling me that in his life he'd never met his 'soulmate'.

'*Moi non plus*,' I replied. 'Me neither.'

André told me not to worry. I still had plenty of time. He pointed to the heavens and said that, for him, his soulmate was probably up there, waiting.

As I bade him goodbye and continued on my 'not so aerobic' walk, I wondered if that's how it really worked. Maybe when you miss out on meeting your soulmate down here on earth, then you get to meet them up in heaven. Maybe it's the first thing that happens when you arrive.

'Welcome to heaven,' Peter probably says at the Pearly Gates. 'I expect you're dying for a cup of tea. The canteen's just on the left over there − and your soulmate is waiting for you at table five.'

In my experience French trains are much more punctual than their British counterparts. Certainly the 15.50 for Toulouse rolled into the deserted station exactly on time, almost to the second.

I was making a day trip to visit the city's range of furniture retailers. I'd been told that Toulouse had some great stores, and I knew that the time was fast approaching when the furniture I'd brought from England would need supplementing. As for the stuff

I'd purchased from Conforama and assembled with Brad, well, this could surely be bettered for style and potential longevity. I'd chosen the train over the car so that I could use the hours of travel to read through the work I'd done on the new draft of the screenplay. I didn't know it as I boarded the impressively pristine train, but on the outward journey at least I wasn't going to get a stroke of work done. Mind you, it couldn't have been for a nicer reason.

Just as I sat down in the fairly empty carriage and began to arrange my belongings, I saw a familiar young woman making her way up the aisle of the train. She looked flustered, perhaps because she'd only made the train by a matter of seconds. However, as she drew closer I noted that she was looking prettier than I'd ever seen her before.

'*Bonjour, Christine,*' I said, flagging her down, rather hoping that she might take advantage of the empty seat next to me.

'*Ah, bonjour, Tony,*' she said, with a big smile.

To my delight, the deputy mayor's daughter, waitress, card player and photographer set her small bag in the overhead rack and sat down to join me.

I had to switch my brain into 'French mode'. I wanted to speak the language well right now. I knew that this was a fine opportunity to spend some time with an attractive, intelligent and versatile young woman, and I didn't want to let myself down by constantly asking Christine to repeat things. It wasn't easy given that mentally I wasn't prepared. I'd been geared up for a nice comfortable time reading through my own work and I wasn't at all ready for the speed of Christine's speech, or indeed her strong regional accent.

Things began well enough with a brief chat about what I was going to do in Toulouse and a discussion about what kind of furniture we both liked. Soon, though, we had meandered onto the subject of how she loved horses and how her family kept two on their land. As she continued to speak, I ceased to concentrate so much on her words and instead I was lazily offering up nods of the head along with the odd routine '*oui*'. And the reason? Well, I was focusing on just how lovely she looked today. But what was it? What was so different? I looked at her as she talked, concentrating not on her words, but on the detail of her appearance. Was it her hair? No, that was the same. More make-up? No, if anything she was wearing less than usual. Different clothes? No, I'd seen her in jeans and T-shirt plenty of times. Then it occurred to me that the big difference was the context. This was the first occasion that I'd seen Christine outside the village environment.

For the first time I wasn't thinking in terms of her being the daughter of Leon, the deputy mayor. I was seeing her as a young woman, on her way to Toulouse, probably to continue her studies. How old was Christine, I wondered. Somewhere in her early twenties, that was for sure. Yes, she was a bit young for me, but there'd been countless examples of this kind of relationship working out. Christine was a catch, too. Bright, witty and not short on womanly charms. It wasn't ridiculous to consider this as a possibility either. There are plenty of young women who like the older man, enjoying the stability and wisdom they can often offer. Could Christine, I speculated, be one of these?

She continued to chatter away about how both of her horses were rather wild, and how neither of them was really suitable for riding. I mostly nodded and made little in the way of response. My mind was too full of calculations to offer meaningful replies, mainly because a very big question had just popped into my head. Was I old enough to be Christine's father? I did some mental arithmetic, trying hard not to let my face reveal what was on my mind. Oh dear. The sums weren't providing the desired outcome. In fact, there was even a moment when I began to wonder whether, had I made an extremely early start to my sex life, I might even be old enough to be her grandfather. It didn't bear thinking about.

I looked up to see Christine waiting for a response from me. But what had she just asked me? Something about horses, I reckoned.

'*Oui,*' I said, hoping that this would do the trick.

Christine smiled, and inwardly I sighed with relief. However, I now thought it best to take the conversational initiative and switch from a subject which had not received anything like my best attention.

'So, Christine, are you going to Toulouse to continue your studies?' I asked.

'I'm not going to Toulouse,' she replied. 'I will get off at St Gaudens, the next stop.'

'Oh. What are you doing in St Gaudens?'

'I'm going to visit my boyfriend.'

'Ah. I see.'

I tried hard not to go a bit quiet, but failed. I did manage a few further exchanges but frankly I was quite relieved when, five minutes later, Christine kissed me goodbye and headed for the train door. Perhaps it was for the best. Maybe things wouldn't have worked out between us. Besides, she would never have been accepted by Roger, what with her not being *une petite Anglaise*. No, I was pleased that Christine had a boyfriend.

Just so long as he wasn't over fifty.

17

I'm So Glad You Called

I was quite excited by the prospect of a bingo night. I'd never been to an 'eyes down' session in England, but thanks to the village social committee I would now have the opportunity to do so in France.

'It's quite a big thing out here,' said Malcolm as he shared a beer with me on the balcony, having dropped by to say hello. 'Autumn here is bingo season. Most villages will put on a night of their own, and lots of people will drive around and go to all of them.'

'So they're virtually professionals?'

'Exactly.'

'Can they expect big prizes?'

'Too right they can. If they get on a winning streak they can end up with a huge joint of meat and quite a lot of paint. Not to mention our big prize.'

'What's that?'

'Twenty baby chickens.'

'Bloody hell, that's amazing! I'm going to win those chickens tonight,' I said confidently. 'Just you wait and see.'

I was late for the event, having once again misjudged the time it took to walk to *la mairie*. The problem was that I could see it from my house. This meant that it looked close, and I would forget that the road to it wound all over the place and that there was a long, steep climb the other side of the valley.

The hall was packed. Roger greeted me at the door – well, not so much greeted me as admonished me. He tutted, shook his head, tapped his watch, frowned and then quickly sold me four bingo cards before hurrying me to the only vacant seat in the house. The second game was just about to begin, and I hardly had time to absorb the atmosphere around me. Trestle tables filled the hall, around which eager players sat with heads down and eyes fixed on their cards. There was an air of seriousness that I hadn't been expecting. No one was chatting or smiling. Most people had similar expressions to athletes just before a race is about to begin. Absorbed, focused, intense.

On the stage sat the bingo caller, who was none other than Christine. Was there no end to her talents? She looked assured as she addressed the room, clutching the microphone almost with the casual swagger of a club singer. Her assistant was Letitia, daughter of Rene the Mayor. She was in charge of taking out the numbered balls, handing them to Christine to be called out, and then placing them in the neat little 'ball holder' that lay on the table before her. Rene himself patrolled the tables like a vigilant traffic cop, ready to assist whenever a query arose and to respond with lightning speed when someone shouted 'House!', or '*Maison!*', or whatever it was that they shouted over here.

I didn't recognise any of the other players on my table. These were out-of-towners, the pros who travelled from village to village hoping to be the ones who proudly walked away with the meat, cheese or paint. I noted that they had brought their own little counters to mark off the numbers on their cards. The rest of us used the small pieces of dried sweetcorn that had been piled up in the middle of each table for use by the non-professionals.

It was only as the game began that the size of the task ahead of me became apparent. The first number was called.

'*Cinquante-sept.*'

There was a beat whilst I made the translation in my head. OK, that's 57. Then I scanned one of my cards for the number. No, 57 wasn't there. Then I realised I had four cards in total. That meant that the three other cards needed scanning for 57, too. I picked up my second card to check it over, only to be interrupted by Christine's voice.

'*Vingt-trois.*'

Vingt-trois? That's 23, isn't it? Right, I'll check for that just as soon as I'm sure that there's no 57 on any of the other cards. Right: 57 – no, nothing on the second card; 57 – yes – one on the third card.

I quickly marked it off with a sweetcorn kernel . . .

'*Quarante-neuf*,' called Christine.

Wait! I'm not ready yet! I've got one more card to check for 57. Then there's the 23 to do. I can't cope with a 49 just yet!

'*Douze*,' announced Christine.

That was it. I lost my cool and pushed the cards away from me, knocking the only piece of corn that was covering a number onto the floor. The lady opposite took a brief moment to give me a short, sharp glare. A brief moment was all she could spare. She was running no fewer than ten cards. And with some ease by the look of things. I sighed.

'Where is the fun in this?' I mumbled to myself. I'd had more fun at meetings with my accountant. At least there were moments of rest in between the endless number crunching.

I gave up before the end of the game and wandered over to the back of the hall to join up with Roger, Malcolm and Anne, who seemed to be observers of the proceedings.

'You didn't last long,' commented Anne.

'No,' I replied. 'I need a beer. It's making me feel ill. When are the twenty baby chickens up for grabs? That's all I'm interested in.'

'I think that's the prize for the fifth game,' said Malcolm. 'Do you mind me asking what you'll do with them if you win?'

'*When* I win. Oh, I haven't decided yet. Maybe I'll take them back to London with me and give them a new start. There aren't many prospects for the young in these parts.'

Roger smiled and shook his head at the same time. '*Tonneee! Tu n'es pas Monsieur Bingo!*'

He was dead right, I was not Mr Bingo. I bloody hated it, in fact. There was no joy for me in a room full of people not saying a word to each other, just sitting with their heads down and ticking off numbers. What made it even more annoying was that I couldn't complain about it being a mindless activity. I'd tried to apply my mind to the task but it had begun to hurt after only a few minutes.

I began to talk with Roger in hushed tones, but soon there came a noisy cry of victory and he had to rush off to join Rene in checking the validity of the claim. I turned to speak with Malcolm and Anne but as I did so they disappeared off to prepare some snacks for the interval. I was left alone. Alone and watching. Alone and watching people listening to numbers and then marking them off. It really was no fun at all. There was nothing for it but to engage in a mild sulk which, though I say so myself, I did rather well. Rather better than I played bingo, certainly.

I returned to my seat for the big fifth game. The twenty baby chickens were finally on offer and I felt good about my prospects. Christine kicked things off.

'*Seize.*'

Sixteen. Good, yes. I've got that on two cards. Excellent news. What a very good start. Stay calm.

'*Neuf.*'

Nine. Great, I've got that too. On the bottom left of my third card. This is going well – and I'm keeping up. The lay-off has served me well. It's important to pace yourself, Tony.

'*Quatre-vingt-huit.*'

Quatre-vingt-huit? What's that? Come on . . . what number is *quatre-vingt-huit?* Ah yes – 88. Quick! Look for 88. Quick before she calls the next—

'*Trente-trois.*'

I was in trouble again. And so soon. I battled on, but I realised that a combination of incompetence and ill luck was going to mean that the baby chickens would remain beyond me. My growing frustration was compounded when a large woman near the front screamed with delight and claimed the treasured prize. My prize. Like she needed chickens.

I returned to the back of the hall and began chatting with Irish Mary who had returned from playing an early evening gig at her hotel in Lourdes. It had been a quiet night and Mary didn't have much to tell me that she hadn't told me before, but I hung on her every word. Anything was better than this bingo. This godforsaken bingo. As I listened attentively I vowed never to play it again in my life.

'Will you play the last game, Tony?' asked Mary as Christine announced the biggest prize of the night – a holiday for two in Spain.

'Er . . . I'd rather not. I was thinking that—'

'Ah come on, Tony! You have your cards there. You may be a winner, you never know.'

'It's just that—'

'Don't be so silly, Tony. There, get your cards out in front of you. I'll help you, if you like.'

'Right,' I said, wondering if I'd just set a new record for breaking a vow.

Christine began calling out the numbers.

'*Seize.*'

'Sixteen. You have that. Twice,' said an enthused Mary.

'*Soixante-quinze.*'

'Oh God, what's that?' said Mary. 'That's a hard one.'

'Seventy-five,' I said.

'Oh yes, seventy-five. Good. You've got that one. This bottom card is filling up nicely.'

Another good start. This time, however, the run of luck continued and soon Mary and I were beginning to get rather excited by the prospect of actually winning: 66, 35, 14, 4, and 97 were all filled. All we needed were 54 and 90. We were on the verge of an extraordinary victory.

'*Cinquante-quatre*,' called Christine.

'Fifty-four!' I said, just at the last minute managing to mute an exalted cry. 'This is unbelievable. All we need now is number ninety. That's *quatre-vingt-dix*. Listen out for *quatre-vingt-dix*, Mary, and bellow if you hear it.'

'*Soixante-deux*,' announced Christine.

'Damn,' I said. 'Maybe the next one.'

'*Trente-trois*.'

'No! Come on, Christine.'

'*Quatre-vingt-dix*—'

'*OUI! OUI! OUI!*' I bellowed.

I couldn't believe it, I'd actually won. Well, a couple of us had anyway – because someone else had screamed with delight at the same time as me. Did that mean we'd have to share the prize? Would I have to go on holiday with the other winner? I hadn't seen who the other victory claimant had been, but an earlier glance around the room hadn't revealed many suitable-looking holiday partners amongst the other players.

The lady opposite me looked sick. She'd played her ten cards with exquisite skill all night but she hadn't won any of the electric drills, clocks, DVD players or fondue sets that had been on offer. And now I had a holiday. In disgust she tipped her counters from the cards and onto the table before her. Other disgruntled players did the same.

Serves her right for bringing her own counters, I thought to myself as I waited for Roger to arrive and verify my card.

When he reached me, Christine repeated the numbers and Roger enunciated a crisp, clear '*oui*' as each number matched up on my card.

Soon there was just the last number to check – *quatre-vingt-dix*.
'*Quatre-vingt-dix-huit,*' said Christine, much to my astonishment.
'*Non,*' said a deadpan Roger.

Oh no. I immediately realised what had happened. It was the
bloody silly way the French say their numbers that had caused the
problem. I mean – what a stupid way of saying ninety-eight.
Quatre-vingt-dix-huit translates as 'four–twenty–ten–eight'. Absurd.

And very embarrassing.

But it could have been a lot worse. Had it not been for the other
victory claimant (and they did have '*quatre-vingt-dix-huit*' on their
card), then there could have been a major international incident.
All the disappointed players who had thrown their counters or
pieces of corn from their cards and onto the table would have been
enraged. They would have rightly complained that victory could
have been theirs with the calling of the next number had it not
been for the idiotic Englishman shouting out when he did. The
lady opposite would have almost certainly given me a good old-
fashioned punch on the nose.

'I think it's time for bed,' I said to Mary.

'I agree, Tony,' she replied. 'I'll give you a lift home.'

And with those words Mary and I tiptoed off into the night, my
first and last night of bingo behind me.

The following few days provided me with a comprehensive lesson
in French music. At dinner with Michel and his wife, the other
Christine, I had mentioned that I would be interested in learning
more about French songwriters. Michel's eyes lit up immediately.
Our relationship was about to change. We were no longer to be
neighbours, but instead we would become tutor and student. For
the following three evenings I was invited round to listen to CDs
and watch videos and I did my best to assimilate all the information that was thrown at me. Much of it, however, went sailing over
my head. At times I couldn't help but glaze over as Michel
explained the finer points of a French lyric. One thing was

abundantly clear, however, and that was that Michel had two favourite artistes: Georges Brassens and Jacques Brel. Although neither would have been my choice for the CD in the car, I could appreciate that both were exceptional artists and that they'd been a huge influence on the next generation of songwriters. Brel, in particular, had been responsible for songs that had become big worldwide hits when translated into English.★

On the sleeve notes of *Scott Walker Sings Jacques Brel*, I learnt that the chansonnier was the Belgian-born son of a cardboard-carton manufacturer. After many years of working in his father's factory, for some inexplicable reason Jacques upped and left for the bright lights of Paris. Mysteriously, he chose to exchange the daily joy of the cardboard carton for the drudgery of singing in Left Bank cafés and writing passionate songs about death, timid suitors, Dutch fishermen, and even one about a bull dying under the hot Spanish sun. (There were none about cardboard cartons, but this is understandable enough since, even in French, the words 'cardboard' and 'carton' are buggers to find rhymes for.) He was a dynamic performer, too, and the video that Michel showed me of his performance in a Parisian club singing 'Amsterdam' suggested that Brel's doctor would have been concerned for him at the time, such was the vigour and extraordinary passion of his rendition. I'm no medic, but I'm of the opinion that it can't be good for you if your veins stick out that far on your neck.

The good thing about these music sessions with Michel was that they put me back in touch with the reason why I'd bought my house here in the first place. The piano. Admittedly, the next time I sat down to play, it wasn't to practise. I wanted to write a song that could match the raw force and meaningful lyrics of the restless, creative spirit that was Jacques Brel.

The attempt wasn't a huge success. Initially I sat there uninspired, gazing out of the window. Nothing. No creative spark

---

★'If You Go Away', 'Seasons In The Sun', 'Jackie'.

whatsoever. I tried to force it, but I should have known better. After close to an hour I had a half-decent tune, but the lyrics just didn't hit the mark. I guess Brel didn't have to look out over an unfinished swimming pool in his garden whilst he waited for the muse to come.

I doubted that I'd be playing this new song to anyone in the near future. 'Oh Unsightly Hole' would have to be one of those songs that remained in the drawer forever. Unless, of course, I needed to get rid of someone in a hurry.

The problem of the unfinished pool was solved when I had Fabrice and Marie-Laure over for dinner. I treated them to an exotic spaghetti bolognaise for which they arrived a cool two hours late. They were quite the opposite of a couple who were beside themselves with regret for their tardiness. There was no 'God, we're so sorry, you'll never believe the journey we've just had!' In fact, there was no comment at all until I looked rather wistfully at my watch, and this prompted Marie-Laure to apologise and Fabrice to make a facetious comment about them being on 'Bigourdian time'. I wondered how these Bigourdians ever made it on time to catch flights.*

I noted, too, that Fabrice, like Marie-Laure, had kissed me on both cheeks upon arrival. Quite what this meant I wasn't sure. Did he do this when he felt guilty about being late? Was it because he liked me so much now that a handshake wasn't a sufficient salutation any more? Whatever it was, I rather liked it. It made me feel like I'd come a long way in the short time I'd been here.

During dinner we covered many subjects and I was pleased to find that my French was coping well with most of them. Living alone and without fellow English folk, I'd now begun to think in French rather than forming the sentence in English and then

---

*The answer was revealed later in the evening when Fabrice explained that he'd never been overseas or flown anywhere in his life.

translating it. Ironically, it was a sentence in English from Fabrice
that was the most memorable of the evening.

'I can finish your pool!' he suddenly claimed, after he'd spent a
few moments studying the hole in the ground at the back of my
house.

'Really?'

'*Oui. Avec mon ami Philippe.*'

Fabrice explained that he was now doing more and more free-
lance work and that he and his chum Philippe could cope perfectly
well with the remaining tasks required to complete my pool. I was
rather excited by the prospect. Fabrice was younger, slimmer and
more enthusiastic than Ron. He also spoke better French. The only
downside would be if he operated on Bigourdian time on working
days.

'OK, let's do it!' I said. 'You're hired.'

The following Monday Fabrice arrived with Philippe, a good-
looking chap of about my age, who certainly seemed to know his
stuff when it came to swimming pools. Around him, Fabrice
became a subordinate figure, but he took to this role with relish
and if anything it helped to accentuate his playful side. He danced
to the music that he pumped out at volume from the cab of his
van, and he played air guitar when Santana got into full flow.
Virtually every time I saw him he made me laugh with either a
comment or a piece of slapstick mime. Fabrice was a natural
comic, but the kind who'd had the good sense not to ruin his life
by trying to become a comedian.

On the second morning, two other mates turned up to help
them out – Laurent and Stéphane. These two reminded me of a
kind of French Laurel and Hardy. Stéphane was wide and serious
to Laurent's slight and cheeky. Laurent spoke excellent English,
having lived in London for several years. Stéphane had a go at
English but I noted that he had an unusual approach, beginning
each sentence with a few English words and then reverting to

French for the rest of it. His English was inconsistent, but consistently so.

Soon the four men were demonstrating a refreshing approach to the jobs in hand with dynamism and a real sense of purpose. Philippe orchestrated things with an occasionally quick-tempered authority, and the others responded vocally. For several days the garden was filled with Bigourdian banter. The work, however, was getting done, and at a fair lick. Most mornings all four of them turned down the offer of a coffee, and even when they accepted, they'd take sips in between tasks rather than stop and make a break of it. All in all, Ron would have found their approach rather distasteful.

Laurent took on the role of translator whenever the group discussion became technical. He and I also began to share nice little snatches of conversation throughout the day and I found him to be smart and witty. And restless too.

'Don't you find it boring around here?' he asked one day, during a rare coffee break.

'Not at all. I find it peaceful and relaxing.'

'Yes,' he replied. 'But that is only because you are not here all the time. If you were here all the time, you would find it boring – believe me.'

'You think so?'

'I know so. I am going to Paris at the weekend. I need some life. Stéphane, Fabrice, Philippe – they like it here. But I cannot stand how quiet it is.'

'But it's precisely the peace and quiet that I love.'

'Yes, and when you are bored of it – you can fly back to London. It is perfect for you.'

Laurent probably had it right. Knowing that the energy and excitement of London was within easy reach for me had made this oasis of calm all the more attractive. I didn't feel trapped. I felt liberated. Laurent's restless search for a balance was some way from being realised.

* * *

One evening, after the comedy quartet had put in an exceptionally long day and when progress with the pool was at its most visible to the naked eye, I asked an optimistic question.

'When will I be able to swim in it?'

'Soon, *bientôt*, soon,' said Philippe.

'It needs water first,' said Fabrice.

'Yes, thank you, Fabrice, I was aware of that.'

I licked my lips in anticipation at the promise of a pool that would be ready 'soon', choosing to ignore the fact that there was probably such a thing as a 'Bigourdian promise' as well as 'Bigourdian time'.

Later that night, after my diligent workers had made their way home, I made myself a herbal tea and sat down on the balcony and looked across the valley. It was dark, but I knew it all so well. Each contour of the land, every large tree, the bend in the road as it snaked its way up the hill, the outlines of the distant peaks against the skyline – it was all vividly there for me, even though I wasn't actually seeing it. Below me, the once unsightly 'Serge's hole' was finally beginning to resemble something that visitors might perceive to be the shell of a swimming pool. Slowly the dream of the perfect peaceful home where I could work and practise piano was becoming a reality.

I was still positively glowing with a feeling of well-being as I climbed the stairs on my way to bed. Then the phone rang. Funny, I thought. It's late. Who could be calling at this time?

'*Allô*,' I said.

It had been one of the first things I'd truly mastered in French – answering the phone with an '*allô*' rather than a 'hello'.

'Hello, is that Tony?' came the voice at the end of the line.

It sounded familiar. It was female, English, but I couldn't quite identify it.

'Yes, it's Tony,' I replied. 'Who's that?'

'Well – it's been a while. . . Don't you recognise my voice?'

'I do, yes.'

'Well – who am I then?'

'You need to say some more – I'm nearly there.'

'I'll give you a clue – I'm not Cherie Blair or Gwyneth Paltrow.'

'Shit! Wait, it can't be . . . is that you – Fi? Fiona?'

'Well done. How are you?'

My mind was racing. This was Fiona. Fiona for whom I'd written a song thirteen years previously. Fi, who I'd told Tim and Matt about in the long drive down through France in a white van. Fiona, who'd nearly gone out with me but who had chosen a life in Ibiza with someone else instead. Fi, who I'd fallen in love with.

'I'm . . . I'm fine, I think. I'm just a bit thrown by hearing from you out of the blue. How did you get this number?'

'From your answerphone in London.'

'Oh yes, I forgot that.'

'Are you in France?'

'Yes. I've got a house here.'

'Do you live there?'

'Some of the time. I'm coming here to write. And play the piano. And to finish building a swimming pool.'

'Cool. Where abouts?'

'In the French Pyrenees. Lovely views of the mountains.'

'Fab.'

'Where are you calling from – Ibiza?'

'No, London. Things didn't work out with Steve. What about you? Last time we spoke you were seeing an Irish girl . . .'

'That didn't work out either.'

It had never really been anything much in the first place. I remembered now that all those years ago I'd tried to give Fiona the impression that this fling with the Irish girl had been more than it actually was, in a pathetic attempt to show her that I was over her.

'Oh, that's a shame,' she said. 'That sounded like it was going well.'

'It was . . . for a while. Anyway, it all finished a long time ago.'

'So. Are you seeing anyone now?'

'No, I'm not. How about you?'

'No.'

There was a slight pause, and finally the conversation began to move on to what we had both been up to in the thirteen years since our lives had drifted apart. Before that could happen we'd been like teenagers, establishing, not altogether subtly, whether each other was single or not. Only now could we chat like adults.

And how we talked. We had always made each other laugh and we certainly hadn't lost the knack. The conversation flowed so easily. It seemed like thirteen years had just evaporated. I felt exactly as I'd done all those years ago whenever I spoke to Fi. Energised, animated, excited. The only difference was that I had a few grey hairs that she didn't know about.

'I'm so glad you called, Fi,' I said as the conversation finally drew to a close. 'I'll call you in a few days.'

'Great.'

'Maybe you should come out to France . . .'

'Maybe.'

'Bye then.'

'Bye.'

I didn't sleep too well that night. I just couldn't shut down my mind. From time to time I kept saying out loud, 'This is it.' What 'it' was I couldn't necessarily define, but this definitely had an 'it' feel.

'Yes, this is it,' I repeated, before rolling over onto my side with the intention of curtailing these agreeable but sleep-preventing thoughts.

And all this from one phone conversation?

The mountain air must have got to me.

18

I Drove All Night

As it turned out, Fi and I didn't have our magnificent reunion in either France or Britain. Spain was to host the event. The next time I'd called her, she said that she was going to spend the following weekend in Spain visiting her parents who had retired out there fifteen years previously, and who were about to celebrate their fortieth wedding anniversary.

'I could drive down and see you if you like,' I'd said.

'Isn't it a bit of a way?'

'No, I'm right on the border with Spain. It would be fun to meet your parents anyway. I'll drive down on Friday evening.'

'Great. But I still think it's a bit of a way.'

'Nonsense.'

It was bloody miles. Five hundred miles, to be precise. A glance at the map revealed Spain to be a needlessly substantial body of land, and the journey from Bagnères-de-Bigorre to Valencia to be quite some undertaking.

Clearly I needed to hire a car. The red Peugeot 106 had served me well but it wouldn't survive the kind of pounding that this weekend was going to give it. Also I reckoned that I needed to break the journey, so I booked myself into a credit-card-operated hotel situated in some industrial estate a few hours into Spain. Well, I thought, if I'm going to a new country, I may as well experience the culture.

As I loaded my bags into the car and prepared to wave goodbye to the view that had revived me in the mornings and soothed me at night, I was struck by a worrying thought. Wasn't rushing down to see Fi exactly the same mistake as I'd made when I'd hastily put the offer in for this house in the first place?

'It makes you appear too keen,' Kevin had clearly stated.

I tried to reassure myself that a ten-hour drive in a hire car with an overnight stop wasn't keen at all, merely committed. And didn't women like commitment? And anyway, keen or not, hadn't it all worked out rather well with the French house in the end? Perhaps my initial response to Kevin had been the right one.

'Well, I am keen. What's the point of not appearing keen if I am?'

I set off in the late afternoon, and as I crossed the Pyrenees, following the same route that had been used by political dissidents, smugglers and soldiers for generations, I watched the landscape change from the lush greens on the French side to the barren, rusty reds of Spain. As darkness fell I began to sing Roy Orbison's song, 'I Drove All Night To Be With You'. I liked the romance of this. I knew that Fi was worth this drive, and in a way I wanted her to know it.

I didn't tell her that, though, when I called her from the soulless hotel that was to provide me with rest (and very little else) before the second leg of my journey began at daybreak. Instead we made playful small talk.

I hung up the phone and made my way back to my cheap and distinctly uncheerful hotel room where I sat on the hard bed and prepared myself mentally for sleep. I needed to be fresh in the morning.

I was fully expecting it to be a big day.

Normally I don't like long drives. Actually I'm not crazy about short ones, and medium-length ones get on my nerves. This morning, however, I was getting quite a buzz out of nailing each passing kilometre. I was dominating the fast lane, and I was getting ever closer to the moment when I would see Fi again.

It was going to be a roadside rendezvous.

'There's a little bit where you can park just after you've paid your motorway toll,' she'd said. 'I'll meet you there at midday.'

It was one minute to twelve. My heart was pounding. I didn't know what car she'd be driving so I had to scrutinise each one. She shouldn't be difficult to spot. She was gorgeous with beautiful long blonde hair. Unless, of course, she'd cut it off – or perhaps she'd dyed it? Suddenly I was struck by how long thirteen years is. A new fear grabbed me. Perhaps the telephone conversations we'd shared had been deceptive? Could it be that when we met in the flesh we'd find that we'd both changed so much that the magic wasn't there any more?

Six minutes past twelve and no sign. Fi was late but that was OK. It was a woman's prerogative.

Twelve minutes past twelve and still no sign. Still OK – this was Fi's prerogative. Wait a minute! What was going on here? Wasn't this whole thing ringing some ominous bells? I was struck by a terrible thought. Maybe this was Salamanca all over again. I was in Spain, after all. Arantxa and Mercedes had left me and Tim forlornly sitting on those church steps all those years ago. Was Fi about to do much the same? Maybe this was my destiny. To be the 'nearly man' of love.

Twenty past twelve and still no sign. Just as the worries were about to turn into genuine pain, an old Ford Escort pulled over with a flustered but beautiful woman at the wheel.

'Sorry! I got lost. They've built a few more roundabouts since I was last here,' said the driver, who looked just as good as I'd remembered.

Fi got out of the car and we hugged. It was a warm hug, a special hug, but it wasn't without its tension. We were both clearly still a little nervous.

'Hello again!' I said.

'Yes, hello again to you too.'

'You look great.'

'Rubbish. You look good, though.'

'I know.'

She laughed.

'Come on. We have to go to the supermarket to buy lunch. My mother expects guests to grasp the concept of self-catering.'

Maybe it wasn't the most romantic of starts to our weekend but it was certainly fun.

'I love coming here,' said Fi as we walked the aisles looking for her father's favourite cheese. 'I like playing Spot The Spaniard.'

'What do you mean?'

'Well, look around you.'

I followed Fi's instructions and I soon saw what she meant. For the first time I noticed a lot of sunburnt faces, and men in socks and sandals.

'God, the place is crawling with Brits,' I said.

'Yes. And we get a point for every Spaniard we spot.'

'OK. Well, there's one over there!'

'She's behind the delicatessen counter. Staff don't count.'

Fi won Spot The Spaniard. It had been a close game. It had been 4–4 for a long time, but Fi snatched victory when she spotted a young family of three by the soap powder.

'Seven–four,' she boasted proudly. 'A fine victory. Although I'm a good deal more experienced in this than you.'

For a moment I wondered if the French Pyrenees would ever become overrun with Brits in the same way as southern Spain. I hoped not. Its Frenchness was what made it special. I wanted more than the Britain in the Sun that this part of the world seemed to have become.

'Mum, Dad, this is Tony,' said Fi as we reached the front door of the modest Spanish villa. 'Tony – this is John and Arlene.'

The pretty house was set on a small hill and had pleasant views of the neighbourhood (largely made up of pretty houses on small hills with pleasant views of the neighbourhood). I wasn't nervous about meeting Fi's parents. Getting on with girlfriends' parents had always been my forte. It had been the 'getting on with the girlfriends' bit that I'd found hard.

'Hi there, pleased to meet you,' I said, confidently.

'Good to meet you, Tony,' said Arlene.

'Come and have a beer,' said John. 'You must be dying for one after that journey.'

The tall, slim John waved us through to the terrace, looking a little like I might imagine myself in another twenty-five years. Arlene tagged along beside him, jovial and giggly, and clearly delighted to have their daughter around. Soon we were all laughing together, and it became apparent that we were going to get on just fine.

With each passing minute, the initial nervousness between Fi and I dissipated and we began to share the odd brush of hands, or affectionate touch on the shoulder. How I'd longed for fleeting moments of intimacy like these all those years ago.

The closest I'd got had been in Manchester. It had been Fi's first producing job in television – filming a comedy benefit for the *Big Issue*. I'd hosted the show and as a result we'd worked closely together, rehearsing in the afternoon. At one point we'd both been down in the auditorium and we were needed up on the stage. The stage hands hadn't put the movable staircase in just yet, and so I took it upon myself to put my arms around Fi's waist and hoist her onto the stage. As I did so, there'd been a definite moment of frisson between us. But, alas, that's all it had been. A moment.

Perhaps it was because I'd been thirty-three to Fi's twenty-five. At that point I was beginning to reach a period in my life where I was ready to slow down a bit, whereas Fi still had her foot pressed down hard on the accelerator. Maybe things would be different now. After all, you know what they say.

Good things come to those who wait bloody ages.

We played tennis in the afternoon. This gave me the chance a) to show off a bit, and b) to stand behind Fi with my arm across her midriff whilst showing her the topspin forehand. Afterwards we swam in the sea, and I admired her body, taking good care to make these examinations when Fi was preoccupied with gazing at the view or observing fellow swimmers. We talked about old times, we laughed and we shared the occasional affectionate touch. As we walked back to the car from the beach I wanted to hold her hand, but like a nervous teenager I couldn't summon the courage. What if this was a step too far? What if I'd been misreading the signs? I remembered my 'date' with Monique, back in France. She'd appeared keen enough – but things, it seems, are never that straightforward.

Our first evening together for over a decade was no ordinary meal. We were joining John and Arlene at a favourite restaurant in celebration of their fortieth wedding anniversary. As we sat down at the table I had to smile at the unconventional nature of my relationship with their daughter. Having initially got close to each other, we had introduced a thirteen-year hiatus – and then, having re-established contact, I'd travelled miles from one country to another in order to share in a unique family occasion. Shouldn't we have at least kissed each other before this happened? Oh well, rules are there for breaking, I suppose.

'So, Tony, how do you like living in France?' asked John, as we tucked into our fish soup starters.

'I like it,' I said. 'I'm not there all the time, but when I am, I definitely feel the stresses of London life peeling away.'

'Will you be taking Fi there?' enquired Arlene, who I'd already learned was someone who liked to race straight to the point.

'I hope so,' I said, throwing a glance at Fi. 'I'm going to make a formal invitation later.'

'Good,' said Arlene.

I looked at John and Arlene. Forty years together. God, how impressive is that, I thought. To be married for forty years. To live in the same house, share the same bed, bathroom, holidays, anecdotes and dreams. Well, maybe you don't share the same dreams. Perhaps that's how you survive. I guess that they'd had their ups and downs. What couple hasn't? I suppose the secret to longevity is to have more ups and fewer downs. That would be the challenge ahead for me and Fi, if we ever managed to get our act together and actually start something.

'Where's Tony going to sleep?' asked Arlene, as we staggered back into the house, filled with excellent food, wine and festive champagne. 'Shall I make up the sofabed in the lounge?'

'It's all right, Mum,' said Fi. 'He can come in the guest room with me. There are two beds in there.'

My mind began to race. This was good. Very good indeed. I would deal with the problem of the twin beds later. One step at a time.

Five minutes later I was offering my final congratulations to Fi's parents before being led by the hand towards the guest room by their beautiful daughter. She opened the door, pushed me into the room, shut the door behind her with her foot and pulled me towards her.

And at that moment our friendship ended. Fortunately something rather lovely took its place.

The weekend was all over so quickly. Just as Fi and I had finally begun the relationship that had been so long in gestation, we were parting again. I was driving back to France and she was flying back to the UK.

I drove Fi to Valencia airport, only freeing my hand from hers when I needed to change gear. All too soon I was pulling the car into the departures drop-off point where we would have to say goodbye. The two of us got out of the car and hugged. The hug intensified and soon we became locked in a deep embrace. I knew that we were creating the kind of amorous spectacle that I'd watched so often with envy when I'd been at airports travelling on my own. It was my turn now to be the leading player in what could have been the final shot of a romantic movie. The trouble was that this wasn't a film and that our lives would continue the moment this embrace was over. Just as soon as the credits had rolled and the audience had filed out of the movie theatre, Fi would have to queue up at check in, and I would have to drive for bloody hours on a dull Spanish motorway.

Why do they never put that bit in films?

As I motored north towards the relatively lush greens of France I thought of Fi flying home and wondered if at any point she'd be directly above me in the air. One thing was for sure. She'd be travelling much faster than me. By the time I checked into the same charmless hotel that had housed me on the outward journey, she would have been in London and on her way back to her flat. She'd have crossed seas and mountain ranges, whilst I was still stuck in Spain.

I slept soundly, though, and with a deep contentment that felt somehow new to me. In the morning I would complete the final leg of the journey and face the inquisition of the four Frenchmen who would be working at my house. I'd mentioned the reason for my Spanish excursion to the boys just before I'd left and there'd been a good deal of unintelligible Bigourdian banter on the subject.

Fabrice was working alone when I made it back to the house.

'*Bonjour, Monsieur Tonny!*' he exclaimed. 'And how is Casanova?'

He was standing near the would-be swimming pool, beaming cheekily. I started to tell him the story of the weekend, and I soon discovered that now his chums weren't around him, he was happy to talk more seriously to me. He seemed anxious to know more about the background to my new relationship, and when he heard the details he couldn't quite believe it.

'*Mais non!*' he said, shaking his head. 'After thirteen years! This is *incroyable.*'

He wanted to know still more. How did I feel?

It was no good, though. I just couldn't find the French words to sum up what I was really feeling, however hard I tried. I wanted to communicate how I felt sure that this was the start of something significant, even though I only really had some history and a weekend in Spain to base it on. I struggled to convey to him how the usual doubts that surrounded the beginning of a relationship just didn't seem to be there. I attempted to explain that I had no explanation.

Fabrice, power drill in hand, looked at me with an expression that suggested I was overcomplicating things. Then he shook his head and said a few English words, no doubt gleaned from the American films he'd watched.

'Tony, you are in love.'

Then, in a masterful display of bathos, he began drilling.

In the days that followed I felt more alone in the house than I had done before. The peace and quiet of which I'd grown so fond now only served as a reminder that something was missing. Suddenly this house didn't feel like the best place to complete the work on my screenplay and I started to contemplate heading back to England earlier than I'd planned. After all, I had Roger to think about. How would he feel if he knew that I'd met a potential perfect *petite Anglaise* and then I'd failed to go back to England to pursue her?

So it was, days later, that I stood in my garden and attempted to lecture Fabrice, Philippe, Laurent and Stéphane on what work needed to be done in my absence.

I had booked myself on a flight back to London.

★ ★ ★

'How are you coping?' I said to Brad as we sipped coffee in Covent Garden.

The heating in the café didn't seem to be working very well and we were both still wearing our thick coats. The British winter had just begun its long slow assault on the disposition of its people. They weren't fully fed up with it yet – but give them another three months.

'I'm better than expected,' an upbeat Brad replied. 'It's almost like losing my mother has been a wake-up call to me. It's made me re-evaluate my life. It's made me really think about what I do and don't enjoy.'

'And as a result of this thinking, have you drawn any conclusions?'

'I've done more than that. I'm in the process of winding up my project-management business.'

'Wow. And what will you do instead?'

'I don't know.'

'And that doesn't bother you?'

'Nope. The right thing will come along. All I have to do is be ready and waiting. In the meantime I'm helping Ron out with the odd bit of building work.'

'That's great news. How is the old bugger?'

'He's on fine form, Tony. I really think he's turned the corner with that depression thing that he battles with.'

'Let's hope so.'

'And what about you, Tony? Anything to report on the love life?'

'Ah. I'd better order two more coffees. This might take a little time.'

We were still talking about it as we left the coffee bar half an hour later. Brad was thrilled at the news. He'd not met Fi when the two of us had first been spending time together but he claimed that he'd heard me talk so much about her that it felt like he knew her.

'It feels like we've been going out for ages,' I said.

'That's because you've known each other such a long time.'

'Maybe.'

'But the big question is – when are you going to take her to the house in France?'

'Immediately after Christmas. I want her to see the house when there's snow on the ground.'

'Excellent romantic work,' said Brad, looking most impressed. 'I wonder what the house looks like in a winter wonderland.'

'Why don't you come out for New Year and find out for yourself?'

'That sounds fantastic. I'm definitely up for that.'

'Well, let's see, but I think we can make it happen.'

I started dating *la petite Anglaise* in London and we nearly overdosed on fun. We were clearly enjoying the golden period of euphoria in a new relationship when both parties look adoringly at their partner, firmly believing that the sun shines out of every available orifice. Experience had shown me, though, that what comes next is a trickier period when it begins to cloud over a bit. Each party discovers, somewhat to their horror, that their partner doesn't agree with them on absolutely everything, and actually dares to quarrel with them on some matters too. Worse still, they don't always want to do the same things as the other one, or at the same time, or whilst wearing the skimpy outfit they've just bought. People, it seems, can be inconsiderate.

Then there are the additional problems created by the fact that men and women are completely different creatures. I had to keep reminding myself that Fi was from Venus and that I was from Sussex. We began to have the occasional quarrel, but we did so healthily, and more often than not we both ended up apologising to each other by the end of it. There was every sign that we were making it through the tricky cloudy period, and that we were ready for the sun to burn its way through, making way for us to start thinking about what it might be like to have a fortieth wedding anniversary attended by our daughter and her new boyfriend.

The future, in so far as it ever can, looked rather rosy.

19

Nature Boy

'Hey, it's so beautiful!' said Fi, as we drove down the narrow lane that had first led me to this haven of tranquillity a year before. 'Look at the snow just nestling on the trees. It's heaven on a stick.'

A fresh fall of snow had deposited a white blanket over the green fields, and the trees looked like they'd been touched up with white paint by an over-exuberant decorator. Brad hadn't been far off the mark when he'd referred to it as a winter wonderland.

'Snow is amazing stuff, isn't it?' I said, gazing out across the whiter than white horizon. 'You know, scientists say that no two snowflakes are the same.'

'I've heard that too, but quite how they can be sure of that I don't know. I mean, unless someone checks every snowflake that falls, then how can they be entirely certain?'

'That's a fair point, Fi. I don't think scientists should make bold statements like that until they've found an enthusiastic enough team of volunteers to check every snowflake.'

'It's only fair.'

'I agree.'

It felt good to have found someone who was also a heavyweight thinker on matters of such importance.

Fi liked the house. Thank God for that. I don't know what would have happened to our relationship if she'd turned up and said, 'It's horrid. Looking at mountains gives me a headache, and swimming pools make me sick.'

Not that there was a swimming pool yet, of course. Just a hole that was more sophisticated than it had been before, and which had been lovingly prepared for the imminent fitting of the blue liner by Fabrice and the Three Musketeers. The water would be added shortly afterwards. My project-management skills had ensured that I would have a pool just in time to be able to take advantage of January's arctic conditions.

We awoke on our first full day in the house together to be greeted by a healthy dose of December sun. Somehow the sky seemed clearer than it ever had before, and bluer too. The light was crisper, the definition of the snow-capped peaks more pronounced. The mountains were majestic. I felt proud – almost as if this being such a beautiful day was somehow down to me.

'Can we ski today?' asked Fi.

'Oh all right, if we must,' I replied, with mock reluctance.

One of the many things I liked about Fi was that she was as keen on skiing as I was. I hoped that she could last longer than Kevin had done almost a year before, because I wanted more than half an hour on a day like this. I looked at Fi and saw someone who looked likely to deliver just that. She was younger, fitter and considerably prettier than Kevin. Pleasingly, too, she collected less wood.

'So what are you like at skiing then?' asked Fi, just as the sense of excitement was building as we viewed the white peaks in the distance.

'I'm pretty good actually,' I said.

'Oh. You're "pretty good actually", are you?' said Fi, mockingly.

'Well, I can't see the point in false modesty. I'm pretty good, so I may as well say I am.'

I could tell that Fi thought I was cocky. I didn't mind, though. I reckoned that over the years I'd developed enough skiing technique to be able to fulfil the description of my skiing that I'd just given.

'What about you?' I asked. 'What are you like?'

'Crap. But I can get down most slopes.'

'Great. In the end, that's all that matters.'

Bizarrely enough, downhill skiing was invented by the British. Pretty impressive, given the amount of snow-capped mountains available to them at home. Having learnt how to 'Telemark' from the Norwegians, adventurous (and wealthy) Brits headed off to Switzerland where they came up with the idea of the downhill race. Lord Roberts of Kandahar introduced the first one ever at Montana-sur-Sierre in 1911. The result was a marvellous 1st, 2nd and 3rd place for the British − a dominance that we continued to hold over the sport until the following year when we let some other countries have a go.

Fi and I followed in these historic footsteps, and having got together all our paraphernalia − skis, boots and poles, gloves, goggles and salopettes − we then had half an hour of queuing for our lift passes before we were ready to take on the slopes. I was excited. I love this sport. However, I wasn't without nerves as Fi and I set off for the first chairlift of the day with a spring in our ungainly, ski-boot-laden steps. I'd talked up my skiing prowess and perhaps this had been a mistake. Maybe false modesty would have been the better option after all. At least then I would have had nothing to lose. I could warm up slowly. Now, thanks to my big mouth, I would have to look good from the word go, and that might not be easy given that I hadn't skied for nearly a year, and that had been for only half an hour thanks to Kevin's needless five-a-side-football ankle injury.

There was only a small queue for the lift. It moved much faster than we'd expected and we were happily chatting away when suddenly it was our turn to jump on the next chair as it was whizzed round. We were bellowed at by the burly ski–lift attendant and he hurriedly manhandled us into position. Something went wrong and I seemed to get a ski caught somewhere, so instead of being in position for the chair to sweep me up neatly, I was sideways on when the chair arrived and I fell directly on top of Fi.

'Ouch!' she said, appropriately enough.

'Sorry.'

'Can you get off me, please? This isn't the time or the place.'

'You're right. I'll just haul myself back into position.'

By this stage the burly chairlift attendant had seen the mess we had made and had hit the button that stopped the chairlift so we could sort ourselves out. He had obviously taken an executive decision that it wasn't safe to send the chair to the top of the mountain with a man dangling precariously from it, holding onto his girlfriend for dear life. By the time he'd halted the lift we were already thirty feet in the air, though, so I was finding it very hard to manoeuvre myself off Fi, not having the ground to use for leverage.

'The problem is that your left foot seems to be stuck under mine,' said Fi. 'Pull.'

'I am pulling.'

Boy was I pulling. But nothing was happening. Meanwhile the chairlift attendant had decided that the best thing to do was to shout at us in French. Good, that would help. Just what I needed right now.

I pulled some more but to no avail.

'I don't believe it!' said Fi, who had managed to lean forward into a position that meant she could see what had caused me to become trapped. 'Your ski seems to be caught underneath mine. If you spin yourself round to the left you should be able to see for yourself.'

I contorted myself in mid-air, ignoring the unintelligible instructions that were being bellowed to me from the burly man below. And then I saw what the problem was.

'God. It's even worse. I don't believe what's happened. It doesn't seem possible,' I said to the woman lying beneath me.

'What's happened?'

'We appear to be joined at the feet.'

'What do you mean?'

'Well, there's a gap between the bottom of your ski boot and the top of your ski.'

'And?'

'Unbelievably, the tip of my ski seems to have found its way between that gap and it's wedged in there.'

'No!'

'Yes. Honest.'

'So you can't pull it free just by moving?'

'No. You'll have to take my ski off or I'm stuck like this.'

'But I can't take your ski off – you're in the way.'

'Yes. This seems to be the root of the problem.'

It was a problem that had now been identified by the chairlift man below.

'YOU MUST TAKE OFF ZE SKI!' he shouted in English, having realised that I'd not been overly responsive to his French.

'I KNOW!' I shouted back. 'BUT IT'S NOT THAT EASY!'

The worst thing about this situation was that our entanglement had brought the entire chairlift to a grinding halt. People who were anxious to get out there on the slopes were being held up by the daft English couple. Time was of the essence or we might be close to causing an international incident.

'You must be able to get it off,' said Fi.

'I'm trying. Honest. The problem is that I can't get myself into the right position. I'm too tangled up with you.'

'I thought you liked being tangled up with me.'

'I do. But I'd prefer it if there were less people inconvenienced by it.'

Others further up the chairlift had begun to shout at us. Great. That really made the process of releasing my ski from the binding that much easier. And more help was at hand below.

'YOU MUST TAKE OFF ZE SKI!' repeated the burly one.

One thing was certain. If we ever got out of this mess, we wouldn't be using this chairlift again today. I couldn't face seeing the burly man again for quite some time. To be fair, he probably wouldn't be overly anxious to see me either.

I exerted all my efforts into one big shove against the binding, nearly falling from the lift to guaranteed hospitalisation as I did so. I grunted and I strained and finally I got the result. The ski binding released and I was able to pull my leg free. An ironic cheer went up from those who were looking on anxiously from above us on the chairlift. I managed to hold onto my ski, slide myself sideways and, with a helping hand from Fi, hoist myself back up into the conventional position for chairlift transportation.

'That was all quite embarrassing,' giggled Fi. 'Do you reckon we can get through the day without further incident?'

'I'm not confident,' I replied, as the chairlift started up again. 'The trouble is that it's quite a fast lift, this one. I could have a problem if the lift guy at the top doesn't see that I'm carrying one of my skis and slow the thing down when it's time for me to get off.'

Needless to say he didn't. He was too engrossed in reading *OK* magazine to notice that I was anything but OK. We undid the bar of the chairlift and I attempted to ski off on one ski. As a matter of routine I fell over, taking a bash on the head from Fi's ski pole as I did so.

The couple coming up in the chair behind ours arrived and landed in a heap on top of me. Only then had we created enough chaos to distract the lift operator from his reading, and he duly stopped the lift so that the pile-up wouldn't become bigger, giving us time to disentangle ourselves. I apologised profusely to the couple, who had already spent more of their morning than they would have liked watching me contorted on the chair in front of them. They mumbled something that was almost certainly derogatory and then they skied off.

Fi was laughing hysterically.

'So this is "pretty good actually" is it?' she managed to say between convulsions.

'It gets better.'

'I do hope not. This is much more fun. Are you always this funny?'

'Tragically, no,' I said, remembering some of the tougher gigs I'd done to late-night crowds in comedy clubs. 'Now let's get out of here. I can't handle any more dirty looks.'

And finally we skied off – thankfully into a day without any further incidents that would have made Lord Roberts of Kandahar turn in his grave.

The next three days were made up of a blissful combination of amusing tumbles in the snow, warm hugs by the open fire and evenings whiled away by the piano. The summer's practice schedule, ill disciplined though it may have been, was finally paying me dividends. I indulged in shameless showing-off. A bit of boogie-woogie and some blues, interspersed with the occasional self-penned composition, left Fi suitably impressed.

'How do you do it all without any music?' she asked.

'Well, when I was sixteen I used to spend hours just messing around on the piano and experimenting with chords – and I've done it ever since.'

'Will you teach me?'

'Of course.'

The piano, it seemed, was going to perform a new and unexpected role.

Our guests arrived on the morning of New Year's Eve. Fi and I were being joined by two couples – Nic and Kevin, and Ron and Brad. Not that the latter were an item as such, but they'd developed an affectionate banter that may well have been misinterpreted by anyone meeting them for the first time.

'What's on the agenda for tonight, the big night?' asked Kevin, as I drove the eager new arrivals from airport to mountain retreat.

'There's a dinner at the village hall.'

'But of course!' said Kevin's fiancée Nic. 'As if they'd let an occasion go by without a dinner at the village hall.'

'I've bought us tickets,' I explained. 'And Fabrice and Marie-Laure are driving up to join us. It should be a good night.'

'Are you coming along with us, Ron?' asked Brad, tentatively.

'Nope. You lot go. I'm happy enough back at the house.'

'Really? That's a shame,' I said, disguising the fact that I'd been so sure that he wouldn't come that I hadn't bothered to buy him a ticket. Ron's improved state of mind didn't yet mean that he was ready to cope with more than two or three humans at a time.

'Fi is back at the house, I take it?' asked Nic.

'Yup. And there's an outside chance she might have a salad ready for us when we get there.'

'Will this be the first time everyone in the village gets to meet Fi?' asked Brad.

'Yes. I hope they like her.'

'Of course they will,' said Kevin. 'And you'll be well on the way to losing that *célibataire* label.'

About time too.

As usual we turned up too early for aperitifs at the village hall. Fabrice and Marie-Laure, predictably enough, were running late and had told us that they'd join us later. Only the old guard were there – Odette and André. Fi began speaking to them in her rusty school French, and I looked on proudly as I watched her charm them with each laboured and disjointed sentence. Like many a rusty French speaker, Fi claimed that she could 'understand much better than speak'. Later in the evening, however, I was to discover that her powers of comprehension left something to be desired when she returned from a brief chat with a lady from a neighbouring village.

'That's amazing,' she said. 'That lady's husband used to be a nightclub singer in Paris.'

It wasn't until half an hour after when I began chatting with the lady in question I learned her husband had in fact worked for the French railways in a ticket office. The mind boggles as to how great a misapprehension could have occurred, but the reality was that this was just an exaggerated example of the kind of thing that had happened to me on a daily basis. The number of times I had ended conversations with only the faintest grasp of what had been said must have run into the hundreds. The levels of concentration involved made it all so tiring, too. Sometimes an evening of French speaking left my brain feeling like it had undergone a frontal lobotomy. I knew that this linguistic barrier would prove a huge obstacle if I ever decided to live in the Pyrenees permanently. Being a student in the language means that you miss out on the witty asides, the plays on words, the cultural references and the subtle nuances in the repartee. All this passes you by, leaving you feeling like a child at an adults' party.

The room began to fill with guests. Aperitifs continued to be poured and there was not the remotest sign of any intention by anyone to sit down and eat, even when the clock passed ten. There was too much chatting to be done. I looked around me and saw Nic and Kevin babbling away in French to Fabrice and Marie-Laure, flanked by a furiously nodding Brad, who had developed the admirable skill of being able to have a good time even though he was totally oblivious to what was going on around him.

Satisfied though I was to see everyone getting on so well, I was still slightly on edge. Someone very important had failed to show up thus far.

He rolled in at ten past ten.

'*Bonsoir, Roger!*' I said, confronting him after he'd barely made it though the door. '*Je veux te presenter à la petite Anglaise!*'

His eyes lit up, and I quickly called Fi over. When she arrived I popped my arm around her and forced her into some kind of unnatural pose in front of Roger, a little like we were entering a 'Couple of the Year' competition.

'Aha! Yes!' said Roger, with a broad smile on his face. '*Magnifique*. You have done well!'

He then slapped me on the back and moved off to greet his fellow villagers.

It had been a short exchange, but it had meant a lot. Quite why I needed the approval of my choice of woman from a part-time mechanic in a Pyrenean village I'm not entirely sure, but require it I did.

Moments later further approval was forthcoming from Fabrice when he took me aside and gave me a pat on the back.

'I did not know that there were girls this beautiful in England,' he said.

'Otherwise you would have gone there by now, right?'

'*Exactement*,' he said laughing, before quickly adopting his more serious face. 'Tonny, I am sorry to tell you that we will not finish your pool as quickly as we said.'

'Oh?'

'No. Philippe and I were talking and we think that it makes no sense to put the water in at this time of year. It will freeze at night and this will damage the liner. Can you wait a few more months?'

'I suppose so,' I said, wondering slightly why they hadn't told me this weeks ago. 'I guess if I've waited this long, then I can hold out a little longer.'

'It is better like this,' he said. 'It will be ready soon.'

'OK. I understand.'

And I did understand. This wasn't the place to be if you wanted things done quickly. Had Bigorre been a sovereign state then its national anthem would have been called 'Ready Soon'. (Either that, or the composer would have been still working on it.)

After what seemed like an age, Rene the Mayor invited us all to be seated, and the meal began. As ever, it was a long-drawn-out affair – oysters, foie gras and scallops were all served as starters. Needless to say, we were nowhere near having the main course by the time midnight came around. In fact, had it not been for the deputy mayor's son Mikael, we might have missed it. He happened to glance at his watch and notice that the magical moment was only a few minutes away, and then immediately alerted the group. We were all ushered to our feet whilst Guy, the village technical bod, tuned the PA into the radio. Soon we were counting down to the hour of midnight, along with some fatuous French DJ. (All of us except Brad, that is, who possibly thought we were praying – perhaps for the arrival of our main course.)

The kissing and the shaking of hands then began in earnest. Bizarrely we'd already done this to each other when we'd all arrived, the only difference this time being that we got to kiss and embrace the people we'd arrived with. That meant hugs for Nic, Kevin and Brad. Oh yes, and one other.

God, she looked lovely.

'God, you look lovely, Fi,' I said.

'I don't.'

'You do.'

'I don't.'

'Well, whatever. This is no time for an argument. Give me a kiss.'

And she obliged. I found myself swept into a place where things felt different. For a moment, the village hall and its revellers seemed to be a long way away. I felt pleasantly disorientated, lost in a momentary sense that this embrace was everything. Warm, sensuous, secure – spiritual even. I longed for it to last forever. One thing was certain. I never could have found a moment like this in Ron's arms.

Van Halen brought me back to the real world. Rather rudely, I thought. A deafening burst of wailing guitar made everyone in the hall nearly jump out of their boots. Guy had pressed the wrong button on the music system and subjected us to several seconds of heavy metal. Fi was whisked away from me by a grinning Roger, and I continued on the salutatory circuit of the room, suddenly reunited with who I was, what I was up to and where it was that I was doing it. It may not have been as extraordinary a world as the one from which I'd just been untimely plucked, but as worlds go, it wasn't too bad. I was soon engulfed in a three-way hug with Fabrice and Marie-Laure, before everyone in the room was swept into a huge circular dance that seemed to involve a lot of whooping and a certain amount of lateral movement, but little else. The perfect dance for slightly drunk English folk, of whom there were now more than one or two.

We all walked back from the village hall at four in the morning. It had been one of the best New Year's Eves I'd had for ages. Never mind that we hadn't eaten our main course until after one in the morning. It didn't matter that the latter part of the evening had been dominated by the traditional introduction of pea shooters, and that the wanton firing of pellets around the room had led to a couple of stinging blows to the back of my neck. I didn't even mind that the radiators had packed up working at 2am and that for much of the remaining festivities guests had seen fit to don their winter coats. None of this had bothered me in the least. I was amongst friends – both new and old – and simple though it was, this meant more than it ever had before.

The night wasn't over yet, though. When we got back to the house, Brad and I got the guitars out. The noise disturbed Ron, who made his way down to join us, sleep still in his eyes, flies undone and shirt on the wrong way round.

'It's the first day of the New Year, mate. I hope you have a good one!' said Brad.

'I doubt it,' said Ron, deadpan and laconic as ever.

'What shall we play?' I asked, guitar poised for action.

'Do you know "Nature Boy"?' enquired Kevin.

I certainly did. It's a classic song that has been covered by artists as diverse as Nat King Cole and George Benson.

'Ah yes, that's fab,' said Fi. 'It ends with just the best line ever.'

'And what's that?' asked Kevin.

'Listen up, they'll get to it in a minute.'

Kevin, Nic, Fi and Ron all fell silent in anticipation of the great line as Brad and I sang our way towards it. And then the moment arrived:

'The greatest thing you'll ever learn is just to love and be loved in return.'

The warm applause that followed the song felt like it was more for that line in particular than for our interpretation of the piece. Immediately all of us began to discuss the meaning of the words and, somewhat inevitably for the time of night, soon we were involved in a discussion about why there was so much suffering in the world.

'It's difficult to believe in a benign deity when there are so many natural disasters in the world,' said Brad.

'Yes, but most of the world's suffering is man-made, don't you think?' suggested Nic.

'I agree,' I said. 'And I think it all stems from fear. Man's fear of not having enough for himself and his family leads him to become greedy, and when greed takes hold, then suffering surely follows. What do you think?'

'You may be right,' mumbled Brad, while Kev, Nic and Fi nodded quietly.

'What about you, Ron? What do you think?' I asked.

'Me? I think that if you're all going to talk bollocks then I'm off to bed,' he said, immediately acting on his words.

His comment seemed to alert the rest of us to the futility of trying to set the world to rights in the early hours of the morning. Slowly but surely the remaining sages made their way upstairs to bed, until only Fi and I remained.

'It was a wonderful evening, wasn't it?' said Fi.

'It certainly was.'

'Different to a London night.'

'Very.'

'It's late, though, and I'm tired. Are you coming to bed?' she asked.

'I'll be up a minute. I just want a little longer looking at the sky.'

'OK.'

I poured myself a nightcap and moved out onto the balcony and peered towards the heavens. The stars were shining. Really shining. The sky was so vibrant – so alive. In stark contrast I looked down at the mess we'd created in my garden. Yes, Serge's hole was less of an eyesore than it had been, but it was still far from becoming the pool of which I'd dreamt.

The rest of the garden resembled a cross between a building site and an archaeological dig. This job was far from over, and there would surely be plenty that wouldn't go to plan. I knew that, and I didn't mind one bit. Why did the place have to be perfect? Whatever went wrong from here on in would be a joyous idiosyncrasy – not a cock-up. Whatever we created, however botched it might appear, would contain within it a happy memory.

Perhaps it was prompted by the warmth of the evening that had just passed, or maybe it was because I was now on my second nightcap after a long night of festivities, but I started to see 'love' in every stone, each pile of mud, every abandoned shovel, each mound of sand. I began to think about the year that had just passed. So much seemed to have happened. It was here that I'd struggled so hard to practise the piano, and where Kevin had piled his useless pieces of wood and proposed marriage to Nic. This was where Brad had received the news of his mother's passing, and where Ron had enjoyed countless siestas, developed a taste for courgettes and found a way to pull himself out of his malaise. This had been the location for me to receive a life-changing phone call when I'd least expected it – the call that had finally enabled me to deliver *la petite Anglaise* to the expectant Roger.

Right now, Fi was only a climb of the stairs away. That made me feel good. However, I was well aware that we'd only just got things together and that there were still plenty of things that could go wrong. I also knew that I would have felt just as warm and happy at this moment even if she hadn't yet telephoned her way back into my life. Why? Because I was already lucky in love. I had friends who I loved and who loved me. If that wasn't enough, then I surely would have been a greedy man.

I sipped the final dregs from my glass, and under my breath, sang the refrain quietly back to myself.

'The greatest thing you'll ever learn is just to love and be loved in return.'

That would do for me.

That, and having a bin with my name on it.